PSIFI
Psychological Theories and Science Fictions

Jim Ridgway & Michele Benjamin

To Anne

To the continuing inspiration of science fiction writers

THE BRITISH PSYCHOLOGICAL SOCIETY

PSiFi

PSYCHOLOGICAL THEORIES AND SCIENCE FICTIONS

Jim Ridgway
and Michele Benjamin

Erratum: The last line on page 65 is missing. It should read:

'Was it there an hour ago? I mean, wasn't that a view of Mount Hood, when I

First published in 1987 by The British Psychological Society, St Andrews
House, 48 Princess Road East, Leicester LE1 7DR, UK.

British Library Cataloguing in Publication Data

Ridgway, Jim
  PsiFi : psychological theories and science
  fictions.
  1. Psychology and literature   2. Science
  fiction—History and criticism
  I. Title   II. Benjamin, Michele
  III. British Psychological Society
  150'.1   PN56.P93

  ISBN 0-901715-62-X

Set in Linotype Plantin
by Communitype, Leicester
Printed and bound in Great Britain by A. Wheaton & Co. Ltd, Exeter
Cover design by Jeremy Thistlethwaite

CONTENTS

ACKNOWLEDGEMENTS

The editors are grateful to Chris Leach, Guy Fielding, Anne Ridgway and Hermi Däuker for detailed comments on earlier drafts and to members of the Books and Special Projects Group of The British Psychological Society for guidance on this project.

Hermi Däuker, Sylvia Sumner, Sheila Whalley and Shelagh Whytock put in valiant efforts typing and preparing documents.

FOREWORD

Bob Shaw

I started to read science fiction in the mid-1940s, long before it became popular, at a time when even being seen with such magazines automatically earned one a reputation as an idiot. Parents, teachers and friends felt it their bounden duty to ridicule me out of the strange addiction – and, believe me, they worked hard at their task – but I refused to give it up. You see, I *knew* that men would someday walk on the Moon, that radios would be small enough to wear on the wrist, that artificial intelligence was on the way.

I had been enduring the well-meaning persecution (the worst kind) for some years when I discovered Robert Heinlein's famous short story, *They*. Its ending took me completely by surprise, and it also filled me with an unexpected mixture of emotions. Pure joy was dominant among them, mingled with satisfaction, a sense of vindication and – oddly(?) – relief and pride. For hours afterwards I had a lump in my throat caused by sheer *gladness*.

Many times since that aureate occasion I have wondered how common was my reaction to the story. Was it fairly typical, or was it a sign that I was in need of psychiatric help? My conclusion is always, of course, that there is nothing wrong with me, that most people who read *They* will respond to it as I did. My reaction may have been a bit extreme, but surely – I keep telling myself – that was because of its message that an activity (like reading SF in the mid-1940s) which society regards as irrational can be fully justifiable within a wider frame of reference.

The above anecdote – as well as offering The British Psychological Society the chance to carry out an interesting survey via the pages of this book – illustrates the unique, intimate relationship which science fiction has always had to psychology. It is difficult to produce a succinct but comprehensive defintion of science fiction, but *They* meets one of the main criteria in that it is a story which in essence could not be told in any other genre. Science fiction writers are not more concerned with psychology than are practitioners in some other branches of literature – we bow respectfully towards Virginia Woolf and Patricia Highsmith – but nevertheless the special relationship exists.

It took many centuries for the experimental method to establish itself as a principal tool of science, but once it was in it was *in*, and in science fiction the author has unique facilities for creating analogues of fully controlled laboratory conditions. Just as the researcher in the lab uses ingenuity to eliminate every factor which might adulterate the results of an experiment, the science fiction writer is free to shine a laser-pure light on any aspect of human behaviour which interests him. Furthermore, he can manipulate the fictional environment in such a way as to excise every extraneous or clouding factor which might contaminate the experimental data.

Undoubtedly, literary purists will frown on the science fiction writer's methods. The classic seal-of-approval technique for creating a mainstream story is to take a group of characters, throw them together, let them interact and report what happens. But if one tries this technique in science fiction *nothing* will happen. That is to say, nothing of much interest to a science fiction buff. The genre has often been accused of featuring cardboard characters, but – philistine though it may sound – with certain kinds of story there can be a case for arguing that extensive characterization would get in the way of the story's legitimate objectives.

In other words, the idea is always an important and sometimes principal element in a science fiction story. Like it or not, when writing SF one has to start with an idea/situation/environment, and then devise a set of characters whose activities will interact with the idea/situation/environment in a way that explores all the intellectual potentials. That may not sound too promising from the point of view of the psychologist, who is primarily concerned with people, but in real life environment and circumstances play major roles in the formation of character and personality. Who is to say that the science fiction writer's method is not the best, the most fruitful, the most relevant to life itself?

The seven stories in this volume are adult science fiction – in contrast to space pantomimes like *Star Wars* – and in one way or another they deal with people under threat. Not the impersonal and unreal menace of invaders from Mars or giant ants, but with the genuine and far more disturbing threat which comes directly from within ourselves or, at a single remove, from products embodying our desire to impose our will on Nature.

In 40 years of reading and writing science fiction I have come across many notions which were supposed to be alarming, but I am no longer frightened by stories about ecology, death or deranged politicians with their fingers on the nuclear trigger. I don't like those ideas, but I don't lose any sleep over them. What does bother me is that old threat from *within*.

Possibly the most depressing words I've ever heard came from a mild-mannered Richard Attenborough, telling what he regarded as an amusing anecdote about the making of his *Oh What A Lovely War*. There were hundreds of extras in the film and they were issued with uniforms from wardrobe on a totally undiscriminating basis, the main concern being to give each an outfit which fitted reasonably well. Sir Richard went on to relate that during tea breaks the few who had been given officer uniforms, purely by chance, stood apart in little groups and didn't drink their tea with the 'other ranks'.

The story *is* funny, but it chilled my blood because it showed how easy it is for a dictator in any part of the world to modify ordinary people's behaviour in a radical way. What was even worse was that I understood the psychology involved and – for one vulnerable instant – almost sympathized with it. *If my behaviour could be altered by a few scraps of cloth and tawdry emblems*, I wondered, *what am I? Does what I regard as 'me' genuinely exist?*

That is one kind of threat from within, effective death of the personality, but another incident connected with war showed me that things could go even further.

During the evacuation of Dunkirk some of the rescue boats could not get as close to the beach as others, so the soldiers were told to divide into three groups: strong swimmers, moderate swimmers, and non-swimmers. Eyewitness reports show that some men, who would otherwise have been saved, drowned while trying to reach the boats because they had placed themselves in the wrong categories. They had died because some wayward element of their personalities, stalking the shadowy hinterland beyond rationality, would not allow them to admit that they were poor swimmers!

Again, I was horrified by those accounts – because I instinctively knew that I might have done the same thing. That's the real threat facing all of us. We might die next month, not as a consequence of war, crime, disease or accident, but because we don't understand what is going on inside our own heads.

Each of the following science fiction stories forms the starting point for an apposite commentary written by a psychologist. I found the commentaries interesting, informative and illuminating, and I was grateful for the opportunity to read them.

The insights I gained may, in some small way, help me to stay alive.

June 1986

1

COME TO VENUS MELANCHOLY

Thomas M. Disch

Is that you, John? Did someone just come in the door? Of course, it wouldn't be John. Not after all this time. It was because I was startled I said that. If you're there, whoever you are, do you mind if I talk to you?

And if you're not there?

Then I suppose you'll mind even less.

Maybe it was just the wind. Can the wind lift a latch? Maybe the latch is broken. Though it feels all right now. Or maybe I'm hallucinating. That's what happened, you know, in the classic sense-deprivation experiments. But I guess my case is different. I guess they've rigged me up some way so that can't happen.

Or maybe – Christ, I hope not! Maybe one of those hairy caterpillar things has got inside. I really couldn't stand that – thinking of the whole house, thinking of *me* crawling with those things. I've always hated bugs. So if you don't mind, I'll close the door.

Have you been trying to talk to me? I should have told you it's no use. I can't hear and I can't see. I'm broken. Do you see, there in the larger room, in each corner about five feet from the floor, how they've been smashed? My eyes and ears. Can't they be fixed somehow? If it's only a matter of vacuum tubes and diaphragms, there should be things of that sort downstairs. I'm opening the trapdoor now – do you see? And I've turned the lights on in the storeroom.

Oh hell, what's the use.

I mean *you're* probably not there, and even if you are, *he* probably thought to smash any spare tubes that were left. He thought of everything else.

Ah, but he was so handsome, he was really so handsome. He wasn't tall. After all, the ceiling here isn't much over six feet. But he was well-proportioned. He had deep-set eyes and a low brow. Sometimes, when he was worried or puzzled, he looked positively neanderthal.

John George Clay, that was his name. It sounds like part of a poem, doesn't it? John George Clay.

It wasn't so much his features – it was his manner. He took himself so seriously. And he was so dumb. It was that combination – the earnestness and the stupidity – that got to me. A sort of maternity syndrome I guess you'd call it. After all, I couldn't very well be his wife, could I?

Oh, when I think ...

Excuse me, I must be boring you. I'm sure you can't be that interested in a machine's love life. Perhaps I could read some aloud? He wasn't able to get at the microfilm library, so there's still plenty of books. When I'm by myself I don't do anything but read. It gets to seem as though the whole world was made of print. I look at it not for what's written there but as though it were a landscape. But I digress.

What do you like; poetry? novels? science textbooks? the encyclopaedia? I've read all of it so many times I could puke, if you'll excuse the expression. Whoever selected those books never heard of the Twentieth Century. There's nothing later than Robert Browning and Thomas Hardy – and would you believe it? – some of *that* has been expurgated? What did they think? That Browning would corrupt my morals? Or John's? Who can understand the bureaucratic mind?

Personally, I prefer poetry. You don't get tired of it so quickly. But maybe there's something you need to know, a point of information? If you could only *talk* to me. There must be some way to fix one of the mikes, there has to. Oh, *please!*

Oh hell.

I'm sorry, but it's just that it's so hard to believe that you're there. It gets to seem that I only talk to hear myself speak. I wish to God I *could* hear myself speak.

Maybe I just sound like static to you. Maybe he smashed the speakers too, I wouldn't be surprised. I don't know. There's no way I can tell. But I try my best, I think each word very slowly and try to enunciate mentally. And that way the caterpillars won't be confused. Ha!

I'm really glad you've come. I've been so long without company that I'm grateful even for the illusion of it. Don't take offence: since I can't ever be sure that you're there, you can't be more than illusion to me, whether you're real or not. A paradox. I welcome you in either case. With my doors wide open.

It's been fifteen years. Fifteen years, four months, twelve days – and three hours. I've got this built-in clock connected to what used to be the nerves of my stomach. I'm never in doubt about the time. It's always right there – like a bellyache. There've been whole days when I just listen to myself tick.

I was human once, you know. A married woman, with two children and a Master's in English Lit. A lot of good that ever did. My thesis was on some letters Milton wrote when he was Cromwell's Latin Secretary. Dull? You'd better believe it. Only I'll ever know *how* dull.

And yet ... now ... I'd give this whole damn planet to be back there in the academic squirrel cage, spinning that beautiful, dull wheel.

Do you like Milton? I've got the Complete Works, except for the things he wrote in Latin. I could read you something, if you'd like.

I used to read things to John, but he didn't much appreciate it. He enjoyed mysteries now and then. Or he'd study an electronics text under the scanner. But poetry bored him. It was worse than that: he seemed to hate poetry.

But maybe you're not like that. How can I tell? Do you mind if I just read it aloud for my own sake? Poetry's meant to be read aloud.

Il Penseroso. Do you know it? It gives me goosebumps every time. Figuratively.

Are you listening caterpillars?

How did you like that?

These pleasures, Melancholy, give,
And I with thee will choose to live.

Well, it's all a lot of gas. That's what dear John called it. He called it other
things too, and in each case I've come at last to agree. But such lovely gas. John
couldn't see that. He was a very simple sort, was John, and blind to the beauty of
almost anything except a rip-snorting sunset. And nude women. He was
uncomplicated. Without a sense of dialectics. He probably didn't understand half
the things I said to him. If ever there was a mismatched couple, it was us.

Spacemen and pioneers, you know, are supposed to be brighter than average.
And maybe John's IQ was a bit over one hundred but not by much, not by half a
sigma distance. After all, what did he need intelligence for? He was only a
glorified fur-trader. He'd go out into the swamp and hunt around for the slugs
the caterpillars laid there. He'd find one, maybe two, a day and keep them
undernourished so they'd grow slower. Every three weeks the ship would come
along, pick up the slugs and leave supplies.

I don't know what the slugs were for. They secreted something hallucinogenic,
but whether they were using it to cure psychoses or produce them, I never found
out. There was a war going on then, and my theory was that it all had something
to do with bacteriological warfare.

Maybe the war is still going on. But my theory – my *other* theory, I have lots of
them – is that the war is over and both sides have killed each other off.
Otherwise, wouldn't someone have come here for me by now?

But maybe they have – maybe that's why *you're* here! Is it?

Or maybe they don't care. Maybe I'm considered expendable.

Maybe, maybe, maybe! Oh God I could scream!

There now, I'm better again. These things pass.

Let me introduce myself. I've lost my good manners living out here alone like
this. My name is Selma Meret Hoffer. Hoffer's my maiden name. I use it now
that I'm divorced.

Why don't I tell you my story? It will pass the time as well as anything.
There's nothing much to tell about the time I was human. I won't say I was
ordinary – nobody ever believes that of themselves – but I probably didn't stand
out in a crowd. In fact, I tried very hard not to. I'm the introvert type.

I was only thirty-two when I found out I had leukaemia. The clinic gave me
six months. The alternative was this. Of course I chose this. I thought I was
lucky I could qualify. Most people don't have an alternative. Of those who do,
few refuse. In a way it seemed like an afterlife. The operation was certainly a
good facsimile of death.

After the surgery, they used fancy acids that attacked the body tissues
selectively. Anaesthetics didn't help much then. They whittled me down to the
bare nerves and dumped me into this tank and sealed me in.

Voilà – the Cyborg!

Between the sealing-in and shipping off there were months and months while I
was being wired up with the auxiliary memory banks and being taught to use my
motor nerves again. It's quite a traumatic experience, losing your body, and the
tendency is to go catatonic. What else is there to *do* after all? Naturally, I don't
remember much of that time.

3

Thomas M. Disch

They brought me out of it with shock treatment, and the first thing I remember was this room. It was stark and antiseptic then. I suppose it still is, but then it was starker and more antiseptic. I hated it with passion. The walls were that insipid creamy-green that's supposed to prevent eye-strain. They must have got the furniture from a fire sale at the Bauhaus. It was all aluminium tubes and swatches of bright-coloured canvas. And even so, by some miracle of design the room managed to seem cramped. It's fifteen feet square, but then it seemed no bigger than a coffin. I wanted to run right out of that room – and then I realized I couldn't: I was the room, the room was me.

I learned to talk very quickly so I could give them directions for redecorating. They argued at first. 'But, Miss Hoffer,' they'd say, 'We can't take an ounce more payload, and this furniture is Regulation.' That was the name of their god, Regulation. I said if it took an act of Congress they'd redecorate, and at last I got my way. Looking back on it, I suspect the whole thing was done to keep me busy. Those first few months when you're learning to think of yourself as a machine can be pretty rife with horror. A lot of the cyborgs just go psycho – usually it's some compulsion mechanism. They just keep repeating the Star-Spangled Banner or say the rosary or some such thing. Like a machine.

They say it's not the same thing – a cybernetic organism and a machine, but what do they know about it? They're not cyborgs.

Even when I was human I was never any good at mechanical things. I could never remember which way you turned a screwdriver to put in a screw – and there I was with my motor nerves controlling a whole miniature factory of whatsits and thingumabobs. My index finger powered a Mix-master. My middle toe turned the tumblers that locked the door. My ...

That reminds me: have I locked you in? I'm sorry, when I closed the door I locked it without thinking. You wouldn't want to go out now though. According to my stomach, it's the middle of the night. You're better off in here for the night than in a Venusian swamp, eh?

Well, that's the story of my life. When I had the reflexes of a well-trained rat, they packed me up and shipped me off to Venus at the cost of some few million dollars.

The very last thing I learned before leaving was how to use the microfilm scanner. I read direct from the spindle. By the time I learned how poorly the library had been stocked it was too late to complain. I'd been planted out in the swamp, and John George Clay had moved in. What did I care about the library then? I was in love.

And what do *you* care about any of this? Unless you're a cyberneticist doing a study on malfunction. I should be good for a chapter, at least.

Excuse me, I'm probably keeping you awake. I'll let you get some sleep. I have to sleep sometimes myself, you know. Physically I can go without, but I still have a subconscious that likes to dream –

Of forests and enchantments drear,
Where more is meant than meets the ear

And so goodnight.

Still awake?

I couldn't go to sleep myself, so I've been reading. I thought maybe you'd like to hear a poem. I'll read you *Il Penseroso*. Do you know it? It's probably the

4

finest poem in the language. It's by John Milton.

Oh dear, did I keep you up with that poem last night? Or did I only dream that I did? If I was noisy, you'll excuse me, won't you?

Now if you were John, you'd be raging mad. He didn't like to be woken up by –

> *Such notes as, warbled to the string,*
> *Drew iron tears down Pluto's cheek*
> *And made Hell grant what Love did seek!*

Indeed he didn't. John had a strange and fixed distaste for that wonderful poem, which is probably the finest in the language. He was, I think, jealous of it. It was a part of me he could never possess, even though I was his slave in so many other ways. Or is 'housekeeper' a more polite expression?

I tried to explain the more difficult parts to him, the mythology and the exotic words, but he didn't *want* to understand. He made fun of it. He had a way of saying the lines that made them seem ridiculous. Mincingly, like this:

> *Come, pensive Nun, devout and pure,*
> *Sober, steadfast, and demure.*

When he'd do that, I'd just ignore him. I'd recite it to myself. He'd usually leave the house then, even if it was night. He knew I worried myself sick when he was away. He did it deliberately. He had a genius for cruelty.

I suppose you're wondering if it worked both ways – whether he loved me. The question must have occurred to you. I've given it quite a lot of thought myself, and I've come to the conclusion that he did. The trouble was he didn't know how to express it. Our relationship was necessarily so *cerebral,* and cerebration wasn't John's *forte.*

That was the idea behind throwing us together the way they did. They couldn't very well send a man off by himself for two years. He'd go crazy. Previously they'd send married couples, but the homicide rate was incredible. Something like 30 per cent. It's one thing for a pioneer family to be off by itself in, say, the Yukon. It's something else here. In a social vacuum like this, sex is explosive.

You see, apart from going out for the slugs and nursing them in the shed outside, there's nothing to do. You can't build out here. Things just sort of sink into the mud unless, like me, they're built like a houseboat. You can't grow things – including children. It's a biologist's paradise, but they need hundreds of slug stations and there aren't biologists available in that quantity. Besides, all the *good* biologists are in Venusburg, where there's research facilities. The problem then is to find the minimum number of personnel that can man a station for two years of idleness without exploding. The solution is one man and one cyborg.

Though, not, as you can see, an infallible solution. I tried to kill him, you know. It was a silly thing to do. I regret it now.

But I'd rather not talk about, if you don't mind.

You've been here for two days now – fancy that!

Excuse me for keeping to myself so long, but I had a sudden acute attack of self-consciousness, and the only cure for that is solitude. I invoke Milton's lovely Melancholy, and then everything is better. The beasts quiet down. Eurydice is set free again. Hell freezes over. Ha!

5

But that's a lot of nonsense. Let's not talk always about me. Let's talk about *you*. Who are you? What are you like? How long will you be staying here on Venus? Two days we've been together and still I know nothing about you.

Shall I tell you what I imagine you to be like? You're tall – though I hope not so tall as to find that low room uncomfortable – with laughing blue eyes and a deep spaceman's tan. You're strong yet gentle, gay yet basically serious. You're getting rather hungry.

And everywhere you go you leave little green slugs behind you that look like runny lime Jell-O.

Oh hell, excuse me, I'm always saying excuse me. I'm sick of it. I'm sick of half-truths and reticences.

Does that frighten you? Do you want out already? Don't go now – I've just *begun* to fight. Listen to the whole story, and then – maybe – I'll unlock the door.

By the way, in case you are getting hungry there may still be some rations left down in the storeroom. I don't want it to be said that I'm lacking in hospitality. I'll open the trapdoor and turn on the light, but you'll have to look for them yourself. Of course, you're worried that I'll lock you in down there. Well, I can't promise that I won't. After all, how do I know you're *not* John? Can you prove it? You can't even prove you exist!

I'll leave the trapdoor open in case you should change your mind.

For my next number I'd like to do *Il Penseroso* by John Milton. Quiet down, caterpillars, and listen. It's the finest poem in the language.

How about that? Makes you want to go right out and join a Trappist monastery, doesn't it? That's what John once said.

I'll say one thing for John: he never tattled. He could have had me taken away and turned to scrap. All he had to do was give the word when the ship came down to pick up the slugs, but when there was company he could always put a good face on things. He was a gentleman in every sense of the word.

How did it happen then – if he was a gentleman and I was a lady? Whose fault was it? Good God, I've asked myself that question a hundred times. It was both our faults and neither's. It was the fault of the situation.

I can't remember now which of us was the first to start talking about sex. We talked about everything that first year, and sex is very much a part of everything. What harm could there be in it, after all, with me sealed in a steel tank? And how could we *avoid* the subject? He'd mention an old girlfriend, or tell a slightly shady joke, and I'd be reminded of something by degrees ...

The thing is that there's an immense curiosity between the sexes that almost never is satisfied. Things that men never know about women, and *vice versa*. Even beween a man and a wife, there is a gulf of unmentionables. Maybe especially between a man and a wife. But between John and me there seemed to be nothing to prevent perfect candour. What possible harm could it do?

Then ... the next thing ... I don't remember which of us started that either. We should have known better. The borderline between perfect candour and erotic fantasy is no wider than an adjective. But it happened imperceptibly, and before we knew quite what we were doing, it had been done. It was already a habit.

When I realized exactly what we were doing, of course, I laid down the law. It was an unhealthy situation, it had to stop. At first John was agreeable. He was embarrassed, like a little boy who's been found out in some naughtiness. We told each other it was over and done with.

But it had become, as I've said, a habit. I have a rather more vivid imagination than John and he had grown dependent on me. He asked for new stories, and I refused. He got angry then and wouldn't speak to me, and finally I gave in. I was in love with him, you see, in my own ectoplasmic way, and this was all I could do to show it.

Every day he wanted a new story. It's hard to make the same tired old tale seem new in every telling. Scheherazade was supposed to have stood up for a thousand and one nights, but after only thirty I was wearing thin. Under the strain I sort of retreated into myself.

I read poetry, lot of poetry, but mostly Milton. Milton had a very calming effect on me – like a mil- town if you'll excuse the pun.

The pun – that's what did it. It was the last turn of the screw, a simple pun.

It seems that when I read, I sometimes read aloud without realizing it. That's what John has told me. It was all right during the day when he was off in the swamp, and when he was here in the evenings we'd talk with each other. But he needed more sleep than I did, and when I was left on my own, after he'd gone to bed, I'd read. There was nothing else to do. Usually I'd read some long Victorian novel, but at the time I'm speaking of I mostly read *Il Penseroso*.

He shouldn't have made fun of it. I guess he didn't realize how important it had become to me. It was like a pool of pure water in which I could wash away the grime of each day. Or else he was angry for being woken up.

Do you remember the part, right near the beginning, where it says:

> But hail, thou goddess sage and holy.
> Hail, divinist Melancholy

Of course you do, you probably know the whole thing as well as I do by now. Well, when John heard that he broke out laughing, a nasty laugh, and I, well, I couldn't really stand that, could I? I mean Milton means so *much* to me, and the thing was that he began to sing this *song*. This awful song. Oh, it was a clever idea, I suppose, when first he thought of it, but the combination of that vulgar tune and his perversion of Milton's noble words – though he claims that's how he understood the words when I first read them to him. And I still maintain that the second *i* in divinist is pronounced like a long e – it was aggravating in the extreme, I can't tell you how much it upset me.

Do I *have* to reapeat them?

> Come to Venus, Melancholy Baby
> Cuddle up and don't be shy.

And so on. It's not only a bad pun – it's a misquotation as well. It should be *Hail*, not *Come*. So vulgar. It gives me goosebumps even now.

I told him to leave the house right that minute. I told him not to come back till he was ready to apologize. I was so angry I forgot it was the middle of the night. As soon as he was out of the door, I was ashamed of myself.

He came back in five minutes. He apologized outside the door, and I let him in. He had the large polyetheline bag over his shoulder that he uses to gather up the slugs, but I was so relieved I didn't think anything of it.

He put them on the visual receptors. There must have been twenty, all told, and each one was about a foot long. They fought each other to get right on the lens because it was slightly warmer there. There were twenty of them, foul, gelatinous slugs, crawling on my *eyes*, oh God! I shut off my eyes and I shut off my ears, because he was singing that song again, and I locked the doors and I left him like that for five days while I recited *Il Penseroso*.

But when I come to that one line, I could never say it.

It was perhaps the hallucinogens, though he might just as well have done it in his right mind. He had every reason to. But I prefer to think it was the hallucinogens. He had been all that time with nothing to eat. I've never been five days without food, so I don't know how desperate that would make one.

In any case, when I came to myself again and opened my eyes I found I had no eyes to open. He'd smashed every receptor in the room, even the little mobile attachment for cleaning. The strange thing was how little I cared. It seemed hardly to matter at all.

I opened the door for five minutes so he could get out. Then I closed it so no more caterpillars could get in. But unlocked. That way John was free to come back.

But he never did.

The supply ship was due in two days later, and I guess John must have spent that time in the shed where he kept the slugs. He must have been alive, otherwise the pilot of the supply ship would have come in the door to look for him. And nobody ever came in the door again.

Unless you did.

They just left me here, deaf and blind and half- immortal, in the middle of the Venusian swamp. If only I could starve to death – or wear out – or rust – or really go insane. But I'm too well made for that. You'd think after all the money they spent on me, they'd want to salvage what they could, wouldn't you?

I have a deal to make with you. I'll let you out the door, if you'll do something for me. Fair enough?

Down in the storeroom there are explosives. They're so safe a child could use them. John did, after all. If I remember rightly, they're on the third shelf down on the west wall – little black boxes with DANGER written on them in red. You pull out the little pin and set the timing mechanism for anything from five minutes to an hour. It's just like an alarm clock.

Once they're set, just leave them in the storeroom. They'll be nearer to me down there. I'm over the storeroom. Then run like hell. Five minutes should be time enough, shouldn't it? I'll only want to read a bit of *Il Penseroso*.

Is it a deal? The trapdoor is open, and I'm opening the outside door now just to show you I'm in earnest.

While you set to work, I think I'll read something to pass the time.

Hello? I'm waiting. Is everything all right? Are you still there? Or were you ever there? Oh please, *please* – I want to explode. That would be so wonderful. Please, I *beg* of you!

I'm still waiting.

Why was my breeding ordered and prescribed
As of a person separate to God,
Designed for great exploits, if I must die

8

Betrayed, captive, and both my eyes put out?
John Milton, *Samson Agonistes*.

We can look at the story of Selma Meret Hoffer from a number of viewpoints. We could examine the surface narrative of her progress from married English graduate with a master's degree in Milton, through disease, translation to cyborg, relationship with John Clay, slughunter, and eventual abandonment, damaged and deprived on Venus. A literary analysis might view the story as a seventeenth century moral tale updated and moved to Venus, with enough clues to let us untangle the main themes of moral choice, compatibility of partners, and the need to understand a failed author (Hoffer, the cyborg, acting as a failed Milton). If you know about Milton – the moral themes of his poetry, his political work as Cromwell's Latin secretary, his struggle with blindness – you can explain the events on Venus perfectly well. Or can you?

Analyses like this are common among people who study literature. They require quite a lot of information about the authors concerned – about their personal experiences, and ideas, as reflected in the whole spectrum of their writing. Reading about people's lives, and discussing their ideas on morality, education, politics and human relationships can be a good stimulus for our own thinking. It challenges us to review our ideas – to account for happenings and events which we might not yet have given any attention to. This, of course, is some of our attraction to literature of all sorts – from Milton's poems and essays to science fiction stories. Talking and reflecting about things is essential if we are to clarify our ideas, and to produce accounts and explanations which are reasonably self-consistent. When we haven't spent much time thinking about a topic, we are likely to have contradictory ideas about it – if indeed we have much to say at all.

But does this really help us to *know* more about the issues themselves? An account that doesn't contain contradictions is probably better than the one before it that did, but consistency isn't the same as being right. We all have expectations about human behaviour ('she shouldn't have got involved – I knew it would end in tears') and explanations for it, too ('It's the way he was brought up'; 'his father was just the same'; 'anyone that reads as much as she does ...'). When different people put forward different explanations or predictions about some aspect of human behaviour, it is important to study the behaviour itself, rather than just to talk about it. Talking might well result in agreement between the discussants, but as long as we confine ourselves to discussion, we can have no real idea whether our agreed views really have much to do with anything in the world outside our discussion. To progress beyond chat, we must begin to relate our words and ideas to particular events, and to things that we can observe.

We need to be sure about what we mean by the words we use (when can two people be said to be 'compatible'?; what is an 'hallucination'?; what is 'melancholia'?); we need to be sure about the pattern of events that we are trying to explain (are murder victims more likely to have been killed by people they live with than by strangers?; what happens to our senses in deprived environments?; what happens when people live together for a long time in a close confinement?); and we need to evaluate different explanations by either examining evidence that is already available, or by carrying out experiments which produce relevant new evidence. Unless we can produce explanations and predictions based directly on systematic observation of the behaviour and events we are interested in, we can have little faith in our abilities to make reliable predictions about future events, or about the likely utility of any suggestions for changing current practices.

Psychology is the study of human behaviour. Most people who study psychology are committed to a process of observation, explanation, and prediction. We differ a good deal in the aspects of human behaviour which we find most interesting to study; in the sorts of things we choose to observe; in the kinds of explanations we put forward; and in the kind of things we make predictions about, and indeed, in the kinds of predictions we make. Even so, there is general agreement amongst psychologists about the need to observe, and to explain, and to predict, rather than just to discuss and reflect.

We can analyse *Come to Venus Melancholy* by an explanation of the *story*, or by a discussion on topics such as: being melancholy; working in confined situations; becoming friends or lovers or enemies; hallucinogenic substances; sensory deprivation; or free will. All of these topics occur somewhere in the story, but none of them, exclusively, *is* the story. We often read stories, or see films, because they raise interesting issues for us to think about. The focus of the rest of this commentary, and of all the commentaries which follow this one, is about a few of the *issues* raised in each story. We *won't* be concerned about what the story 'really' means; or why the author wrote it; or whether the style needs to be polished; or indeed with any analysis of the story *as* a story. Instead, we will review issues from a psychological viewpoint, and describe some of the studies which psychologists have carried out in order to extend their knowledge beyond the stages of discussion and reflection.

When you discuss stories, it becomes clear that each story raises a host of issues; we each find different aspects of the stories fascinating, and want to talk about the topics which interest us most. It is impossible to cover more than a few of the issues raised by any story, without volumes! Each commentary offered here covers just a few of the themes raised in each story; so there is a danger that you will be dissatisfied with commentaries which fail to discuss issues that *you* want to see explored! Hopefully, though, by the time you have read all the stories and commentaries, you can begin to approach these other themes, using a more psychological approach than you could have done at the start.

In this commentary we consider two main themes: the development and dissolution of close personal relationships, and the problems posed when people work in hazardous environments. Both themes are relevant to the real problems faced by humans working together in dangerous environments, such as the deep sea, the Antarctic, and space, as well as to the disasters which befell Clay, and Hoffer the cyborg.

CLOSE PERSONAL RELATIONSHIPS

A central theme in *Come to Venus Melancholy* is the relationship between Selma Meret Hoffer and John George Clay. Almost everyone needs the support of others; the mutual needs of Hoffer and Clay in the story are quite obvious (Hoffer would not have had the opportunity to become a cyborg unless humans working in remote and hostile places needed cyborg support; Clay needed the physical support system provided by Hoffer). The idea of sending a cyborg and a human arose, we are told, because 'They couldn't very well send a man off by himself for two years. He'd go crazy'. We know that there are people who can tolerate long periods of isolation from others, but such people are quite rare; for almost everyone, other people are extremely important for maintaining both physical and mental health.

In very close personal relationships, such as marriage, when one partner dies we find that the bereaved spouse is far more likely to die shortly after the death of their partner (i.e. within two years) than would be predicted from tables of life expectancy. This observation cannot be explained away by attributing the higher death rates to contagious diseases and the like. Marital breakdown is often associated with complaints such as ulcers, heart disease and depression. It is also associated with a higher suicide rate and with problems of alcohol abuse, as has been shown by Bloom and co-workers in 1978. These findings cannot simply be attributed to something like 'worry' because one can identify people within marriages who spend a good deal of time worrying, yet who do not develop medical problems. Coronary patients, considered as a group, have been shown to have a relatively small number of friends. 'Loners' are more likely to have heart attacks. Their work patterns can create health problems – overwork can give rise to a range of stress-related illnesses. 'Significant life events' like starting a family, getting married, getting divorced, the death of a spouse, children leaving home, and retiring, carry risks and are stressful. All of these are characterized by changes in close relationships, which can make us re- evaluate our personal worth, and place in the world.

Why do we need friends so much? Try to list some of the reasons why you have friends, and add to the list any reasons why friends have you! Here is our list. It isn't complete, or true for every friendship:

11

- for conversation and to avoid loneliness
- to provide a sense of belonging
- to share beliefs and attitudes; to support our views about the world
- to talk about ourselves
- to provide mutual support – for instance to help each other to achieve common goals, or to provide emotional support
- to offer a chance to help other people
- to reassure ourselves of our own worth.

Making lists of things is quite easy to do, and is part of the reflecting and discussing process which helps us clarify our ideas. All the reasons in our list add up to a common theme of 'psychological propping up', for example. But can we study friendship, and other social relationships, directly? Only relatively recently, say in the last ten years or so, have we begun to look at social relationships by carrying out careful studies of human behaviour. Why should this be? One reason is that everyone 'knows' all about social relationships anyway. We all engage in them; we all have personal views about them; it somehow is 'natural' to let things roll along, and 'unnatural' to interfere with them to bring about any kind of change. Interestingly, we do not have such qualms about interference in a person's health, or their state of knowledge, or the degree of skill they have. In all these cases it is socially acceptable to consult some professional person with a view to improving things. Yet we all go through difficulties in our close relationships. Most of us lose friends at some time that we would rather have kept up with; most of us have experienced friendships going wrong, or simply failing to mature beyond a certain level of intimacy. (In the case of Selma Hoffer and John Clay, the breakdown in their relationship proved to be almost fatal for him, and emotionally disastrous for her.) Making and keeping friends requires a certain degree of social skill: friendships have to be started off; they must develop; they have to be made to work, and from time to time they need some repair. Few of us take time to study and improve these skills. Let us consider some of the skills which are necessary for friendship formation. We can consider these in terms of the time sequence of the relationship.

Meeting People
Before friendships begin, there must be opportunities for meeting people who are likely to be good future friends. This involves some skill in selecting situations where such people are likely to be found. For example, if one's primary interests are fell walking, ornithology and botany, then structured meeting places such as parties and discos are probably best viewed as places to go just to have fun rather than to meet kindred spirits.

First Impressions
How important are first impressions, for example physical appearance? Do

physically attractive people have better relationships and more opportunities for attracting? The research evidence shows that people *do not*
approach the most physically attractive people, rather we approach people
who are as attractive as we think can be approached without fear of
rejection.

How do we go about deciding who it is worth trying to be friends with?
First we should recognize whether the person has any interest at all in
extending their current circle of friends. Some people are quite satisfied
with a small intimate circle of friends, others prefer a large number of less
intimate acquaintances. In either case, we need to know whether the person
has any intention of widening their current circle by including us in it. Lots
of other good friendships will deter them from being involved. At the other
end of the scale, research evidence shows that people with a low estimate of
their own value seek out the friendship of others less. Let us suppose that
we progress beyond this stage and find someone that has not ruled out the
possibility of increasing their circle of friends. We now need to make
judgements about each other to decide whether a friendship is desirable or
indeed possible.

Finding out about People: Showing What We Are Like

Finding out about people comes far more naturally to us than we are often
aware of. Think about the way we introduce each other. It is quite common
for a mutual acquaintance to introduce two people along these lines: 'John
come and meet Selma. John Clay. Selma Hoffer. Selma and I both studied
English Literature at college. John here is Chairman of the local Action
Group trying to stop them running that damn road through the forest – he
teaches biology at the High School'.

We commonly introduce people in terms of the jobs which they do.
Knowing that somebody is, say, a teacher provides a lot of information
about their income, social standing and the like. It allows us to bring a good
deal of knowledge that we have about schools and teachers to the fore, to
prepare for the conversation. These frames of knowledge are extremely
useful to us. They remind us that teachers have all had a college education
(which might suggest some intellectual starting points for the conversation); teachers usually have long school holidays (which opens up a series of
starting points on interesting hobbies, and outdoor pursuits); teachers are,
by and large, interested in young people and educational matters in general
(so we can talk about particular young people, particular schools, and about
educational topics which are currently the subject of political discussion).
Conversely we may have frames of knowledge about teachers which are all
rather negative. We might view them as being overprivileged, underworked
and oppressive of the young people put into their care. This latter frame of
knowledge is likely to lead to us terminating the interaction rather quickly.

So even brief verbal descriptions provide us with a good deal of information about people based on our past experiences and our stored knowledge. We obviously also gather a good deal of information about people from the clothes they wear, and from the gestures they make. In England at least, it is possible to pick up information from people's accents. Accents label regional origins, and sometimes social origins too.

As soon as people strike up a conversation they provide a whole range of cues, sometimes intentionally, sometimes not, about themselves which are available for subsequent comment, for example 'When I lived in Manchester'.

People differ a good deal in their abilities to find out about others in a friendly and reassuring way. Phrases like 'you made an interesting remark about ... would you tell me more about it?'; our use of nods, smiles and gestures to show interest in the remarks which a new acquaintance is making, and other gambits can all smooth our social relationships. There is a large range of bodily gestures we make when we talk to people, as you will know if you have ever seen a film of people meeting which is played back fast. People appear to dance together and to move in synchrony. As well as these gross body movements there is a whole range of behaviour associated with looking patterns, such as looking people straight in the eye, breaking off gaze, and the like. (For obvious reasons, these gestural devices cannot be shared by a cyborg, and would form a considerable barrier to their social relationships.)   The process of extracting and providing information is critically important to friendship formation. There needs to be a good deal of turn taking. For example, people who talk too much about themselves are labelled boring; people who talk too little are viewed as being socially gauche. Asking people for lots of intimate information at an early stage is viewed as being nosy and pushy; providing too much information about oneself is viewed as being indiscreet. We are also likely to interpret such an interaction as a sign that such a person tells everyone rather than just us.

So, to summarize this early meeting phase, both the people getting acquainted need a range of skills for exploring the other person, with a view to making a judgement about whether they are likely to be a satisfactory friend or not. As well as the content of what is said, such as attitudes expressed about particular topics of mutual interest, the ways in which we find out about each other are also very important. Most people have had experience at a social gathering of feeling they are being grilled by a perfect stranger; similarly most of us have had the experience of trying to initiate a conversation with somebody who is quite unforthcoming in their responses. Both of these circumstances arise because of a mismatch between the two people in their expectations about what reasonable levels of personal exposure are.

Getting the Relationship Going
Birds of a feather flock together. Opposites attract. Do you agree with

either, neither or both of these sayings? And where do they leave our view of friendship formation? Steve Duck reports that research results cluster neatly into three piles; one pile shows that people who are similar are attracted (birds of a feather flock together); another pile shows that people who are dissimilar to each other become friends (opposites attract); the third pile shows that neither similarity nor dissimilarity seems to be the sole basis of friendship formation.

How can we make sense of these apparent contradictions both in our folk sayings and in a large collection of research studies? Suppose we think about the features of people that we judge to be important for similarity or complementarity to work. Try and write down a few things to illustrate the proposition that similarity is attractive; now try and write down a few things to illustrate the assertion that opposites are attractive. Generating a list of attributes likely to show neither similarity nor complementarity is easy to do – so we will do it for you! Shoe size; front door colour; eye colour; number of teeth ... How did you get on with your list of similarities? The research literature shows that friends usually have the same skin colour, similar social backgrounds, the same religion, and similar attitudes and beliefs to each other. They usually have a rather similar view of the world. We can see that this is quite consistent with our early views of the roles which friendship fulfils for us. Associating with people who have the same ideas as our own about issues that we are concerned with can give us important emotional support. If the people that we choose to associate with view the world in the same way that we do, it supports and reinforces our belief that we have a view of the world that is appropriate. On the other hand if we associate with people routinely who have quite different attitudes and beliefs to our own we are likely to find this emotionally and cognitively distressing.

This early association between people who share similar attitudes and beliefs has been widely found in the area of friendship research. Much of the initial interaction between people is concerned with the exploration of attitudes because of their importance in maintaining our views about the world. Our judgements about the similarity of other people's attitudes to our own are far more wide reaching than one would expect on the basis of common-sense analysis. They pervade our judgements about people in a number of areas quite unrelated to attitudes themselves. Byrne has conducted a great deal of research on the roles which attitudes and beliefs play in personal judgements, and has produced a number of interesting results.

- Jurors impose lighter sentences on convicted persons whom they judge to have similar attitudes to their own.
- Teachers pay more attention to children with similar attitudes to their own.

- Bank managers give bigger loans to people they perceive to have similar attitudes to their own.
- Studies of psychotherapists show that patients whose attitudes are similar to those of the therapist recover faster than those with different attitudes to the therapist. The latter group are judged to have relatively intractable problems by the therapists.

There is a lot of research which shows that the more similar two people's attitudes are, the more they will like each other. This is enhanced if the attitudes on which they are similar are of particlar importance to the person and if these attitudes are rare. So two people who are both adamant in their belief that they have been visited by people from outer space are likely to be attracted strongly to each other, because of both the strength of their belief and of the rarity of this belief. In our initial dealings with people we spend a good deal of time reading and interpreting other people's attitudes, and displaying our own. As well as extracting information on particular topics we also extract information on what we might call personal cognitive style – that is to say things like their tolerance for other people, openness, extent of personal passions, and the assumptions that they make about life in general.

What about notions of complementarity? Studies on married couples have shown that many couples are opposite in major personality characteristics and show complementary needs. For example a dominant partner and a submissive partner; a helpful partner and a needy partner, and the like. This sounds as if it could apply to Selma Hoffer and John Clay, doesn't it? Again, this idea of complementarity makes sense in terms of our original list of functions of friendships. Here long-term friends are satisfying each other's personality needs as well as providing support for individual world views.

Uncovering information about personality requires yet a further range of skills; again we must know what to look for, and what information to provide ourselves in exchange. Frank, open, honest disclosure about one's most intimate thoughts early on in a conversation with someone can be acutely embarrassing for the listener! Similarly, never expressing feelings about events and circumstances to friends can be unrewarding for the relationship and can be seen as showing a closed and defensive personality. Both these styles of behaviour lead to withdrawal of the partner. As we disclose information about ourselves, and find out more about each other, we need to be able to judge how best to present information about ourselves. Information needs to be leaked out over a period of time rather than presented all in a mass, if it is to be useful to the person receiving it. This process of presenting and obtaining information, beginning with surface features, then uncovering attitudes and beliefs, and later making discoveries about personality and personal needs, can be likened to two onions peeling layers each off the other; it can be seen as an extensive exploration

16

and evaluation of the likelihood of mutual psychological support.

Increasing Intimacy

For close friends most social distances are reduced. This reduction in physical distances could hardly be better demonstrated than the relationship between Clay and the cyborg! Let's consider the way that friendship develops into love and the formation of intimate relationships, so that we can reflect on the problems experienced by John Clay and Selma Hoffer.

Friends are likely to sit closer to each other; to touch more frequently; to have more prolonged periods of eye contact; and to be generally far less formal in their body postures and gestures than they would be with people with whom they are less acquainted. Friendship, of course, is a way of acting; friends need to demonstrate affection to each other. As well as physical proximity, there is a range of verbal cues about friendship relationships. Consider for example the range of ways of addressing a person: 'Sir'; 'Mr Smith'; 'Ronald'; 'Ron'; 'You old so and so'. Each of these conveys a different level of intimacy between the speaker and recipient. Of course these cues are available for others to detect; the cues therefore are signals not only between the partners but also to others outside the relationship about the degree of friendship and intimacy which exists between the partners.

Rubin has studied loving couples, and reports a very consistent pattern of non-verbal behaviour which develops as the relationship develops. These signals reveal both to the partners and to the outside world the developing level of intimacy between the couple. Where such patterns were absent these were seen to cause problems for outsiders about how to treat the partners.

When Friends Become Lovers

Why do friends turn into lovers? Surveys about people's approval for, and frequency of, engaging in pre-marital sexual intercourse have shown that these attitudes and behaviours are related to a whole range of social factors such as one's religious beliefs; the age at which one first engaged in intercourse; friends' sexual practices and the like. In a study by Cate and Christopher in 1982, they asked people about the factors which mattered most in their own decisions to have pre-marital sex. These responses could be classified into a number of headings as follows.

- Positive feelings: couples who loved each other and felt committed to the relationship were more likely to have discussed their feelings and the role that sex would play in their relationship. If they both felt that sex was a positive step forward, deepening their relationship, then they were more likely to sleep together.

17

- Arousal: level of sexual arousal was often a significant factor in the decision to engage in pre- marital sex!
- Obligation and pressure: different social groups have different patterns of sexual relationships. In some societies pre-marital sex is extremely rare; in others very common. This generalization is also true of different social groups within any society. Decisions to engage in pre-marital sex were often reported to be coloured by expectations of friends; boys were more likely to report pressure from friends than were girls.
- Circumstances: a range of other social circumstances such as whether or not the partners had been consuming alcohol; or whether they were meeting for a particular social event of some significance were also reported to contribute to their decision to embark on sexual relationships.

Girls were more likely to report positive feelings as being a major factor in contributing towards their decision to engage in pre-marital sex, as were relatively sexually inexperienced people of either sex.

Once a sexual relationship has been initiated the problem changes to one of managing both the social and physical consequences. Sex obviously is not a simple physical event but is something of great significance to personal relationships. Sexual pleasures and problems reflect and are reflected by the nature of these relationships between people. This is illustrated by studies on American couples carried out by Markman and his co-workers in 1982 which showed that three out of five females and two out of five males who were dissatisfied with their marriage reported no sexual pleasure for about a year before they complained about the social aspects of their marriage. We can conclude that sexual adjustment and marital adjustment are strongly related.

This sort of finding, of course, is not constrained to sexual activities. The quality of a relationship in general relates to the quality of the activities which the partners engage in. Our feelings and our actions are interdependent. If we do things in the company of a friend which provide mutual pleasure this is likely to lead to a good relationship; on the other hand, if our mutual activities are rather unrewarding then we interpret the friendship as being rather unrewarding. This interdependence of feelings and behaviours is illustrated in a study by Peplau and co-workers in 1977. Again the topic of this study was sexual relationships. The researchers were interested in the role of sexual behaviour in the development of the relationship. Couples who engaged in sexual activities within one month of meeting usually attributed their behaviour to sexual desire; couples who waited six months or more, usually attributed the onset of sexual relationships to love. The first group often argued that sexual behaviour facilitated their loving relationship; the latter group often argued that love preceded and led up to their sexual relationships. The reported closeness of the relationship was about the same for both groups, as was the break-up rate. This study illustrates the inter-dependence of feelings and actions. Feelings lead to actions; actions lead to feelings.

Getting Married

Newcomb reviewed the national census data for 1977 in the USA and reports that between 2 and 5 per cent of the adult population were cohabiting. In a survey sent to part of the sample, about one quarter of people reported that they never discussed it, just did it!

Let's consider the situation where dating couples decide to get married. At this point their relationship becomes socially recognized and becomes a formal one. They live together and are committed to a relationship which has implications that they might well raise a family together. People who marry have expectations about a prolonged relationship which will conform to many formal and informal rules. When people are married they need to work out the roles each partner will perform; and need a good deal of forward planning. In addition, the relationship will need a good deal of maintenance as it progresses and as the personalities of the partners slowly evolve.

Huston in 1981 and his co-workers identified four tracks to marriage:

- Accelerated–arrested. These couples plan marriage within two to three months of meeting; and carry it out a year or so later.
- Accelerated: these couples plan marriage within five months of meeting and are married within a further five months.
- Intermediate: these couples plan marriage after about a year and marry within eight months.
- Delayed: these couples delay both the planning and carrying out stage.

Couples in the intermediate and delayed stages are the ones who experience most problems in their marital relationships. The accelerated–arrested and the accelerated group both reported greatest closeness and affection. The intermediate couples reported the lowest levels of affection and were least likely to work together on tasks.

The shortest courtships are characterized by the couples working out good ways to work together fairly quickly. They cope with problems in adjusting to every- day tasks and collaborate by joint decision making. They do not necessarily report more love in the early stages of their relationships. In contrast the longer courtships are characterized by higher levels of love and affection. However, partners have great difficulty in sustaining their relationship.

Mental problems are strongly associated with a poor fit between partners' expectations and beliefs about their roles, as demonstrated by Newcomb and Bentler in 1981. Rigid role specialization is associated with lower marital happiness; relationships in which activities and mutual responsibilities and duties are negotiated are more successful.

It should be clear from all this discussion that love is not everything in a relationship. The relationship is the behaviour of the partners; high levels of affection will not in the long term compensate for inabilities to handle the realities of everyday living. These activities in themselves must be mutually pleasurable. For this to take place couples must negotiate roles and patterns of activity.

Maintaining Relationships

Aquaintance leads to the swapping of attitudes and beliefs, and in turn leads to exchanging information about feelings and personality; secrets, and past life events of significance are exchanged. At this point there is a good deal of mutual exposure and mutual vulnerability. As friendships develop there is a need to focus on the relationship itself and on its development. Then development and repair skills come to the fore. One key to this maintenance is the notion of fairness, according to Walster and co-workers in 1978. We give up relationships which seem to be one way: if we seem to be getting too much out of a relationship we typically feel guilty; if we get too little we typically feel angry. So benefiting too much from a relationship can be just as destructive as benefiting too little.

Each partner makes a contribution of some sort to the friendship and reaps rewards. Contributions and rewards might be exchanging information; offering help; love; esteem and the like. Relationships are likely to crumble if partners feel that their contribution is out of scale with the rewards they obtain. Relationships need to be reviewed regularly to assess their equality, and to resolve any conflicts, arguments and tensions that may exist. Kaplan in 1976 showed that the commonest response to stress within a relationship is to suppress feelings – thus ignoring the problem. Presumably partners hope the stress will pass. What seems to happen though is that suppression leads to anger, hostility and resentment, so that the trouble is bottled up – perhaps to explode later. A better approach is to discuss feelings gently and to try actively to resolve differences in a constructive manner.

When relationships are in crisis, other people such as friends and family can be very important in helping each partner to see the other's viewpoint and helping bring about some self-evaluation; and in emphasizing structures and the legality of the situation; and in the event of a breakdown in the relationship, to provide support during the period of emotional upset and distress for each partner.

Obvious kinds of advice are to suggest that people who are troubled within their relationships should explain their feelings to their partners and look for ways in which difficulties can be resolved. If negative feelings towards partners have developed then the partner needs to be re-evaluated in a far more global sense, away from short-term niggles and in terms of their general more positive attributes. The theme of joint activities should also be borne in mind. If relationships seem to be foundering, then partners should actively engage in activities which they know will provide mutual pleasure, and desist from activities which are either boring, or are not enjoyed by one or other partner.

Halting the Process

So far, we have described the development of friendship from the initial stages of acquaintance right through to the establishment of lifelong intimate relationships. Our friendships, though, develop to markedly different extents. Some develop to the extent of forming lifelong partnerships where couples spend the majority of their lives together; others build up and decay; others build up to certain levels and then progress no further. What factors are involved in these different relationships? In the case of long-term relationships we have argued that the kind of support that the partners provide for each other changes over the course of the relationship starting out with attitudinal support and developing into complementarity of personal needs. Partnerships can fail to develop if complementary needs are not present, and can crumble if needs are similar rather than dissimilar; friendships can simply hang in a state at which both partners are getting adequate rewards to keep the friendship maintained but see little reward in extending it further.

A common theme in the break-up of relationships, especially for courting couples, is the different expectations which the partners have about the relationship, reflected in comments like 'it is getting too intense' or 'it's getting nowhere'. At these points partners come to make major decisions about whether to change the nature of the partnership into a more permanent one or to abandon it. The break-up of a relationship is not necessarily a disaster for either partner; we all make and break friends from time to time. Most commonly this is triggered when the relationship no longer satisfies one or both partners or if it stifles the personal growth of either partner (which may well have been brought about by the other partner). Repair to the relationship is not the only strategy. Social networks can help partners disengage from each other, and can attempt to minimize the emotional damage done through this disengagement process. This idea takes us back to the start of this section, when we pointed out the need for a network of friends to help each to cope with life's crises!

This review of the work that has been done to investigate the formation of friendships by social psychologists, medical researchers, criminologists and marriage guidance counsellors and others, offers quite a rich view of the way we make friends and lovers, and the way in which these relationships can be nurtured or dissolved. Is this view really any better than a common-sense view, or the views of a great thinker like John Milton on marriage? How does the view developed here differ in the advice it offers to people who have problems either making or maintaining relationships? How can we explain what happened to Venus? What could be done to prevent social disasters from happening in the exploration of space?

Offering Advice about Personal Relationships

We all have intuitions about what makes friendships work and what inhibits the development of good social relationships. Even if we do not trust our own intuition, we can find advice about personal relationships in a wide range of places such as magazine problem pages, and even in the doctor's surgery!

Advice given by problem pages along the lines of 'join a club and meet people' is probably worse than useless. First, this is a very obvious idea and almost no one will fail to think of it for themselves. Second, the problem is likely to be located in the social skills which the person brings to each situation. Meeting more people will simply reinforce the idea that their social skills are inadequate, and that, through some deep-rooted personal fault, they cannot make friends.

A number of professional groups receive training in communication skills. Examples are nurses and doctors who receive instruction in appropriate ways of meeting and interacting with sick people; salesmen; personnel managers; and airline personnel. What sort of instruction do these professional groups receive? Well, they certainly aren't shown how to change their appearance in easy ways by, for example, removing spots or by buying a particular manufacturer's jeans, or drinking Auld Liver Salts Scotch – social skills training is learning to behave in a different sort of way when we meet people.

To offer advice, it is necessary first to diagnose the problem accurately. From our descriptions of the skills necessary to foster friendship, it is clear that things can go wrong in all manner of ways. People might choose inappropriate places to look for friends; they may spend all their time trying to engage with people who find them unattractive; their gestures and patterns of contact might be inappropriate; they may seek and offer personal information about attitudes and beliefs too quickly, or too slowly or too dogmatically; they may find the transition from aquaintance to friendship hard to manage, because they fail to negotiate an appropriate meeting place, or because chosen activities fail to give pleasure to their new acquaintance; they may foster friendships that decay because of lack of maintenance; and so on.

Blanket advice on personal relationships is unlikely to be much use to anyone. Once an area of difficulty has been established, we are in a position to offer some help. This help probably *won't* be just a cosy discussion, but will involve watching videotapes of friendly behaviour (own and others) and discussing them; and practising specific skills until they are more acceptable to others. Social skills are rather like other kinds of skills such as cycling and swimming, in that it helps to be told where we are going wrong, but we improve our faults most efficiently by practicing new techniques and reviewing our own progress.

So our systematic study of the growth of friendship has led to the situation where we can offer direct help to people who have difficulty forming personal relationships. We have gone far beyond common-sense ideas and remedies, and far beyond Milton's views, too. His emphasis on the need for different kinds of compatibilities between marriage partners was a good partial insight into loving relationships. His ideas on the need for physical and intellectual compatibility are in broad agreement with research findings on the things that are important for initial attraction between people. Social psychologists might find it worthwhile to explore his ideas about the need for spiritual compatibility. The Miltonian theme about the need to struggle against adversity to achieve one's goal is also useful when we consider relationships which are in disarray. Interesting and stimulating though his ideas are, they are in no sense a plan for action. They have nothing to say about the development of intimate personal relationships; his ideas offer no suggestions for people who have difficulties in making friends; he offers little direct advice on how to repair relationships (except perhaps 'try harder' and 'divorce if you are incompatible in any way').

REFLECTIONS ON VENUS

There are several implications for our story in this brief look at research on friendship formation. We can spell out a large number of reasons why Selma Hoffer and John Clay were ill suited, as Hoffer herself remarked. Their relationship was doomed from the outset. It is clear that anyone wishing to have an interaction with a cyborg has a difficult task ahead. All the usual range of postures, gestures and eye movement are removed from the interaction. (Although perhaps Mission Control might be able to do something about this in terms of some elaborate visual display.)

A working relationship was forced on both Hoffer and Clay. They both needed human company of some sort on Venus, but had little choice of partner. We would hope that the usual phases of exploring each other's attitudes, beliefs, and approaches to life, which are the common basis of friendship formation, would have led each to reject the other as a possible partner. The story shows quite clearly that John Clay and Selma Hoffer had little in common. Hoffer had hoped for some complementarity of relationships ('the earnestness and the stupidity – that got to me. A sort of maternity syndrome I guess you'd call it.') which failed to emerge.

Nor was there any scope for them to negotiate. The relationship is defined for them by their physical circumstances – Hoffer must support Clay. From Clay's viewpoint Hoffer is no more than an intelligent house.

The range of activities open to Hoffer is rather limited, and includes things such as reading, conversation, and the like. None of these are rewarding to Clay. The only activity which they did find mutually rewarding – telling erotic stories – served simply to emphasize the long-term sterility of their relationship. In Hoffer's words 'if ever there was a mismatched couple, it was us'. Neither Clay nor Hoffer was equipped with skills to repair their deteriorating relationship.

Milton on Venus

John Milton would also have expected this relationship to go wrong. A brief look at some aspects of Milton's life shows that themes similar to those uncovered in the research on friendship formation might emerge from a literary analysis, albeit from a different perspective.

A strong theme which runs through many of Milton's works is his notion about the compatibility of partners. He argued that the basis of a true marriage is compatibility. The partners in a marriage must be compatible physically, intellectually and spiritually. If they are not, then this incompatibility should be sufficient grounds for divorce.

The sixteenth and seventeenth centuries were times of great change. The Renaissance produced a new science, new political schemes and new religions: in short, a new view of our role in the world, and indeed a new view of the nature of humanity. In England, in Milton's time, there was great religious and political unrest. Milton wrote several pamphlets against the bishops in the English church before the Civil War, and sided with the puritans in the war against Charles I. His first official connection with the new government began in 1649, four years after the end of the war, and the year in which Charles I was executed. We know from our cyborg author that he was appointed as Cromwell's Latin Secretary or 'Secretary for Foreign Tongues to the Council of State' to give him his full title. As well as his duties translating and writing letters to foreign governments, Milton viewed himself as having a high calling to write great poetry. He also felt a moral duty to support the new Commonwealth set up after the Civil War, which he saw as a great moral advance after the country's long serfdom under kings. It was during his time as Latin Secretary that Milton became progressively blind. He says that he sacrificed his health and his eyesight to 'his duty'. In February 1652 he became totally blind. He gave up the chief duties of his Secretaryship three years later. We see Milton himself as a man of great genius struggling against enormous difficulty and rising above it.

How are Milton and Hoffer linked? We are given strong clues that Hoffer on Venus identifies herself with Milton in his time as Latin Secretary. The links are that Hoffer studied his letters during this time; the clear theme of 'duty', where both Milton and Hoffer were working on activities which took them away from things closer to their souls; and the obvious link that Milton went blind during this time, as did Hoffer. Milton's wife died in the same year in which he went blind; John Clay left the cyborg (who can't really be sure he is alive). Milton rose above his crushing disability; it seems unlikely that the cyborg will.

Let's return to Milton's three key components for two people to be happily married ('After all I couldn't very well be his wife could I?') – physical, intellectual and spiritual compatibility. This disagreement over *Il Penseroso* and poetry in general shows a complete lack of spiritual compatibility. The cyborg is most unflattering about John Clay's intellectual abilities. Their physical incompatibility is obvious. So we see a strong Miltonian theme being acted out, namely the divorce of two people who are incompatible in too many ways.

But what about the mechanism of the split? How did their relationship fracture and break? Again, we can see another Miltonian theme emerging: the destruction of an individual as the result of a wilful choice of a series of unsavoury, easy alternatives rather than a series of moral ones. Frustration at the inability to generate more erotic stories led to mutual aggression. Aggression escalated and perhaps led to Selma's breakdown, or perhaps her breakdown was the trigger for her aggression to John Clay (waking him up with *Il Penseroso*) and for his counter-aggression. In any event, the escalating aggression resulted in a great deal of damage to the cyborg: we don't really know what happened to the slug hunter.

Human Factors Problems of Working Together in Hazardous Environments

There are still two major problems to solve. How can you choose people who are likely to get on well with each other? What can you do if the relationships do begin to go wrong? Neither common sense nor John Milton have much to offer here, other than to suggest that 'compatible' people be sent together. But isn't that 'answer' just restating the problem?

We have traced through the development of acquaintance to loving relationships, to show some of the problems posed by Selma Hoffer falling in love with John Clay. The task of any Human Factors Group isn't really to find crew members who will form stable life- long relationships; rather, it is to find people who can work together effectively, for periods of months at a time. This is rather easier! So what could the psychologists at Mission Control have done?

Can we predict which people are likely to get on well with each other? Compatibility involves a good deal more than just choosing friendly people who have similar values to each other. We can talk about the need for compatibility both at early stages of a relationship in terms of similarity of attitude, and compatibility at later stages of the relationship in terms of the complementarity of personal needs. We will obviously need a great deal of careful personnel selection if we are to put together effective work teams in space. Social psychologists claim that they *can* predict people who will get on well together on the basis of fairly short-term assessment of each person. For example, Murstein in 1977 has been able to make good predictions about successful partnerships; Duck and Allison in 1978 had a good degree of success predicting which groups of flat mates would survive and which would break up over the course of a college year. Similarly, on the basis of observation of early interactions over the first few weeks it should be possible to use studies like the one of Huston (which we described earlier) where he related the progress of people in the early steps of their relationships to their long-term stability, to make predictions about those people who can work together to maintain their relationships. From the basis of this start, by selecting combinations of people who are likely to get on well together, we can hope that events on Venus will not recur too often.

All this has a rather deterministic ring to it though. We are talking as if choosing compatible partners is like picking a good horse and a good jockey to win a race (or at least stay the distance). Relationships are active processes, and should not be seen as things which have foregone conclusions. A good deal of skills training in the maintenance and repair of social relationships would obviously be an essential part of any training for groups who are socially isolated from other groups. These maintenance and repair skills might well be a matter of life and death.

People who have to work closely together in hazardous environments such as space, the deep sea, or the remote research stations of the Arctic and Antarctic pose a challenge to human factors teams. It is far harder to find out about social patterns and personal relationships than to design instrument controls or study the effects of extreme fatigue. In the last two examples, we can conduct experiments which are easy to explain to people taking part. It is rather like asking people to behave like machines so that we can see how they work. But suppose we wanted to study the effects of social isolation, for example, what could we do? Obviously, we could keep people apart and see what happens. But is this valid? Can we really assume that 'social isolation' is something that an outsider (or outsiders) can impose on the individual? Isn't social isolation more something that people must feel about their situation? A lone sailor may feel part of a community of adventurers and not feel isolated at all whereas old people living in city flats may see themselves as isolated while living in the midst of the cosmopolitan bustle. A member of a closed religious order is likely to feel differently to a prisoner, even though their physical conditions may appear similar.

People changing their environment often take great care to carry reminders of their social identities. Travellers may carry photographs of their families, or less obvious reminders of their roots. Astronauts have taken some strange things with them (or are golf clubs standard issue on Moon missions?). Selma Hoffer was quite right to insist on having herself redecorated; more personal souvenirs of her earlier life might have helped too. Do you think that her fixation with Milton was a desire to establish links to her past life, old friends and memories? Difficult to tell.

The studies of groups of people working together with no outside contact have ranged widely from the anecdotes of lone sailors and castaways; through detailed 'participant observer' studies in Antarctic stations, diving bells and the like; observing astronauts in space laboratories; together with a wide range of laboratory studies which often set out to simulate some particular 'real world' situation of interest. It isn't easy to offer a quick summary of the findings! The obvious reason is that the situations differ from each in so many different ways that it is very hard to say which situations are 'like' which other situations. Nevertheless, it is possible to summarize effects which have been noticed in a number of different studies. Here are two quotations from a review by S.B. Sells.

When people are asked how they feel after prolonged periods away from ordinary social interaction:

> common complaints are sleep disturbance, restlessness, inability to
> concentrate, fatigue, muscular weakness and soreness, boredom,
> monotony, feelings of dirtiness, headaches, dizziness, psychosomatic
> reactions, apathy, low morale, time disorientation, frustrations, anx-
> iety, irritability, hostility, depression and withdrawal.

It is surprising that people who feel this way can function at all! However, Sells notes that:

> in each situation involving organized and professionally led groups,
> with trained disciplined personnel and in the absence of serious overt
> personal conflict, deterioration of interpersonal behaviour and group
> disorganization, frequently mentioned in the anecdotal literature, has
> been rare.

Which is quite reassuring.

Let us look at some other research findings, and see what they tell us about the events on Venus, and about how members of isolated groups should be chosen, and how the groups should operate.

- People who choose to be isolated usually perform better than those who are isolated either accidentally or against their will. Selma Hoffer saw herself as a slave rather than a recluse in her role as a cyborg life support system for John Clay.
- People tolerate isolation and confinement better if they are there to achieve some purpose. When they are isolated simply because they can't avoid it, like prisoners and conscripted military personnel, coping with the stress imposed is more difficult. For Hoffer, it was a choice between becoming a cyborg and death.
- Simulating the situation helps. Advanced knowledge and pre-training can allow people to adjust far better to isolation than they would other-

wise have done. This doesn't seem to be part of the cyborg conversion process.

- In general, the stress associated with isolation increases the longer the isolation lasts. So a cyborg left permanently on Venus would be expected to be subjected to a good deal of stress. However, we know from the extremely long voyages of explorers like Cook, Drake and Magellan, that teams can function well even after several years in isolation.

- Crowding and confinement are sources of stress. Hoffer perceived the room as being 'no bigger than a coffin'.

- Known and imagined dangers increase feelings of stress. In underwater operations, and in space, the capsule is a shelter from outside dangers. So, too, on Venus. The swamps can hardly be welcoming, but the prospect of a malfunctioning cyborg is likely to have reduced John Clay's ability to act rationally and cope well with Hoffer's problems.

- Groups which have well-defined goals that the group members agree are worthwhile perform better than groups which either have no goals or disagree about their usefulness. Hoffer didn't know what Clay was collecting the slugs for, and describes him disparagingly as 'a glorified fur-trader'. Whatever the reason, she wasn't deeply committed to it!

- The personal compatibility of team members is important as Selma Hoffer discovered for herself. We hope that we can use some of our discoveries about different kinds of compatibility, and about complementarity to select people who are likely to get on well with each other.

THE DIRECTOR'S REPORT: GATHERING THEMES TOGETHER

Well, we have done the easy thing here: we have pulled out a collection of fairly straightforward results, one at a time. We have shown how everything on Venus ran against what we know should have been done to give John George Clay and Selma Meret Hoffer a good chance of working together effectively. Imagine you are Director of Human Factors – you have got a far more difficult job! You must avoid the obvious pitfalls, of course – however, all the factors we looked at are interacting together. The effects of social deprivation, confinement, and possible sensory deprivation all feed on each other.

The relationships between the individuals in the isolated community will not only be complex, but will be constantly changing. Any situation where none of the group members can escape to release tension is potentially explosive. There is a clear need to develop strategies among the team members to handle tension, stress and aggression as they arise. We have seen one method, which is to define each person's role quite tightly, so that interactions between people are limited in scope. It is then up to the individual to handle their own stress, without transferring it to other group members. A second strategy is to define an outside group who are then the focus of aggression. Examples might be a competitive group, or headquarters in the case of military groups, or mission control, in the case of astronauts. This strategy probably has a useful role in dispelling hostility, but obviously can make the communications of the group with headquarters or mission control less and less effective. Another method is to attempt to foster a therapeutic community, where group members actively try to reduce tensions among themselves and to remove the sources of grievance. Presumably, we could train team leaders to recognize stresses within the group, to diagnose them, and to help team members resolve conflicts which have arisen.

Well, Director, it's time to write out a plan for the selection and training of mission personnel, and to make some recommendations about their working environment. By now, you should be able to do better than just giving everyone some Milton to read.

2

BURDEN OF PROOF

Bob Shaw

Harpur peered uncertainly through the streaming windows of his car. There had been no parking space close to the police headquarters, and now the building seemed separated from him by miles of puddled concrete and parading curtains of rain. The sky sagged darkly and heavily between the buildings around the square.

Suddenly aware of his age, he stared for a long moment at the old police block and its cascading gutters, before levering himself stiffly out of the driving seat. It was difficult to believe the sun was shining warmly in a basement room under the west wing. Yet he knew it was, because he had phoned and asked about it before leaving home.

'It's real nice down here today, Judge,' the guard had said, speaking with the respectful familiarity he had developed over the years. 'Not so good outside, of course, but down here it's real nice.'

'Have any reporters shown up yet?'

'Just a few so far, Judge. You coming over?'

'I expect so,' Harpur had replied. 'Save a seat for me, Sam.'

'Yes, *Sir!*'

Harpur moved as quickly as he dared, feeling the cool rain penetrate on to the backs of his hands in his shower-proof's pockets. The lining clung round the knuckles when he moved his fingers. As he climbed the steps to the front entrance a preliminary flutter in the left side of his chest told him he had hurried too much, pushed things too far.

The officer at the door saluted smartly.

Harpur nodded to him. 'Hard to believe this is June, isn't it, Ben?'

'Sure is, sir. I hear it's nice down below, though.'

Harpur waved to the guard, and was moving along the corridor when the pain closed with him. It was very clean, very pure. As though someone had carefully chosen a sterile needle, fitted it into an antiseptic handle, heated it to whiteness and – with the swiftness of compassion – run it into his side. He stopped for a moment and leaned on the tiled wall, trying not to be conspicuous, while perspiration pricked out on his forehead. *I can't give up now* , he thought, *not when there's only another couple of weeks to go … But, supposing this is it? Right*

30

now!

Harpur fought the panic, until the entity that was his pain withdrew a short distance. He drew a shuddering breath of relief and began to walk again, slowly, aware that his enemy was watching and following. But he reached the sunshine without any further attacks.

Sam Macnamara, the guard at the inner door, started to give his usual grin and then, seeing the strain on Harpur's face, ushered him quickly into the room. Macnamara was a tall Irishman whose only ambition seemed to be to drink two cups of coffee every hour on the hour, but they had developed a friendship which Harpur found strangely comforting. He shook out a fold-up chair at the back of the room and held it steady while Harpur sat down.

'Thank you, Sam,' Harpur said gratefully, glancing around at the unfamiliar crowd, none of whom had noticed his arrival. They were all staring towards the sunlight.

The smell of the rain-damp clothing worn by the reporters seemed strangely out of place in the dusty, underground room. It was part of the oldest wing of the police headquarters and, until five years before, had been used to store obsolete records. Since then, except on special press days, its bare concrete walls had housed nothing but a bank of monitoring equipment, two very bored guards, and a pane of glass mounted in a frame at one end of the room.

The glass was of the special variety through which light took many years to pass. It was the sort people used to capture scenes of exceptional beauty for their homes.

To Harpur's eyes, the view through this piece of slow glass had no particular beauty. It showed a reasonably pretty bay on the Atlantic coast, but the water was cluttered with sports boats, and a garishly-painted service station obtruded in the foreground. A connoisseur of slow glass would have thrown a rock through it, but Emile Bennett, the original owner, had brought it to the city simply because it contained the view from his childhood home. Having it available, he had explained, saved him a two-hundred mile drive any time he felt homesick.

The sheet of glass Bennett had used was five years thick which meant that it had had to stand for five years at his parents' home before the view from there came through. It continued, of course, to transmit the same view for five years after being brought back to the city, regardless of the fact that it had been confiscated from Bennett by impatient police officers who had a profound disinterest in his parental home. It would report, without fail, everything it ever saw – but only in its own good time.

Slumped tiredly in his seat, Harpur was reminded of the last time he had been to a movie. The only light in the room was that coming from the oblong pane of glass, and the reporters sat fidgeting in orderly rows like a movie audience. Harpur found their presence distracting. It prevented him from slipping into the past as easily as usual.

The shifting waters of the bay scattered sunlight through the otherwise dismal room, the little boats crossed and recrossed, and silent cars occasionally slid into the service station. An attractive girl in the extremely abbreviated dress of a decade ago walked across a garden in the foreground, and Harpur saw several of the reporters jot some personal angle material in their notebooks.

One of the more inquisitive left his seat and walked round behind the pane of glass to see the view from the other side, but came back looking disappointed. Harpur knew a sheet of metal had been welded into the frame at the back,

31

completely covering the glass. The county had ruled that it would have been an invasion of the senior Bennetts' privacy to put on public view all their domestic activities during the time the glass was being charged.

As the minutes began to drag out in the choking atmosphere of the room, the reporters grew noticeably restless and began loudly swapping yarns. Somewhere near the front, one of them began sneezing monotonously and swearing in between. No smoking was permitted near the monitoring equipment which, on behalf of the state, hungrily scanned the glass, so relays of three and four began to drift out into the corridor to light cigarettes. Harpur heard them complaining about the long wait and he smiled. He had been waiting for five years and it seemed even longer.

Today, June 7th, was one of the key days for which he and the rest of the country had been standing by, but it had been impossible to let the press know in advance the exact moment at which they would get their story. The trouble was that Emile Bennett had never been able to remember just what time, on that hot Sunday, he had driven to his parents' home to collect his sheet of slow glass. During the subsequent trial it had not been possible to pin it down to anything more definite than 'about three in the afternoon'.

One of the reporters finally noticed Harpur sitting near the door and came over to him. He was sharply dressed, fair-haired and impossibly young looking.

'Pardon me, sir. Aren't you Judge Harpur?'

Harpur nodded. The boy's eyes widened briefly then narrowed as he assessed the older man's present news value.

'Weren't you the presiding judge in the ... Raddall case?' He had been going to say the Glass Eye case, but immediately changed his mind.

Harpur nodded again. 'Yes, that's correct. But I no longer give interviews to the Press. I'm sorry.'

'That's all right, sir. I understand.' He went on out to the corridor, walking with quicker, springier steps. Harpur guessed the young man had just decided on his angle for today's story. He could have written the copy himself:

Today Judge Kenneth Harpur – the man who five years ago presided in the controversial 'Glass Eye' case, in which twenty-one-year-old Ewan Raddall was charged with a double slaying – sat on a chair in one of the underground rooms at police headquarters. An old man now, the Iron Judge has nothing at all to say. He only watches, waits, and wonders ...

Harpur smiled wryly. He no longer felt any bitterness over the newspaper attacks. The only reason he had stopped speaking to journalists was that he had become very, very bored with that aspect of his life. He had reached the age at which a man discards the unimportant stuff and concentrates on essentials. In another two weeks he would be free to sit in the sun and note exactly how many shades of blue and green there were in the sea, and just how much time elapsed between the appearance of the first evening star and the second. If his physician allowed it, he would have a little good whisky, and if his physician refused it, he would still have the whisky. He would read a few books, and perhaps even write one ...

As it turned out, the estimated time given by Bennett at the trial had been pretty accurate.

At eight minutes past three Harpur and the waiting newsmen saw Bennett approach the glass from the far side with a screwdriver in his hand. He was wearing the sheepish look people often have when they get in range of slow glass.

He worked at the sides for a moment, then the sky flashed crazily into view, showing the glass had been tilted out of its frame. A moment later the room went dark as the image of a brown, army-type blanket unfolded across the glass, blotting out the laggard light.

The monitors at the back of the room produced several faint clicking noises which were drowned out by the sound of the reporters hurrying to telephones.

Harpur got to his feet and slowly walked out behind the reporters. There was no need to hurry now. Police records showed that the glass would remain blanked out for two days, because that was how long it had lain in the trunk of Bennett's car before he had got round to installing it in a window frame at the back of his city home. For a further two weeks after that it would show the casual day-to-day events which took place five years before in the children's public playground at the rear of the Bennett house.

Those events were of no particular interest to anyone: but the records also showed that in the same playground, on the night of June 21, 1986, a twenty-year-old typist, Joan Calderisi, had been raped and murdered. Her boy friend, a twenty-three-year-old auto mechanic named Edward Jerome Hattie, had also been killed, presumably for trying to defend the girl.

Unknown to the murderer, there had been one witness to the double-killing – and now it was getting ready to give its perfect and incontrovertible evidence.

The problem had not been difficult to foresee.

Right from the day slow glass appeared in a few very expensive stores, people had wondered what would happen if a crime were to be committed in its view. What would be the legal position if there were, say, three suspects and it was known that, five or ten years later, a piece of glass could identify the murderer beyond all doubt? Obviously, the law could not risk punishing the wrong person: but, equally obviously, the guilty one could not be allowed to go free all that time.

This was how tabloid feature writers had summed it up, although to Judge Kenneth Harpur there had been no problem at all. When he read the speculations it took him less than five seconds to make up his mind – and he had been impressively unruffled when the test case came his way.

That part had been a coincidence. Erskine County had no more homicides and no more slow glass than any other comparable area. In fact, Harpur had no recollection of ever seeing the stuff until Holt City's electrical street-lighting was suddenly replaced by alternating panels of eight-hour glass and sixteen-hour glass slung in continuous lines above the thoroughfares.

It had taken some time for a Retardite capable of producing delays measured in years to evolve from the first sheets which held light back at roughly half a second. The user had to be absolutely certain of the time delay he wanted – because there was no way of speeding the process up. Had Retardite been a 'glass' in the true sense of the word, it might have been possible to plane a piece down to a different thickness and get the information sooner; but, in reality, it was extremely opaque material: opaque in the sense that light never actually got *into* it.

Radiations with wavelengths in the order of that of light were absorbed on the face of a Retardite panel and their information converted to stress patterns within the material. The piezoluctic effect by which the information worked its way through to the opposite face involved the whole crystalline structure, and anything which disturbed that structure instantaneously randomized the stress patterns.

Infuriating as the discovery was to certain researchers, it had been an important factor in the commercial success of Retardite. People would have been reluctant to install scenedows in their homes, knowing that everything they had done behind them was being stored for other eyes to see years later. So the burgeoning piezoluctics industry had been quick to invent an inexpensive 'tickler' by which any piece of slow glass could be cleaned off for reuse, like a cluttered computer programme.

This was also the reason why, for five years, two guards had been on a round-the-clock watch of the scenedow which held the evidence in the Raddall case. There was always the chance that one of Raddall's relatives, or some publicity-seeking screwball, would sneak in and wipe the slate clean before its time came to resolve all doubts.

There had been moments during the ten years when Harpur had been too ill and tired to care very much, times when it would have been a relief to have the perfect witness silenced forever. But usually the existence of the slow glass did not bother him.

He had made his ruling in the Raddall case, and it had been a decision he would have expected any other judge to make. The subsequent controversy, the enmity of sections of the press, the public, and even some of his colleagues had hurt at first, but he had got over that.

The Law, Harpur had said in his summing up, existed solely because people believed in it. Let that belief be shaken – even once – and the Law would suffer irreparable harm.

As near as could be determined, the killings had taken place about an hour before midnight.

Keeping that in mind, Harpur ate dinner early then showered and shaved for the second time that day. The effort represented a sizeable proportion of his daily energy quota, but it had been hot and sticky in the courtroom. His current case was involved and at the same time, boring. More and more cases were like that lately, he realized. It was a sign he was ready to retire but there was one more duty to perform – he owed that much to the profession.

Harpur put on a lightweight jacket and stood with his back to the valet-mirror which his wife had bought a few months earlier. It was faced with a sheet of fifteen- second Retardite which allowed him after a slight pause to turn around and check his appearance from the back. He surveyed his frail but upright figure dispassionately then walked away before the stranger in the glass could turn to look out.

He disliked valet-mirrors almost as much as the equally popular truviewers, which were merely pieces of short-term Retardite pivotal on a vertical axis. They served roughly the same function as ordinary mirrors, except that there was no reversal effect. For the first time ever, the makers boasted, you could really see yourself as others saw you. Harpur objected to the idea on grounds he hoped were vaguely philosophical, but which he could not really explain, even to himself.

'You don't look well, Kenneth,' Eva said as he adjusted his tie minutely. 'You

haven't *got* to go down there, have you?'
    'No, I haven't *got* to go – that's why I've got to go. That's the whole point.'
    'Then I'll drive you.'
    'You won't. You're going to bed. I'm not going to let you drive around the city in the middle of the night'. He put an arm round her shoulders. At fifty-eight, Eva Harpur was on a seemingly endless plateau of indomitable good health, but they maintained a fiction that it was he who looked after her.
    He drove himself into the city, but progress through the traffic was unusually slow and, on impulse, he stopped several blocks from the police headquarters and began to walk. Live dangerously, he thought, but walk slowly – just in case. It was a bright warm evening and, with the long day-light hours of June, only the sixteen-hour panels slung above the thoroughfare were black. The alternating eight-hour panels were needlessly blazing with light they had absorbed in the afternoon. The system was a compromise with seasonal variations in daylight hours, but it worked well and, above all, the light was practically free.
    An additional advantage was that it provided the Law enforcement authorities with perfect evidence about events like road accidents and traffic violations. In fact, it had been the then brand-new slow glass lighting panels in Fifty-third Avenue which had provided a large part of the evidence in the case against Ewan Raddall.
    Evidence on which Harpur had sent Raddall to the electric chair.

The salient facts of the case had not been exactly as in the classic situation proposed by the tabloids, but they had been near enough to arouse public interest. There had been no other known suspect apart from Raddall, but the evidence against him had been largely circumstantial. The bodies had not been found until the next morning, by which time Raddall had been able to get home, clean himself up and have a night's sleep. When he was picked up he was fresh, composed and plausible – and the forensic teams had been able to prove nothing.
    The case against Raddall was that he had been seen going towards the public playground at the right time, leaving it at the right time, and that he had bruises and scratches consistent with the crime. Also, between midnight and 9.30 in the morning, when he was taken in for questioning, he had 'lost' the plasticord jacket he had worn on the previous evening, and it was never found.
    At the end of Raddall's trial the jury had taken less than an hour to arrive at a verdict of guilty – but during a subsequent appeal his defence claimed the jury was influenced by the knowledge that the crime was recorded in Emile Bennett's rear window. The defence attorney, demanding a retrial, put forward the view that the jury had dismissed their 'reasonable doubt' in the expectation that Harpur would, at the most, impose a life sentence.
    But, in Harpur's eyes, the revised legal code drafted in 1977, mainly to give judges greater power in their own courts, made no provision for wait-and-see legislation, especially in cases of first-degree murder. In January 1987, Raddall was duly sentenced to be executed.
    Harpur's straightforward contention, which had earned him the name 'Iron Judge', was that a decision reached in a court of law always had been, and still was, sacrosanct. The superhuman entity which was the Law must not be humbled before a fragment of glass. Reduced to its crudest terms, his argument was that if wait-and-see legislation were introduced, criminals would carry pieces of fifty-year Retardite with them as standard equipment.

Within two years the slow-grinding mills of the Supreme Court had ratified Harpur's decision and the sentence was carried out. The same thing on a microscopic scale had occurred many times before in the world of sport; and the only possible, the only workable solution, was that the umpire was always right – no matter what cameras or slow glass might say afterwards.

In spite of his vindication, or perhaps because of it, the tabloids never warmed to Harpur. He began making a point of being indifferent to all that anybody wrote or said. All he had needed during the five years was the knowledge that he had made a good decision, as distinct from a wrong one — now he was to discover if he had made a good decision as distinct from a bad one.

Although this night had been looming on his horizon for half a decade, Harpur found it difficult to realize that, in a matter of minutes, they would know if Raddall was guilty. The thought caused a crescendo of uncomfortable jolts in his chest and he stopped for a moment to snatch air. After all, what difference did it really make? He had not made the law, so why feel personally involved?

The answer came quickly.

He was involved because he was part of the law. The reason he had gone on working against medical advice was that it was he, not some abstract embodiment of Webster's 'great interest of man on earth', who had passed sentence on Ewan Raddall. And he was going to be there, personally, to face the music if he had made a mistake.

The realization was strangely comforting to Harpur as he moved on through the crowded streets. Something in the atmosphere of the late evening struck him as being odd, then he noticed the city centre was jammed tight with out-of-town automobiles. Men and women thronged the sidewalks, and he knew they were strangers by the way their eyes occasionally took in the upper parts of buildings. The smell of grilling hamburger meat drifted on the thick, downy air.

Harpur wondered what the occasion might be, then he noticed the general drift towards the police headquarters. So that was it. People had not changed since the days they were drawn towards arenas, guillotines and gallows. There would be nothing for them to see, but to be close at hand would be sufficient to let them taste the ancient joy of continuing to breathe in the knowledge that someone else has just ceased. The fact that they were five years out of date, too, made no difference at all.

Even Harpur, had he wanted to, could not have got into the underground room. Apart from the monitors, there would be only six chairs and six pairs of special binoculars with low magnifications and huge, light- hungry objective lenses. They were reserved for the state-appointed observers.

Harpur had no interest in viewing the crime with his own eyes – he simply wanted to hear the result; then have a long, long rest. It occurred to him he was being completely irrational in going down to the police building, with all the exertion and lethal tension the trip meant for him, but somehow nothing else would do. *I'm guilty,* he thought suddenly, *guilty as ...* He reached the plaza in which the building was situated and worked his way through the pliant, strength-draining barriers of people. By the time he was halfway across sweat had bound his clothes so tightly he could hardly raise his feet. At an indeterminate point in the long journey he became aware of another presence following close behind – the sorrowful friend with the white-hot needle.

Reaching the untidy ranks of automobiles belonging to the Press, Harpur realized he could not go in too early, and there was at least half an hour left. He turned and began forcing his way back to the opposite side of the plaza. The needle point caught up with him – one precise thrust – and he lurched forward clawing for support.

'What the ...!' A startled voice boomed over his head. 'Take it easy old-timer.' Its owner was a burly giant in a pale blue one-piece, who had been watching a 3-D television broadcast when Harpur fell against him. He snatched off the receiver spectacles, the tiny left and right pictures glowing with movement like distant bonfires. A wisp of music escaped from the earpiece.

'I'm sorry,' Harpur said. 'I tripped. I'm sorry.'

'That's all right. Say! Aren't you Judge ...'

Harpur pushed on by as the big man tugged excitedly on the arm of a woman who was with him. *I mustn't be recognized,* he thought in a panic. He burrowed into the crowd, now beginning to lose his sense of direction. Six more desperate paces and the needle caught him again – right up to its antiseptic hilt this time. He moaned as the plaza tilted ponderously away. Not here, he pleaded, not here, *please.*

Somehow, he saved himself from falling and moved on. Near at hand, but a million miles away, an unseen woman gave a beautiful, carefree laugh. At the edge of the square the pain returned, even more decisively than before – once, twice, three times. Harpur screamed as he felt the life-muscle implode in cramp.

He began to go down, then felt himself gripped by firm hands. Harpur looked up at the swarthy young man who was holding him. The handsome, worry-creased face looming through reddish mist looked strangely familiar. Harpur struggled to speak.

'You ... you're Ewan Raddall, aren't you?'

The black eyebrows met in puzzlement. 'Raddall? No. Never heard of him. I think we'd better call an ambulance for you.'

Harpur thought hard. 'That's right. You couldn't be Raddall. I killed him five years ago.' Then he spoke louder. 'But if you never heard of Raddall, why are you here?'

'I was on my way home from a bowling match when I saw the crowd.'

The boy began getting Harpur out of the crowd, holding him up with one arm, fending uncomprehending bodies away with the other. Harpur tried to help, but was aware of his feet trailing helplessly on the concrete.

'Do you live right here in Holt?'

The boy nodded emphatically.

'Do you know who I am?'

'All I know about you, sir, is you should be in the hospital. I'll call an ambulance on the liquor store phone.'

Harpur felt vaguely that there was some tremendous significance in what they had been saying, but had no time to pursue the matter.

'Listen,' he said, forcing himself to stand upright for a moment. 'I don't want an ambulance. I'll be fine if I can just get home. Can you help me get a cab?'

The boy looked uncertain, then he shrugged. 'It's your funeral.'

Harpur opened his door carefully and entered the friendly darkness of the big old house. During the ride out of town his sweat-soaked clothes had become clammy cold, and he shivered uncontrollably as he felt for the light switch.

With the light on, he sat down beside the telephone and looked at his watch. Almost midnight – by this time there would be no mystery, no doubt, about exactly what had happened in the Fifty-third Avenue playground five years earlier. He picked up the handset, and at the same moment heard his wife begin to move around upstairs. There were several numbers he could ring to ask what the slow glass had revealed, but the thought of talking to any police executive or someone in City Hall was too much. He called Sam Macnamara.

As a guard, Sam would not know the result officially but he would have the answer just the same. Harpur tried to punch out the number of the direct line to the guard kiosk but his finger points kept buckling on impact with the buttons and he gave up.

Eva Harpur came down the stairs in her dressing gown and approached him apprehensively.

'Oh, Kenneth!' Her hand went to her mouth. 'What have you done? You look ... I'll have to call Dr Sherman.'

Harpur smiled weakly. *I do a lot of smiling these days,* he thought irrelevantly, *it's the only response an old man can make to so many situations.*

'All I want you to do is to make me some coffee and help me up to my bed; but first of all get me a number on this contraption.' Eva opened her mouth to protest, then closed it as their eyes met.

When Sam came to the phone Harpur worked to keep his own voice level.

'Hello, Sam. Judge Harpur here. Is the fun all over yet?'

'Yes, sir. There was a press conference afterwards and that's over, too. I guess you heard the result on the radio.'

'As a matter of fact, I haven't, Sam. I was ... out until a little while ago. Decided to ring someone about it before I went to bed, and your number just came into my head.'

Sam laughed uncertainly. 'Well, they were able to make a positive identification. It was Raddall, all right – but I guess you knew that all along.'

'I guess I did, Sam.' Harpur felt his eyes grow hot with tears.

'It'll be a load off your mind all the same, Judge.'

Harpur nodded tiredly, but into the phone he said, 'Well, naturally I'm glad there was no miscarriage of justice – but judges don't make the laws, Sam. They don't even decide who's guilty and who isn't. As far as I'm concerned, the presence of a peculiar piece of glass makes very little difference, one way or the other.'

It was a good speech for the Iron Judge.

There was a long silence in the line then, with a note of something like desperation in his voice, Sam persisted. 'I know all that, Judge ... but, all the same, it must have been a big load off your mind.'

Harpur realized, with a warm surprise, that the big Irishman was pleading with him. *It doesn't matter any more,* he thought. *In the morning I'm going to retire and rejoin the human race.*

'All right, Sam,' he said finally. 'Let's put it this way – I'll sleep well tonight. All right?'

'Thank you, Judge. Good night.'

Harpur set the phone down with his eyes tight-closed, waited for peace.

Legal processes are central to the study of many social scientists who have examined such topics as the relevance of morality to law, the use and abuse of the power of the law and the cost effectiveness of prison (to name but a few) from a variety of perspectives. But the law and legal processes are based on assumptions about causes of behaviour, and the way behaviour can be modified; about the ways we see and remember things and about the ways in which decisions are made. All these are major topics in psychology. Specifically psychologists have been concerned with:

- Eyewitness testimony – is it reliable? Do studies of memory and perception cast light on its value?
- Courtroom procedure and social processes.
- Small group behaviour as exemplified by jury behaviour.
- Decision making by judges and magistrates.
- Criminal motivation, deterrence and rehabilitation.

Each of these topics could form a book in its own right but the story of slow glass allows us to focus on just one – eyewitness testimony. Why should there be so much fuss about slow glass when human eyewitnesses exist to many crimes anyway? What's wrong with people as witnesses?

How would a human witness compare with slow glass? The most obvious difference is that seeing and remembering are both processes that we do actively, not passively. We bring strong expectations about what we are likely to see, and we actively choose what to look at. The way we attend to a scene will determine what we see and what we remember.

How could you show that people attend to different things in the same scene? One method is to show people the same picture, ask different questions about the picture, and record what they look at. Generally, we are not much aware of the movement of our eyes when we view the world. One of the many paradoxical things about our visual system is that when we move our eyes, we usually move them in a series of very rapid flicks, called saccades, each followed by a pause, called a fixation. The system works rather like a very fast moving TV camera which pauses from time to time, to get a decent image. Somehow, we put all this information together, ignoring the blurring that must occur as a result of the movement of our eyes, to give a sensation of a stable world around us, more or less all in focus, which we look at, at will in a smoothly continuous way. We can investigate what people are looking at by recording the position of their eyes, then we can superimpose this on the picture itself. This is exactly what Yarbus did, as part of his research into different viewing patterns. Figure 2.1 shows 'typical' viewing patterns from two people who are shown the same picture, but are asked different questions about it.

One viewer (a) was asked to remember the position of the people and objects in the room; the other viewer (b) was asked to give the ages of the people. The eye movements superimposed on the pictures show us clearly that perception can be directed; we look for particular things in a reasonably ordered way.

The situation of viewing static pictures is a bit artificial; after all, our world is full of movement and change which affects us directly – we don't just sit and scan it. Is there evidence that attention is at work here? In a task like driving our attention (and eye movements) focuses on the most important aspects of the scene – road margins, other cars, pedestrian crossings and the like. As learners, we are made aware of the need to scan different sources of information regularly – such as the rear-view mirror and speedometer, as well as the road ahead. Sure enough, when we record the eye movements of drivers, they confirm our expectations of what the driver looks at. So attention to things which we are engaged in is a major feature of perception. What are the implications for eyewitness testimony? Well, because our potential witnesses are looking at parts of the scene that are relevant to things that they are doing, they may fail to attend at all to details which are important to a criminal event.

Do we have to try to remember details of things we attend to, or are they stored automatically? Time for an exercise. Try some of these:

- Do oak trees or chestnut trees loose their leaves earlier in the autumn?
- Do horses in fields stand with head or tail to the wind?
- In which direction do the seeds of an apple point?
- What is the smallest coin that is legal tender? Try to draw it, both of its sides, then check all the details against the real thing.

Figure 2.1. Different viewing patterns for the same scene.

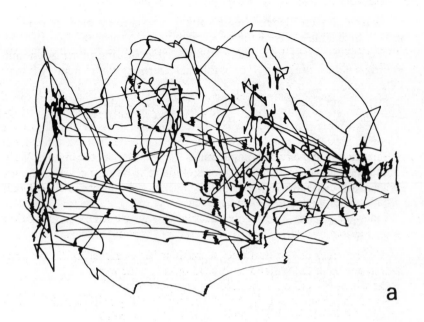

a

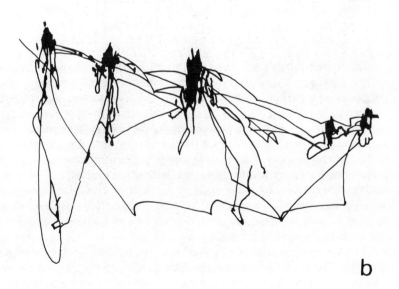

b

Reprinted with permission from R.N. Haber and M. Hershenson (1980) *The Psychology of Visual Perception*, 2nd ed. New York: Holt Rinehart and Winston.

41

- What was the weather, exactly one week ago?

We have all seen all these things many times, yet few people can remember all the details correctly (chestnut; tail; point towards the stem).

There is far more to memory, though, than storing information and pulling it out for use, later. One of the characteristics of our memory is that we store meanings of events, rather than copies of the events that happened. Bransford and Franks conducted one of the classic studies in this area. A series of short sentences were read out, some of which told a story. For example:

The rock rolled down the mountain.
The jelly is sweet.
The rock crushed the hut.
The hut is at the river.
The breeze is warm.
The hut is tiny. Etc.

After each sentence a simple question was asked, for example 'where is the hut?' Five minutes after the last sentence was read, test sentences were presented. The test was simply to say which sentences had been heard before, and which ones were new. Here are some of the test items.

1. The rock which rolled down the mountain crushed the tiny hut at the river.
2. The rock crushed the tiny hut at the river.
3. The rock crushed the tiny hut.
4. The hut is at the river.

Which ones do you think were recognized as having been heard already? Only the last sentence was actually present in the original list; most participants denied that they had heard it before. A large majority of participants claimed to have heard the first sentence – showing that they seem to have abstracted and remembered the meanings of the story rather than the actual sentences presented. Sir Frederick Bartlett carried out a number of studies of memory for stories, pictures and prose passages in which observers were given something to remember, and then were asked to recall it. In different experiments, he looked at the changes that take place as people recall the same passage again and again, over a period of time; at the effects of people passing a story on from one to the next; and at the effect of allowing outsiders to ask for clarifying details.

The most obvious change observed was that the passage got a good deal shorter. Details like proper names were quickly lost; other details were changed, so too were elements of the story that did not seem significant to the reader – and different elements were judged significant by readers from different cultures.

Another major kind of distortion noted by Bartlett is *rationalization*. Subjects add and delete material so that the resulting story 'makes sense'. This effect was particularly marked when people were questioned about their memories.

Bartlett explained these general results by arguing that memory consists of mental frameworks, built up from past experience, which enable us to understand and deal with the immediate present. These frameworks he called *schema*; when we learn something new, we try to fit the new material into our existing schema. If we have very little past experience to go on, learning will be slow, while appropriate schema are built up; if existing schema conflict with the new material to be learned, distortions are likely to occur in the way that the new material is perceived.

Bartlett placed great emphasis on the idea that both learning and remembering are *active* processes, in which we strive to make sense of the new material, or our old memories. When we remember, we don't replay some mental videotape; we reconstruct what must have occurred from the fossil fragments of memory, and the schema they are embedded in!

If the videotape view of perception is wrong, and the active process view is right, then current practices of taking statements, identifying suspects and interviewing witnesses in court could actively cause distortions in eyewitness testimony.
Would this be serious, if it were true?

In 1976 the Devlin Committee analysed all identification parades which had been held in England and Wales during the year 1973. There were over 2000 of them, with 45 per cent of them leading to a suspect being picked out. Of these, no less than 82 per cent were subsequently convicted. In all there were almost 350 cases in which eyewitness identification was the *only* evidence of guilt. Even here, 74 per cent were convicted, indicating the overwhelming weight given to eyewitness testimony.
Baddeley, 1983.

But we are trying to draw grand conclusions on far too flimsy a basis. Let's consider some much simpler questions before we consider these major issues.

How good are we at recognizing people and things that we have seen before? If the initial viewing conditions are good, then our visual memory appears to be quite remarkable. Let's look at some laboratory studies which set out to explore memory for photographs.

Shepard (1967) showed people over 600 pictures of objects and scenes that they hadn't seen before, and asked them to remember them. As soon as they had seen them, they were presented with a series of pairs of pictures. In each pair, one picture was taken from the set they had just seen, and one was new. How well could people tell the old and new ones apart? Shepard

43

showed everyone 68 pairs; people picked the old picture out correctly 98 per cent of the time. How well does this memory last? One week later, faced with the same task, accuracy was about 90 per cent. Other researchers have produced similar results, even using several thousand pictures in the original set to be remembered. What about remembering faces? Hochberg and Galper (1967) showed faces of college students (up to 60), then asked observers to identify the old and new face in a pair of pictures, in the same way that Shepard had done for objects and scenes. Accuracy was about 90 per cent. But perhaps this task of just telling old and new faces apart when one of each is presented in a pair is too easy. What happens when people are asked to sort out new and old faces from a large display? Going and Read (1974) showed people 20 photographs of faces, and then asked people to pick these out from an array of 40 faces, as part of their research on face recognition. Accuracy was about 90 per cent.

People quite commonly claim to have 'a very good memory for faces'. Each of us knows a very large number of people by sight – friends; people we recognize in the local community; television personalities; and more. We don't feel that we make many mistakes in identifying people either. Does all this give us great confidence about our abilities to appear in court as witnesses to crimes? It might, but it shouldn't! The laboratory-based studies took place under almost ideal conditions – participants knew what to attend to, were given plenty of time to study the pictures, and were not stressed by any of the procedures. With familiar faces, we have by definition had many occasions to study them – and we don't really know exactly how good we are at face recognition, because we don't test ourselves very often!

Let's consider the problems faced by a witness a bit more systematically. We have already noted a major problem that we face as witnesses in court is that we are being asked to do something that is quite alien to our normal cognitive functioning – you could even say that we are trying to do things that perception and memory aren't designed for.

The legal process assumes that the witness can act like someone who has taken a video recording of an event, which can then be described to the police during the initial part of the investigation; then to a group of people in court. Of course, the tape can be played repeatedly without changing it in any way, and more and more information can be gleaned by concentrating on different aspects of the tape each time it is replayed. A role of the defending council can be to find questions which show that either the videotape or the recorder are defective in important ways. Is anything wrong with this assumption? Yes. There are lots of ways in which our recollections of an event that was witnessed might be defective. The event is seen only once; the witness isn't usually expecting a criminal event to happen; the actions may last for a very short time; criminals sometimes deliberately try not to be recognized; we might forget things that happened;

and our memories might actually be changed by the processes involved in recall. Let us look at some of these issues in more detail.

Perhaps the most obvious reason for defective recall is that details of the event were not stored in memory at all! We noted earlier that perception is an active, attention-driven process. The world presents us with a huge array of objects and events which all compete for our attention. By and large, things we don't attend to are not remembered well, so if we are present at a crime such as shoplifting, our attention could easily be directed away from the scene of criminal activities – after all, we usually go into shops to look at the goods for sale, rather than at other customers. A second factor related to the perception of events is the *duration* of the events themselves. Seeing things takes a measurable amount of time. A standard research tool for psychologists interested in visual perception is a device called a tachisto-scope. This allows an experimenter to control the amount of viewing time available for any scene very carefully. At short inspection times, very little is recalled, even by observers who know exactly where to look, and roughly what they will be seeing. The popular notion that a fleeting glance can reveal a wealth of information is almost certainly wrong.

Viewing conditions are rarely ideal. Buckhout (1974) describes a case in which he acted for the defence. 'A police officer testified that he saw the defendant, a black man, shoot a victim as both stood in a doorway 120 feet away. Checking for the defence, we found the scene so poorly lit that we could hardly see a person's silhouette, let alone a face; instrument measurements revealed that the light falling on the eye amounted to less than a fifth of the light from a candle'. Jurors visited the scene, and the defendant was acquitted.

Viewing conditions can be less than ideal in other senses than how much light was falling on the scene. Key witnesses – notably victims of crime – usually observe events when they are emotionally roused, for example they may be afraid, or angry or generally upset. What effect will this have on their ability to remember details? We know from other studies that stress can narrow attention to a small part of the scene. A threatened individual may well be concentrating on personal well-being, rather than deliberately trying to record details about threatening individuals. For ethical reasons, appropriate studies have not, as far as we know, been done in laboratories to simulate those emotional states in witnesses. What has been done, though, is to look at the effects of viewing violence on our ability to remember events.

Elizabeth Loftus (1979) asked 500 students for their views; the majority (66 per cent) believed that both men and women would remember scenes involving violence better than non-violent ones. How would you set out to test this belief? Clifford and Scott (1978) tackled the problem by preparing two versions of a videotape in which two policemen were searching for a criminal; one contained a violent passage in the middle, and one had a non–

violent middle part. Groups of 12 men and 12 women watched each tape, and then wrote down their answers to 40 questions about the events shown. Both men and women remembered considerably more in the non-violent version. We have to be very careful not to place too much importance on a single laboratory study where people watch videotapes, and not to generalize the results uncritically to real-world eyewitnessing. Nevertheless, this experiment suggests that our everyday conceptions might well be wrong, and that eyewitness memory may be fallible for yet another reason.

William Stern founded the journal *Beiträge zur Psychologie der Aussage* (*Contributions to the Psychology of Testimony*) around the turn of this century because he was convinced of the need for psychological studies to foster understanding of, and to help improve, the legal process. In his own studies he examined both memory for pictures and memories for events. One of the techniques he described in 1904 has been used extensively since then. Students are gathered in a room as part of their routine learning, and an interruption of some description is staged, which they neither expect, nor feel obliged to attend to. Some time after the event, they are questioned about exactly what took place, the location of objects, the appearance of the actors, and so on.

In the 1904 study, a stooge interrupted a seminar by entering the room, talking to Professor Stern, handing him an envelope, examining the books in the bookcase, one in particular for about 5 minutes, then leaving with the book. Eight days later, all the students in the seminar were asked to write out a report of the event, underlining those parts of the report that they were prepared to swear to in a court of law. Stern then asked them 24 questions which covered the essential features of the event. Fifteen students took part in this study. Stern found that students were able to provide a good deal of information – for example more than half the questions were answered, on average. However, the accuracy of the reports was poor. Overall, about one-third of the subjects' assertions were incorrect – about a quarter of the statements in the initial reports were false, and about half of the responses to the questions! Stern observed:

> The consequence of inadequate attention to an event is not that testimony becomes very brief, but that it becomes very prone to error … we found a much higher error rate (by a factor of two) in the interrogations than in the initial reports. In the present case there were an equal number of right and wrong answers, so the responses to the interrogation have no credibility at all.

This result has been shown over and over again by other researchers.

Stern's stooge removed a book from the seminar room – violating known rules, and a notice to that effect. What was the fate of the book according to the observers? Seven observers said that the stooge replaced the book that he examined; three said that they didn't know; only four said that he had taken it with him. As Stern observes, 'The return of the book was taken for granted; it *must* have happened'.

How well could the observers describe the stooge? Estimates of height ('average') were accurate; so too were estimates of age. Stern notes, 'With respect to all other features of T's (the stooge) appearance, the inaccuracy of the testimony is frightening ... the *true* colour of his suit and hat were never mentioned by anyone ... he had a moustache and a small pointed beard. Nevertheless, three descriptions credit him with a full beard and two others with a moustache alone, while two female subjects described him as clean shaven'. And so on. Stern concludes:

> Descriptions of individuals play an extremely important part in the testimony of witnesses. With respect to such testimony, the outcome of the present experiment leads to a clear conclusion. *Retrospective accounts of people's appearance, especially about hair colour, beardedness, and colour of clothing, should be given no credit whatsoever unless special attention was directed to these features during observation itself.*

An interesting feature of this account is how well it fits in with Bartlett's notions of *schema*. Witnesses report what ought to be the case, not what happened; this effect was most pronounced when observers were questioned directly, when their guesses and rationalizations really had full rein. Unfortunately, we can't claim that this is a great triumph for the model of science in which laboratory-based 'pure' research yields theories about 'the nature of memory' which can then be applied to all sorts of contexts (here: naturalistic laboratory studies). Why not? Because Bartlett knew Stern's original work well, replicated a good deal of it, and borrowed a number of important ideas. Pity though! Still, as we go through a number of studies on recognition and witnessing, think about what they tell us about memory in general – *do* the results fit with the Stern and Bartlett ideas on schema?

Witnesses have more problems than the people who took part in these studies. Leaving aside the viewing conditions, they have to recall where they saw a particular face, and not just identify it as being familiar or not. This might be quite problematic! Have you ever encountered someone you have seen on TV, or in a play, or even in a lecture, and greeted them as a friend to a suitably puzzled response? Or met someone out of the context that you usually see them in, (say meeting the man in the paper shop at a sport meeting, or a neighbour when you are on holiday)? You know that you know them, but searching around in memory for more details can take quite a long time!

Brown, Deffenbacker and Sturgill (1977) decided to investigate these problems – in particular, to look for evidence concerning the Supreme Court report which suggested that exposure to mugshots might change witnesses' memory either for who was seen, or where they were seen (e.g. in the police station or at the scene of the crime).

They showed people photographs of faces in different rooms, and asked them to remember both the faces and where they had seen them. People who took part were able to recognize the faces that they had seen before pretty well (96 per cent of the faces), but of these correct recognitions, people found it much harder to remember where they had seen them, being correct only 58 per cent of the time. Worrying, isn't it?

In their second study, 10 'criminals' appeared before a class who had been told to observe them closely. The class was then shown pictures of some of the 'criminals', together with other photographs of new people. One week later, the class was presented with several 'line-ups', which contained some of the original 'criminals' (both those whose pictures had, and had not been shown), some 'non-criminals' whose photographs had been shown, and some people who were new to those students. Who would be picked out of the line-ups? The results give us cause for concern. The chance of indicting a non-criminal whose mugshot had been shown was one in five; the chance of indicting a criminal whose mugshot had not been shown was only one in two.

Their third study showed up these problems even more dramatically. In preparation for a mid-term class test, students were given a test question by one person, and an answer sheet by another, in the corridor outside the room. These were the 'criminals' that they were later asked to identify. Actually, there were two corridors leading to the test room, so about half of the students saw one pair of 'criminals', while the others saw the other pair. (The answer sheets were coded so that the experimenters could match students and corridors.) Two days after the class test, each of 175 witnesses was shown photographs of 12 people; these included one person who had handed them a sheet; a person from the other corridor that they didn't see, and ten 'innocent' people. Witnesses were asked to look at each photograph, (actually a full-face shot plus a profile) and to say whether or not this person had handed them materials at the mid-term test. Four days later, the witnesses were shown a line-up of four 'criminals' (guess who?), and were asked to say whether each one had handed them materials at the test, and also which ones had been shown in the photograph identification test. Another interesting feature of the study was that each witness was asked to say how confident they were about their decisions.

So the scene is set. We have four 'criminals' on parade. Each witness has seen two of them at the 'crime'. One of these two has also been seen in a mugshot, while the other hasn't. There are two 'innocent' people ('innocent' because they were being 'criminals' in the other corridor!). One of these has been seen in a mugshot, while the other hasn't. Try and predict who will be identified most often. Next, think about confidence ratings. The witness in court who shouts 'That's him! – I'll never forget that face!' is more likely to be believed by judge and jury than someone who says, 'That's him. I think'. But what are these self-ratings of confidence actually worth?

First let's look at who gets identified.

Table 2.1. The effect of viewing crime and seeing the mugshot on the rate of identification

	Criminal	Not Criminal
Mugshot seen	45	29
No mugshot seen	24	18

The table shows that, in this experiment, exposure to the mugshot had as much effect on later identification as actually being there! (Notice that being there, and being seen in a mugshot doesn't do much more than double the chance of identification over a complete stranger.)   What about confidence ratings? Are people who are certain about their identifications also the ones who got them right? In this study and in others we get the clear message that there is *no* relationship between accuracy and confidence! This is rather surprising, don't you think?

So these studies suggest strongly that when people see others briefly, and have no reason to remember them, later accuracy of identification is rather poor. The accuracy can be reduced even further by procedures like examining photographs, because the faces seen are often remembered, but *where* they were seen is not. The lack of any relationship between confidence and accuracy is counter-intuitive, and worrying.

Can anyone remember what the 'criminal' did? The experimenters asked the people who successfully identified either 'criminal' whether the criminal had handed them a test booklet or an answer sheet. The recall was no better than chance.

These studies show that face recognition is much better than the memory of when and where the face was seen, and that witnesses sometimes base their identification on face recognition alone. Witnesses often see suspects in mugshots, so their evidence might be contaminated by this procedure. It seems reasonable to view any testimony which is based on limited exposure to the criminal, or poor viewing conditions, and which is followed by photographic identification as being extremely unreliable.

Buckhout also followed Stern's theme of creating an incident, and examining the responses of witnesses who were unprepared for the event. He and his colleagues staged an attack by a student on a professor in front of 141 witnesses! They then took sworn statements from the witnesses, asking for a description of the incident, together with as many details about the suspect as possible. Of course, they videotaped the incident so that they could check these accounts. As in the Stern study, descriptions were quite inaccurate. The duration of the incident was judged to be more than twice as long as it actually was, for example. Buckhout wasn't just interested in

49

eyewitness recall, though. The main thrust of his study was to examine the ways in which eyewitnesses' reports can be distorted by different interview procedures after the event.

Seven weeks after the staged assault, the witnesses were all tested individually, using a set of six photographs, which included the attacker and a prominent bystander. Witnesses were treated in one of four ways. They received either low or high bias instructions, on either a low or high bias picture set. So a quarter of the witnesses received unbiased instruction and saw the low bias picture set, for example. In the low bias instructions, witnesses were asked simply if they recognized anybody in the photographs; in the high bias instructions they were reminded about the incident, told that the testers had an idea about who the offender was, and were asked to find the attacker in the pictures shown.

In the low bias picture set, all the pictures were of young men with similar, neutral expressions on their faces, presented neatly. In the high bias set, the attacker's portrait was set at an angle, and he was photographed with a distinctive leering expression on his face. What happened? Only 40 per cent of the witnesses identified the attacker correctly. Even the professor who was attacked got it wrong! 25 per cent identified the bystander. You will be dismayed (or perhaps pleased) to learn that using biased instructions and biased photographs, the 'detection rate' improved to 61 per cent! In a subsequent study, using people who *were not present* at the scene, they too were able to pick out the leering, oddly aligned photograph as that of the assailant. Buckhout's study shows clearly that great care must be taken in the way that people are identified using photographs. The same principle can be extended to the use of line-ups. It is easy to show that line-ups can be set up so that the 'correct' suspect is identified – try and design your own study which would let you compare fair and unfair procedures. You will have to decide the ways that you are going to bias your witnesses.

As well as having problems with biases in the way that identification processes are set up, the witness's task can be made appreciably harder by a criminal who adopts a disguise. It isn't too hard to show that disguises make it far harder to recognize people! The size of the effect is quite impressive, though. For example, in a study by Patterson and Baddeley (1975), photographs were taken of a number of people, each wearing a number of disguises, including a wig, a beard, and spectacles, as well as the same person undisguised. Observers were then shown one photograph of each person, in just one combination of disguises. They were shown each photograph until they could recognize and name each photograph correctly. The task the observers were then set was to name these individuals when they were presented with photographs of each person in every disguise, together with an equal number of new faces. The researchers found that each feature of the disguise that was changed (e.g. removed or added) reduced the chance of the observer identifying the photograph correctly. When the face was presented in the same form as it had appeared in the learning trial, the observer's recognition was very good. However, when the maximum number of disguise features was changed, recognition was little better than guesswork.

An interesting subsidiary aspect of this research examined the effect of the camera angle on face recognition presented either full on, or at three-quarters. Patterson and Baddeley found quite clearly that the three-quarters faces were recognized best. Yet both of the two most commonly used schemes for making up suspects' faces from witness descriptions, namely Photo-fit and Identi-kit, use full faces. At present, we can only speculate about possible improvements that might occur if three-quarter faces were used.

Common sense tells us that the use of leading questions will also produce distorted reports from witnesses – use of leading questions in court can lead to objections from opposing council, as we know from court-room dramas on TV! It is easy to demonstrate the effect experimentally.

It has been known for a long time that people have great difficulty in estimating how long events have lasted, and how far and how fast objects (like cars) are travelling. An illustration of this is provided by Loftus and Palmer (1974) who showed different films of car crashes to groups of observers. Observers were first asked to 'give an account of the accident you have just seen', and were then asked to answer a series of specific questions about each incident. If we look at the answer to one question – the actual speed that cars were travelling at, compared with the averages of the observers' estimates (in parentheses), they don't seem to relate at all well: 20 (37.7), 30 (36.2), 50 (39.7), 50 (36.1).

The purpose of this study, though, wasn't just to look at how well people can estimate speed, but the way that the form of the question can affect the estimates given. What happens when the form of the question is varied so that some are more leading than others? Here are the questions, together with the average speed reported.

Table 2.2. The effect of leading questions on speed estimates

Question	Average of speed reported (mph)
How fast were the cars going when they contacted?	31.8
How fast were the cars going when they hit?	34.0
How fast were the cars going when they bumped?	38.1
How fast were the cars going when they collided?	39.3
How fast were the cars going when they smashed?	40.8

What can be concluded from this? Simply that the style of the question has a direct effect on the way speeds are reported, in circumstances where the speed of the vehicle doesn't. Apart from the surprise that vehicle speed wasn't very important to judgement (which does need more thought – would it occur if actual speeds were 5, 20, 40, 80 mph?) this study confirms our common-sense ideas.

Something we might not have good intuitions about though, is the effect that leading questions will have on memory. Is the impact just felt as the testimony is given, or will there be some more diffuse effect on memory for the event, when it is recalled later? In a subsequent experiment, groups of observers again watched a short film in which a car crash occurred. Fifty observers were asked 'About how fast were the cars going when they smashed into each other?'; another 50 were asked 'About how fast were the cars going when they hit each other?'; a further 50 observers weren't asked about speed at all. One week later subjects were asked 'Did you see any broken glass?' (there was none in the accident shown). The group who were asked about vehicles 'smashing' into each other were more likely to wrongly report the presence of broken glass. This is rather worrying from the viewpoint of legal practice - it suggests that not only will the use of leading questions produce distortions in testimony, it might also affect what is actually remembered by witnesses. Elizabeth Loftus has carried out a large number of studies concerned with witnessing and the effects that questioning can have on subsequent recall.

In a study reported in 1977, she showed a number of slides which illustrated an accident in which a pedestrian on a pedestrian crossing was knocked down by a car. In this incident, a green car was shown to drive past the accident without stopping. Observers were asked about the incident; some of these observers were asked a question which referred to the *blue* car which drove by. About 20 minutes after this question, these observers were asked what the colour of the car was which failed to stop. They consistently were more likely to report this car to be blue or bluish green.

How does this result arise? Perhaps observers who fail to pick up the relevant information from the slides are the only ones who are influenced by the information contained in the questions. Loftus looked at this possibility by asking each observer to write down everything they remembered, immediately after the slides were shown. People who included the correct information in the descriptions were just as likely to be influenced by subsequent questioning as those who didn't. So what *is* happening? Well, it appears that the later information which we are given is integrated with the information which is already there, in such a way that the new information cannot be distinguished from the old. So if we draw an analogy with making a wedding cake, adding extra information into memory is like adding brandy to flavour the cake itself – the new ingredient becomes an integral part of the cake, and we have no perception about when it was added. It is unlike the icing on the cake, which can be seen to be a later addition.

We know that there is no such thing as a perfect witness; we know that questioning can actually insert 'facts' into memory, and that seeing a photograph of a 'suspect' can influence a witness about the identity of an assailant. So what can we do? To be 'fair' to everyone concerned, should we abandon *all* questioning by the police, and avoid line-ups, photofits and the like? Try and think about ways that current procedures might be improved, based on what you have read. Here are some starting points:

- encourage free recall of events by witnesses, and avoid directive questioning
- use two identity parades, one of which doesn't contain a suspect, to soften pressures on witnesses to pick *someone*
- ask suspects to move and speak.

Are existing practices completely useless? Of course not. How can courts take account of biases induced in witnesses, though? In a case brought before the United States Supreme Court by Simmons and Garrett, two men who had been convicted of robbery appealed against their sentence, on the grounds that the FBI had biased witnesses against them. Andrews, a third person convicted for involvement in the crime, did not appeal. The FBI had shown family photographs, which included these men, in an informal way to witnesses who were asked if they could recognize any of the faces. Let's go back to the crime. Two unmasked men robbed a bank in the presence of five bank employees. These witnesses wrote out their statements of the incident for the FBI. The FBI searched the house of the mother of one of the suspects, and found incriminating evidence. Photographs of several groups of people, obtained from Simmons' sister – which included Andrews and Simmons as well as others – were shown to each witness individually. Each witness identified Simmons as one of the robbers; none identified Andrews. Later, witnesses were shown other pictures, and three of them identified Garrett. At the trial, the witnesses identified Simmons and Garrett.

What is wrong with that? Well, Simmons and Garrett argued that the way the photographs were used seriously prejudiced the trial. Since Simmons was one of the very few people to appear on all the photographs shown to witnesses, they didn't have to have recognized him from the bank – they could have worked out who they were 'supposed' to identify from the photographs alone.

What would you rule if you were a supreme court judge here?

Mr Justice Harlan reviewed several of the pitfalls of using photographs to identify criminals. He pointed out the dangers of presenting a witness with a photograph of someone who physically resembles the person that he saw; and the attendant dangers that the witness will remember the face in the photograph rather than the one he saw. To balance these warnings, he pointed to the usefulness of photographs; they *can* offer leads to suspects, and spare innocent people from arrest. Sensibly and significantly, the judge asserted 'that each case must be considered on its own facts, and that the convictions based on eyewitness identification at trial following a pretrial identification by photograph will be set aside on that ground only if the photographic identification procedure was so impermissibly suggestive as to give rise to a substantial likelihood of irreparable misidentification'.

In this particular case, the witnesses' viewing conditions were good; witnesses observed the suspect, who was unmasked, for about five minutes; they viewed the photographs the following day, when their memories were fresh; witnesses saw groups of people in photographs, and there is no reason to suppose that they were influenced in their choices about who they were 'supposed' to choose. No witness identified Andrews, who was as prominent in the photographs as Simmons. During cross-examination, none of the witnesses expressed any doubt about their identification of Simmons.

To summarize this view: eyewitness testimony can be error prone, and police procedure can bias witnesses. However, the possibility of errors doesn't rule out its use. Instead, the judicial process must take account of the possibility for error, and weigh the evidence from witnesses along with other kinds of evidence, such as circumstantial evidence, 'incriminating items' and the like.

Now for two problems to think about, one based in fiction, and one on a real event. In the story, we were offered the dramatic irony of Judge Harpur 'recognizing' the man on his way home from the bowling match as Ewan Raddall – the murderer he sent to his death three years before. Is it plausible? Could he make such a mistake?

The second problem comes from a report in Alan Baddeley's guided tour of memory. He recounts an incident which involved Donald Thompson, an Australian psychologist who himself has carried out studies on the reliability of eyewitness testimony. Thompson was picked up by the police, and placed in a line-up, without explanation. A woman identified him and he was told that he was to be charged with rape. The time of the rape coincided with Thompson's appearance in a television discussion, which included an Assistant Commissioner of Police, among others – a watertight alibi by any standards! Try to work out what happened.

Suppose *you* were Thompson, the eyewitness expert, and the television discussion had been recorded, and broadcast on the night of the rape – which you had spent alone, watching TV (predictably!). Now your alibi is distinctly shaky – how will you defend yourself in court?

Two Concluding Remarks
Lord Devlin concluded in 1976 that:

> ... a gap exists between academic research into the powers of the

human mind and the practical requirements of courts of law and the stage seems not yet to have been reached at which the conclusions of psychological research are sufficiently widely accepted or tailored to the needs of the judicial process to become the basis for procedural change.
Devlin Report, 1976.

What do you think, now? In 1977 Paul Meehl offered a psychologist's view.

Unavoidably the law will continue to rely on ... fireside inductions. They should be viewed with that scepticism toward anecdotal evidence and the received belief system that training in the behaviour sciences fosters, but without intellectual arrogance...in favour of overvalued or overinterpreted scientific research.
Meehl, 1977, p.28.

I wonder what the Iron Judge would think?

3

ORR'S DREAMS

Ursula Le Guin

The portal of God is non-existence.
Chuang Tse: XXIII

Dr. William Haber's office did not have a view of Mount Hood. It was an interior Efficiency Suite on the sixty-third floor of Willamette East Tower and didn't have a view of anything. But on one of the windowless walls was a big photographic mural of Mount Hood, and at this Dr. Haber gazed while intercommunicating with his receptionist.

'Who's this Orr coming up, Penny? The hysteric with leprosy symptoms?'

She was only three feet away through the wall, but an interoffice communicator, like a diploma on the wall, inspires confidence in the patient, as well as in the doctor. And it is not seemly for a psychiatrist to open the door and shout, 'Next!'

'No, Doctor, that's Mr. Greene tomorrow at ten. This is the referral from Dr. Walters at the University Medical School, a VTT case.'

'Drug abuse. Right. Got the file here. O.K., send him in when he comes.'

Even as he spoke he could hear the elevator whine up and stop, the doors gasp open; then footsteps, hesitation, the outer door opening. He could also, now he was listening, hear doors, typewriters, voices, toilets flushing, in offices all up and down the hall and above him and underneath him. The real trick was to learn how not to hear them. The only solid partitions left were inside the head.

Now Penny was going through the first-visit routine with the patient, and while waiting Dr. Haber gazed again at the mural and wondered when such a photograph had been taken. Blue sky, snow from foothills to peak. Years ago, in the sixties or seventies, no doubt. The Greenhouse Effect had been quite gradual, and Haber, born in 1962, could clearly remember the blue skies of his childhood. Nowadays the eternal snows were gone from all the world's mountains, even Everest, even Erebus, fiery-throated on the waste Antarctic shore. But of course they might have colored a modern photograph, faked the blue sky and white peak; no telling.

'Good afternoon, Mr. Orr!' he said, rising, smiling, but not extending his hands, for many patients these days had a strong dread of physical contact.

The patient uncertainly withdrew his almost-proffered hand, fingered his necklace nervously, and said, 'How do you do.' The necklace was the usual long chain of silvered steel. Clothing ordinary, office-worker standard; haircut conservative shoulder-length, beard short. Light hair and eyes, a short, slight, fair man, slightly undernourished, good health, 28 to 32. Unaggressive, placid, milquetoast, repressed, conventional. The most valuable period of relationship with a patient, Haber often said, is the first ten seconds.

'Sit down, Mr. Orr. Right! Do you smoke? The brown filters are tranks, the white are denicks.' Orr did not smoke. 'Now, let's see if we're together on your situation. HEW control wants to know why you've been borrowing your friends' Pharmacy Cards to get more than you allotment of pep pills and sleeping pills from the autodrug. Right? So they sent you up to the boys on the hill, and they recommended Voluntary Therapeutic Treatment and sent you over to me for the therapy. All correct?'

He heard his own genial, easy tone, well calculated to put the other person at his ease; but this one was still far from easy. He blinked often, his sitting posture was tense, the position of his hands was overformal: a classic picture of suppressed anxiety. He nodded as if he was gulping at the same moment.

'O.K., fine, nothing out of the way there. If you'd been stockpiling your pills, to sell to addicts or commit a murder with, then you'd be in hot water. But as you simply used 'em, your punishment's no worse than a few sessions with me! Now of course what I want to know is *why* you used 'em, so that together we can work out some better life pattern for you, that'll keep you within the dosage limits of your own Pharm Card for one thing, and perhaps for another set you free of any drug dependency at all. Now your routine,' his eyes went for a moment to the folder sent down from the Med School, 'was to take barbiturates for a couple of weeks, then switch for a few nights to dextroamphetamine, then back to the barbiturates. How did that get started? Insomnia?'

'I sleep well.'

'But you have bad dreams.'

The man looked up, frightened: a flash of open terror. He was going to be a simple case. He had no defenses.

'Sort of,' he said huskily.

'It was an easy guess for me, Mr. Orr. They generally send me the dreamers.' He grinned at the little man. 'I'm a dream specialist. Literally. An oneirologist. Sleep and dreaming are my field. O.K., now I can proceed to the next educated guess, which is that you used the phenobarb to suppress dreaming but found that with habituation the drug has less and less dream- suppressive effect, until it has none at all. Similarly with the Dexedrine. So you alternated them. Right?'

The patient nodded stiffly.

'Why was your stretch on the Dexedrine always shorter?'

'It made me jumpy.'

'I'll bet it did. And that last combination dose you took was a lulu. But not, in itself, dangerous.' He paused for effect. 'You were depriving yourself of dreams.'

Again the patient nodded.

'Do you try to deprive yourself of food and water, Mr. Orr? Have you tried doing without air lately?'

He kept his tone jovial, and the patient managed a brief unhappy smile.

'You know that you need sleep. Just as you need food, water, and air. But did

57

you realize that sleep's not enough, that your body insists just as strongly upon having its allotment of *dreaming* sleep? If deprived systematically of dreams, your brain will do some very odd things to you. It will make you irritable, hungry, unable to concentrate – does this sound familiar? It wasn't just the Dexedrine! – liable to daydreams, uneven as to reaction times, forgetful, irresponsible, and prone to paranoid fantasies. And finally it will force you to dream – no matter what. No drug we have will keep you from dreaming, unless it kills you. For instance, extreme alcoholism can lead to a condition called central pontine myelinolysis, which is fatal; its cause is a lesion in the lower brain resulting from lack of dreaming. Not from lack of sleep! From lack of the very specific state that occurs during sleep, the dreaming state, REM sleep, the d-state. Now you're no alcoholic, and not dead, and so I know that whatever you've taken to suppress your dreams, it's worked only partially. Therefore, (a) you're in poor shape physically from partial dream deprivation, and (b) you've been trying to go up a blind alley. Now. What started you up the blind alley? A fear of dreams, of bad dreams, I take it, or what you consider to be bad dreams. Can you tell me anything about these dreams?'

Orr hesitated.

Haber opened his mouth and shut it again. So often he knew what his patients were going to say, and could say it for them better than they could say it for themselves. But it was their taking the step that counted. He could not take it for them. And after all, this talking was a mere preliminary, a vestigial rite from the palmy days of analysis; its only function was to help him decide how he should help the patient, whether positive or negative conditioning was indicated, what he should *do*.

'I don't have nightmares more than most people, I think,' Orr was saying, looking down at his hands. 'Nothing special. I'm ... afraid of dreaming.'

'Of dreaming bad dreams.'

'Any dreams.'

'I see. Have you any notion how that fear got started? Or what it is you're afraid of, wish to avoid?'

As Orr did not reply at once, but sat looking down at his hands, square, reddish hands lying too still on his knee, Haber prompted just a little. 'Is it the irrationality, the lawlessness, sometimes the immorality of dreams, is it something like that that makes you uncomfortable?'

'Yes, in a way. But for a specific reason. You see, here ... here I ...'

Here's the crux, the lock, thought Haber, also watching those tense hands. Poor bastard. He has wet dreams, and a guilt complex about 'em. Boyhood enuresis, compulsive mother –

'Here's where you stop believing me.'

The little fellow was sicker than he looked.

'A man who deals with dreams both awake and sleeping isn't too concerned with belief and disbelief, Mr. Orr. They're not categories I use much. They don't apply. So ignore that, and go on. I'm interested.' Did that sound patronizing? He looked at Orr to see if the statement had been taken amiss, and met, for one instant, the man's eyes. Extraordinarily beautiful eyes, Haber thought, and was surprised by the word, for beauty was not a category he used much either. The irises were blue or gray, very clear, as if transparent. For a moment Haber forgot himself and stared back at those clear, elusive eyes; but only for a moment, so that the strangeness of the experience scarcely registered

58

on his conscious mind.

'Well,' Orr said, speaking with some determination, 'I have had dreams that
... that affected the ... non-dream world. The real world.'

'We all have, Mr. Orr.'

Orr stared. The perfect straight man.

'The effect of the dreams of the just prewaking d-state on the general
emotional level of the psyche can be – '

But the straight man interrrupted him,. 'No, I don't mean that.' And
stuttering a little, 'What I mean is, I dreamed something, and it came true.'

'That isn't hard to believe, Mr. Orr. I'm quite serious in saying that. It's only
since the rise of scientific thought that anybody much has been inclined even to
question such a statement, much less disbelieve it. Prophetic – '

'Not prophetic dreams. I can't foresee anything. I simply *change* things.' The
hands were clenched tight. No wonder the Med School bigwigs had sent this one
here. They always sent the nuts they couldn't crack to Haber.

'Can you give me an example? For instance, can you recall the very first time
that you had such a dream? How old were you?'

The patient hesitated a long time, and finally said, 'Sixteen, I think.' His
manner was still docile; he showed considerable fear of the subject, but no
defensiveness or hostility toward Haber. 'I'm not sure.'

'Tell me about the first time you're sure of.'

'I was seventeen. I was still living at home, and my mother's sister was staying
with us. She was getting a divorce and wasn't working, just getting Basic
Support. She was kind of in the way. It was a regular three-room flat, and she
was always there. Drove my mother up the wall. She wasn't considerate, Aunt
Ethel, I mean. Hogged the bathroom – we still had a private bathroom in that
flat. And she kept, oh, making a sort of joking play for me. Half joking. Coming
into my bedroom in her topless pajamas, and so on. She was only about thirty. It
got me kind of uptight. I didn't have a girl yet and ... you know. Adolescents.
It's easy to get a kid worked up. I resented it. I mean, she was my aunt.'

He glanced at Haber to make sure that the doctor knew what he had resented,
and did not disapprove of his resentment. The insistent permissiveness of the late
Twentieth Century had produced fully as much sex- guilt and sex-fear in its heirs
as had the insistent repressiveness of the late Nineteenth Century. Orr was afraid
that Haber might be shocked at his not wanting to go to bed with his aunt.
Haber maintained his noncommittal but interested expression, and Orr plowed
on.

'Well, I had a lot of sort of anxiety dreams, and this aunt was always in them.
Usually disguised, the way people are in dreams sometimes; once she was a white
cat, but I knew she was Ethel, too. Anyhow, finally one night when she'd got me
to take her to the movies, and tried to get me to handle her, and then when we
got home she kept flopping around on my bed and saying how my parents were
asleep and so on, well, after I finally got her out of my room and got to sleep, I
had this dream. A very vivid one. I could recall it completely when I woke up. I
dreamed that Ethel had been killed in a car crash in Los Angeles, and the
telegram had come. My mother was crying while she was trying to cook dinner,
and I felt sorry for her, and kept wishing I could do something for her, but I
didn't know what to do. That was all ... Only when I got up, I went into the
living room. No Ethel on the couch. There wasn't anybody else in the
apartment, just my parents and me. She wasn't there. She never had been there.

I didn't have to ask. I remembered. I knew that Aunt Ethel had been killed in a crash on a Los Angeles freeway six weeks ago, coming home after seeing a lawyer about getting a divorce. We had got the news by telegram. The whole dream was just sort of reliving something like what had actually happened. Only it hadn't happened. Until the dream. I mean, I *also* knew that she'd been living with us, sleeping on the couch in the living room, until last night.'

'But there was nothing to show that, to prove it?'

'No. Nothing. She hadn't been. Nobody remembered that she had been, except me. And I was wrong. Now.'

Haber nodded judiciously and stroked his beard. What had seemed a mild drug-habituation case now appeared to be a severe aberration, but he had never had a delusion system presented to him quite so straightforwardly. Orr might be an intelligent schizophrenic, feeding him a line, putting him on, with schizoid inventiveness and deviousness; but he lacked the faint inward arrogance of such people, to which Haber was extremely sensitive.

'Why do you think your mother didn't notice that reality had changed since last night?'

'Well, she didn't dream it. I mean, the dream really did change reality. It made a different reality, retroactively, which she'd been part of all along. Being in it, she had no memory of any other. I did, I remembered both, because I was ... there ... at the moment of the change. This is the only way I can explain it, I know it doesn't make sense. But I have got to have some explanation, or else face the fact that I am insane.'

No, this fellow was no milquetoast.

'I'm not in the judgment business, Mr. Orr. I'm after facts. And the events of the mind, believe me, to me are facts. When you *see* another man's dream as he dreams it recorded in black and white on the electroencephalograph, as I've done ten thousand times, you don't speak of dreams as "unreal". They exist; they are events; they leave a mark behind them. O.K. I take it that you had other dreams that seemed to have this same sort of effect?'

'Some. Not for a long time. Only under stress. But it seemed to ... to be happening oftener. I began to get scared.'

Haber leaned forward. 'Why?'

Orr looked blank.

'Why scared?'

'Because I don't want to change things!' Orr said, as if stating the superobvious. 'Who am I to meddle with the way things go? And it's my unconscious mind that changes things, without any intelligent control. I tried autohypnosis but it didn't do any good. Dreams are incoherent, selfish, irrational – immoral, you said a minute ago. They come from the unsocialized part of us, don't they, at least partly? I didn't want to kill poor Ethel. I just wanted her out of my way. Well, in a dream, that's likely to be drastic. Dreams take short cuts. I killed her. In a car crash a thousand miles away six weeks ago. I am responsible for her death.'

Haber stroked his beard again. 'Therefore,' he said slowly, 'the dream-suppressant drugs. So that you will avoid further responsibilities.'

'Yes. The drugs kept the dreams from building up and getting vivid. It's only certain ones, very intense ones, that are ...' He sought a word, 'effective.'

'Right. O.K. Now, let's see. You're unmarried; you're a draftsman for the Bonneville-Umatilla Power District. How do you like your work?'

'Fine.'

'How's your sex life?'

'Had one trial marriage. Broke up last summer, after a couple of years.'

'Did you pull out, or she?'

'Both of us. She didn't want a kid. It wasn't full-marriage material.'

'And since then?'

'Well, there're some girls at my office, I'm not a ... not a great stud, actually.'

'How about interpersonal relationships in general? Do you feel you relate satisfactorily to other people, that you have a niche in the emotional ecology of your environment?'

'I guess so.'

'So that you could say that there's nothing really wrong with your life. Right? O.K. Now tell me this; do you want, do you seriously want, to get out of this drug dependency?'

'Yes.'

'O.K., good. Now, you've been taking drugs because you want to keep from dreaming. But not all dreams are dangerous; only certain vivid ones. You dreamed of your Aunt Ethel as a white cat, but she wasn't a white cat next morning – right? Some dreams are all right – safe.'

He waited for Orr's assenting nod.

'Now, think about this. How would you feel about testing this whole thing out, and perhaps learning how to dream safely, without fear? Let me explain. You've got the subject of dreaming pretty loaded emotionally. You are literally afraid to dream because you feel that some of your dreams have this capacity to affect real life, in ways you can't control. Now, that may be an elaborate and meaningful metaphor, by which your unconscious mind is trying to tell your conscious mind something about reality – your reality, your life – which you aren't ready, rationally, to accept. But we can take the metaphor quite literally; there's no need to translate it, at this point, into rational terms. Your problem at present is this: you're afraid to dream, and yet you need to dream. You tried suppression by drugs; it didn't work. O.K., let's try the opposite. Let's get you to dream, intentionally. Let's get you to dream, intensely and vividly, right here. Under my supervision, under controlled conditions. So that *you* can get control over what seems to you to have got out of hand.'

'How can I dream to order?' Orr said with extreme discomfort.

'In Doctor Haber's Palace of Dreams, you can! Have you been hypnotized?'

'For dental work.'

'Good. O.K. Here's the system. I put you into hypnotic trance and suggest that you're going to sleep, that you're going to dream, and *what* you're going to dream. You'll wear a trancap to ensure that you have genuine sleep, not just hypnotrance. While you're dreaming I watch you, physically and on the EEG, the whole time. I wake you, and we talk about the dream experience. If it's gone off safely, perhaps you'll feel a bit easier about facing the next dream.'

'But I won't dream effectively here; it only happens in one dream out of dozens or hundreds.' Orr's defensive rationalizations were quite consistent.

'You can dream any style dream at all here. Dream content and dream affect can be controlled almost totally by a motivated subject and a properly trained hypnotizer. I've been doing it for ten years. And you'll be right there with me, because you'll be wearing a trancap. Ever worn one?'

Orr shook his head.

61

'You know what they are, though.'

'They send a signal through electrodes that stimulates the ... the brain to go along with it.'

'That's roughly it. The Russians have been using it for fifty years, the Israelis refined on it, we finally climbed aboard and mass-produced it for professional use in calming psychotic patients and for home use in inducing sleep or alpha trance. Now, I was working a couple of years ago with a severely depressed patient on OTT at Linnton. Like many depressives she didn't get much sleep and was particularly short of d-state sleep, dreaming- sleep; whenever she did enter the d-state she tended to wake up. Vicious- circle effect: more depression – less dreams; less dreams – more depression. Break it. How? No drug we have does much to increase d-sleep. ESB – electronic brain stimulation? But that involves implanting electrodes, and deep, for the sleep centers; rather avoid an operation. I was using the trancap on her to encourage sleep. What if you made the diffuse, low-frequency signal more specific, directed it locally to the specific area within the brain; oh yes, sure, Dr. Haber, that's a snap! But actually, once I got the requisite electronics research under my belt, it only took a couple of months to work out the basic machine. Then I tried stimulating the subject's brain with a recording of brain waves from a healthy subject in the appropriate states, the various stages of sleep and dreaming. Not much luck. Found a signal from another brain may or may not pick up a response in the subject; had to learn to generalize, to make a sort of average, out of hundreds of normal brain-wave records. Then, as I work with the patient, I narrow it down again, tailor it: whenever the subject's brain is doing what I want it to do more of, I record that moment, augment it, enlarge and prolong it, replay it, and stimulate the brain to go along with its own healthiest impulses, if you'll excuse the pun. Now all that involved an enormous amout of feedback analysis, so that a simple EEG- plus-trancap grew into this,' and he gestured to the electronic forest behind Orr. He had hidden most of it behind plastic panelling, for many patients were either scared of machinery or overidentified with it, but still it took up about a quarter of the office. 'That's the Dream Machine,' he said with a grin, 'or, prosaically, the Augmentor; and what it'll do for you is ensure that you do go to sleep and that you dream – as briefly and lightly, or as long and intensively, as we like. Oh, incidentally, the depressive patient was discharged from Linnton this last summer as fully cured.' He leaned forward. 'Willing to give it a try?'

'Now?'

'What do you want to wait for?'

'But I can't fall asleep at four-thirty in the afternoon – ' Then he looked foolish. Haber had been digging in the overcrowded drawer of his desk, and now produced a paper, the Consent to Hypnosis form required by HEW. Orr took the pen Haber held out, signed the form, and put it submissively down on the desk.

'All right. Good. Now, tell me this, George. Does your dentist use a Hypnotape, or is he a do-it-yourself man?'

'Tape. I'm 3 on the susceptibility scale.'

'Right in the middle of the graph, eh? Well, for suggestion as to dream content to work well, we'll want fairly deep trance. We don't want a trance dream, but a genuine sleep dream; the Augmentor will provide that; but we want to be sure the suggestion goes pretty deep. So, to avoid spending hours in just conditioning you to enter deep trance, we'll use v-c induction. Ever seen it done?'

Orr shook his head. He looked apprehensive, but he offered no objection. There was an acceptant, passive quality about him that seemed feminine, or even childish. Haber recognized in himself a protective/bullying reaction toward this phyically slight and compliant man. To dominate, to patronize him was so easy as to be almost irresistable.

'I use it on most patients. It's fast, safe, and sure – by far the best method of inducing hypnosis, and the least trouble for both hypnotist and subject.' Orr would certainly have heard the scare stories about subjects being brain-damaged or killed by overprolonged or inept v-c induction, and though such fears did not apply here, Haber must pander to them and calm them, lest Orr resist the whole induction. So he went on with the patter, describing the fifty-year history of the v-c induction method and then veering off the subject of hypnosis altogether, back to the subject of sleep and dreams, in order to get Orr's attention off the induction process and on to the aim of it. 'The gap we have to bridge, you see, is the gulf that exists between the waking or hypnotized-trance condition and the dreaming state. That gulf has a common name: sleep. Normal sleep, the s-state, non- REM sleep, whichever name you like. Now, there are, roughly speaking, four mental states with which we're concerned; waking, trance, s-sleep, and d-state. If you look at mentation processes, the s-state, the d-state, and the hypnotic state all have something in common; sleep, dream, and trance all release the activity of the subconscious, the undermind; they tend to employ primary-process thinking, while waking mentation is secondary process – rational. But now look at the EEG records of the four states. Now it's the d-state, the trance and the waking state that have a lot in common, while the s-state – sleep – is utterly different. And you can't get straight from trance into true d-state dreaming. The s-state must intervene. Normally, you only enter d-state four or five times a night, every hour or two, and only for a quarter of an hour at a time. The rest of the time you're in one stage or another of normal sleep. And there you'll dream, but usually not vividly; mentation in s-sleep is like an engine idling, a kind of steady muttering of images and thoughts. What we're after are the vivid, emotion-laden memorable dreams of the d-state. Our hypnosis plus the Augmentor will ensure that we get them, get across the neurophysiological and temporal gulf of sleep, right into dreaming. So we'll need you on the couch here. My field was pioneered by Dement, Aserinsky, Berger, Oswald, Hartmann, and the rest, but the couch we get straight from Papa Freud ... But we use it to *sleep on*, which he objected to. Now, what I want, just for a starter, is for you to sit down here on the foot of the couch. Yes, that's it. You'll be there a while, so make yourself comfortable. You said you'd tried autohypnosis, didn't you? All right, just go ahead and use the techniques you used for that. How about deep breathing? Count ten while you inhale, hold for five; yes, right, excellent. Would you mind looking up at the ceiling, straight up over your head. O.K., right.'

As Orr obediently tipped his head back, Haber, close beside him, reached out quickly and quietly and put his left hand behind the man's head, pressing firmly with thumb and one finger behind and below each ear; at the same time with right thumb and finger he pressed hard on the bared throat, just below the soft, blond beard, where the vagus nerve and carotid artery run. He was aware of the fine, sallow skin under his fingers; he felt the first startled movement of protest, then saw the clear eyes closing. He felt a thrill of enjoyment of his own skill, his instant dominance over the patient, even as he was muttering softly and rapidly, 'You're going to sleep now; close your eyes, sleep, relax, let your mind go blank;

you're going to sleep, you're relaxed, you're going limp; relax, let go – '

And Orr fell backward on the couch like a man shot dead, his right hand dropping lax from his side.

Haber knelt by him at once, keeping his right hand lightly on the pressure spots and never stopping the quiet, quick flow of suggestion. 'You're in trance now, not asleep but deeply in hypnotic trance, and you will not come out of it and awaken until I tell you to do so. You're in trance now, and going deeper all the time into trance, but you can still hear my voice and follow my instructions. After this, whenever I simply touch you on the throat as I'm doing now, you'll enter the hypnotic trance at once.' He repeated the instructions, and went on. 'Now when I tell you to open your eyes you'll do so, and see a crystal ball floating in front of you. I want you to fix your attention on it closely, and as you do so you will continue to go deeper into trance. Now open your eyes, yes, good, and tell me when you see the crystal ball.'

The light eyes, now with a curious inward gaze, looked past Haber at nothing. 'Now,' the hypnotized man said very softly.

'Good. Keep gazing at it, and breathing regularly; soon you'll be in very deep trance ...'

Haber glanced up at the clock. The whole business had only taken a couple of minutes. Good; he didn't like to waste time on means, getting to the desired end was the thing. While Orr lay staring at his imaginary crystal ball, Haber got up and began fitting him with the modified trancap, constantly removing and replacing it to readjust the tiny electrodes and position them on the scalp under the thick, light-brown hair. He spoke often and softly, repeating suggestions and occasionally asking bland questions so that Orr would not drift off into sleep yet and would stay in rapport. As soon as the cap was in place he switched on the EEG, and for a while he watched it, to see what this brain looked like.

Eight of the cap's electrodes went to the EEG; inside the machine, eight pens scored a permanent record of the brain's electrical activity. On the screen which Haber watched, the impulses were reproduced directly, jittering white scribbles on dark gray. He could isolate and enlarge one, or superimpose one on another, at will. It was a scene he never tired of, the All-Night Movie, the show on Channel One.

There were none of the sigmoid jags he looked for, the concomitant of certain schizoid personality types. There was nothing unusual about the total pattern, except its diversity. A simple brain produces a relatively simple jig-jog set of patterns and is content to repeat them; this was not a simple brain. Its motions were subtle and complex, and the repetitions neither frequent nor unvaried. The computer of the Augmentor would analyze them, but until he saw the analysis Haber could isolate no singular factor except the complexity itself.

On commanding the patient to cease seeing the crystal ball and close his eyes, he obtained almost at once a strong, clear alpha trace at 12 cycles. He played about a little more with the brain, getting records for the computer and testing hypnotic depth, and then said, 'Now, John – ' No, what the hell was the subject's name? 'George. Now you're going to go to sleep in a minute. You're going to go sound asleep and dream; but you won't go to sleep until I say the word 'Antwerp'; when I say that, you'll go to sleep, and sleep until I say your name three times. Now when you sleep, you're going to have a dream, a good dream. One clear, pleasant dream. Not a bad dream at all, a pleasant one, but very clear and vivid. You'll be sure to remember it when you wake up. It will be about – ' He hesitated a moment; he hadn't planned anything, relying on inspiration. 'About a horse. A big bay horse galloping in a field. Running around. Maybe you'll ride the horse, or catch him, or maybe just watch him. But the dream will be about a horse. A vivid – ' what was the word the patient had used? '– *effective* dream about a horse. After that you won't dream anything else; and when I speak your name three times you'll wake up feeling calm and rested. Now, I am going to send you to sleep by ... saying ... Antwerp.'

Obedient, the little dancing lines on the screen began to change. They grew stronger and slower; soon the sleep spindles of stage 2 sleep began to appear, and a hint of the long, deep delta rhythm of stage 4. And as the brain's rhythms changed, so did the heavy matter inhabited by that dancing energy: the hands were lax on the slow-breathing chest, the face was aloof and still.

The Augmentor had got a full record of the waking brain's patterns; now it was recording and analyzing the s-sleep patterns; soon it would be picking up the beginning of the patient's d-sleep patterns, and would be able even within this first dream to feed them back to the sleeping brain, amplifying its own emissions. Indeed it might be doing so now. Haber had expected a wait, but the hypnotic suggestion, plus the patient's long semideprivation of dreams, were putting him into the d-state at once: no sooner had he reached stage 2 than he began the re-ascent. The slowly swaying lines on the screen jittered once here and there; jigged again; began to quicken and dance, taking on a rapid, unsynchronized rhythm. Now the pons was active, and the trace from the hippocampus showed a five-second cycle, the theta rhythm, which had not showed up clearly in this subject. The fingers moved a little; the eyes under closed lids moved, watching; the lips parted for a deep breath. The sleeper dreamed.

It was 5:06.

At 5.11 Haber pressed the black OFF button on the Augmentor. At 5.12, noticing the deep jags and spindles of s-sleep reappearing, he leaned over the patient and said his name clearly thrice.

Orr sighed, moved his arm in a wide, loose gesture, opened his eyes, and wakened. Haber detached the electrodes from his scalp in a few deft motions. 'Feel O.K?' he asked, genial and assured.

'Fine.'

'And you dreamed. That much I can tell you. Can you tell me the dream?'

'A horse,' Orr said huskily, still bewildered by sleep. He sat up. 'It was about a horse. That one,' and he waved his hand toward the picture- window-size mural that decorated Haber's office, a photograph of the great racing stallion Tammany Hall at play in a grassy paddock.

'What did you dream about it?' Haber said, pleased. He had not been sure hypnosuggestion would work on dream content in a first hypnosis.

'It was ... I was walking in this field, and it was off in the distance for a while. Then it came galloping at me, and after a while I realized it was going to run me down. I wasn't scared at all, though. I figured perhaps I could catch its bridle, or swing up and ride it. I knew that actually it couldn't hurt me because it was the horse in your picture, and not a real one. It was all a sort of game ... Dr. Haber, does anything about that picture strike you as ... as unusual?'

'Well, some people find it overdramatic for a shrink's office, a bit overwhelming. A life-size sex symbol right opposite the couch!' He laughed.

came in – before I dreamed about the horse?'

Oh Christ it had been Mount Hood the man was right

It had not been Mount Hood it could not have been Mount Hood it was a horse it was a *horse*

It had been a mountain

A horse it was a horse it was –

He was staring at George Orr, staring blankly at him, several seconds must have passed since Orr's question, he must not be caught out, he must inspire confidence, he knew the answers.

'George, do you remember the picture there as being a photograph of Mount Hood?'

'Yes,' Orr said in his rather sad but unshaken way. 'I do. It was. Snow on it.'

'Mhm,' Haber nodded judicially, pondering. The awful chill at the pit of his chest had passed.

'You don't?'

The man's eyes, so elusive in color yet clear and direct in gaze: they were the eyes of a psychotic.

'No, I'm afraid I don't. It's Tammany Hall, the triple-winner back in '89. I miss the races, it's a shame the way the lower species get crowded out by our food problems. Of course a horse is the perfect anachronism, but I like the picture; it has vigor, strength – total self-realization in animal terms. It's a sort of ideal of what a psychiatrist strives to achieve in human psychological terms, a symbol. It's the source of my suggestion of your dream content, of course, I happened to be looking at it ... ' Haber glanced sidelong at the mural. Of course it was the horse. 'But listen, if you want a third opinion we'll ask Miss Crouch; she's worked here two years.'

'She'll say it was always a horse,' Orr said calmly but ruefully. 'It always was. Since my dream. Always has been. I thought that maybe, since you suggested the dream to me, you might have the double memory, like me. But I guess you don't.' But his eyes, no longer downcast, looked again at Haber with that clarity, that forbearance, that quiet and despairing plea for help.

The man was sick. He must be cured. 'I'd like you to come again, George, and tomorrow if possible.'

'Well, I work – '

'Get off an hour early, and come here at four. You're under VTT. Tell your boss, and don't feel any false shame about it. At one time or another 82 per cent of the population gets VTT, not to mention the 31 per cent that gets OTT. So be here at four and we'll get to work. We're going to get somewhere with this, you know. Now, here's a prescription for meprobamate; it'll keep your dreams low-keyed without suppressing the d-state entirely. You can refill it at the autodrug every three days. If you have a dream, or any other experience that frightens you, call me, day or night. But I doubt you will, using that; and if you're willing to work hard at this with me, you won't be needing any drug much longer. You'll have this whole problem with your dreams licked, and be out in the clear. Right?'

Orr took the IBM prescription card. 'It would be a relief,' he said. He smiled, a tentative, unhappy, yet not humorless smile. 'Another thing about the horse,' he said.

Haber, a head taller, stared down at him.

'It looks like you,' Orr said.

Haber looked up quickly at the mural. It did. Big, healthy, hairy, reddish-brown, bearing down at a full gallop –
'Perhaps the horse in your dream resembled me?' he asked, shrewdly genial.
'Yes, it did,' the patient said.
When he was gone, Haber sat down and looked up uneasily at the mural photograph of Tammany Hall. It really was too big for the office. Goddamn but he wished he could afford an office with a window with a view!

Methought I heard a voice cry, 'Sleep no more!
Macbeth does murder sleep', – the innocent sleep,
Sleep that knits up the ravelled sleeve of care,
The death of each day's life, sore labour's bath,
Balm of hurt minds, great nature's second course,
Chief nourisher in life's feast.
Macbeth II,ii. 36.

Maybe Shakespeare meant *REM* sleep; then again, maybe he didn't.

Ancient Egyptians thought of dreams as being messages sent from the Gods. Professional interpreters of dreams were available to help the recipient understand the message; examples of such people are referred to in the Old Testament. The Egyptians also believed that in sleep the ka was able to leave the sleeper's body to explore the spiritual world, attached only by a slim silken thread to the dreamer. Dreams, then, could be divine messages, prophecies or simply experiences of the wanderings of one's spirit.

The ancient Greeks also treated dreams very seriously. In the temples of Aesculapius devoted to health and healing, emphasis was placed on the content of patients' dreams. These dreams were used to determine both the treatment and prognosis of particular diseases. In the second centuryAD, Artemidorus of Daldis wrote *Oneirocritica*, a scholarly and sensible approach to the interpretation of dreams. Artemidorus insisted that if dream contents were to be understood then the background of the dreamer had to be noted – such as relationships within the family, the dreamer's occupation and whether any of the elements in the dream were related to events in the dreamer's waking life. He argued that there are no universal dream symbols and that the same symbol can mean different things not only to different observers, but also to the same observer on different occasions.

Artemidorus divided dreams into two groups; prophetic dreams, and those influenced by present or past events with no predictive power. The *Oneirocritica* was written to satisfy this need for an interpretation of prophetic dreams. The idea of the prophetic dream is still around: a few days before he was shot dead at the theatre, Abraham Lincoln reported a dream in which he was walking through the rooms of the White House and saw a

67

coffin as he entered the East Room, which was guarded by soldiers. When he asked one of the soldiers who was dead, he was told that the President had died, shot by an assassin.

In the middle ages Thomas Aquinas attributed dreams to four causes which were: visits by God or demons; the daytime concerns of the dreamer; internal factors such as good or ill health; and external factors.

In this century, Sigmund Freud viewed his *The Interpretation of Dreams* as one of his most important scientific achievements, and referred to dreams as 'the royal road to the unconscious'. For him, dreams represent the emergence of repressed unconscious wishes and desires into conscious thought.

So human beings have been studying and writing about dreams for thousands of years. Dreams of significant people have affected the actions of whole nations, as well as of individuals. Dreams take a major role in much of the world's literature. Some societies view dreams and dream interpretation as major events. Appeals to significant dreams (which may never have occurred) can have a great impact even on the technologically developed nations of the West. Remember Martin Luther King's 'I had a dream ...'?

How can we investigate dreams and dreaming? The traditional approach is for the recipient of a dream to visit an expert who can explain it. In modern times this expert role has fallen to the psychoanalyst. The patient visits the analyst and describes the content of a dream, which the analyst then teases apart in order to arrive at its 'true meaning'. Analysis of such dreams seems a reasonable approach to take, if the purpose of the exercise is to understand the dreamer better. If the point of the analysis is to understand dreams and dreaming better then this method of dream analysis is not very good. It is likely to produce an unrepresentative sample of dreams from an unrepresentative set of people (they have submitted themselves for analysis after all, and they are rich enough to pay for it). The sample of dreams is likely to be distorted in other ways as well – notably by the sort of dream the analyst *expects* to be reported. So let us now look at Dr William Haber and his distinguished predecessors. What do *they* have to offer our understanding of dreams and dreaming?

PHYSIOLOGICAL STUDIES OF DREAMING

Hans Berger was a psychiatrist whose interest in the workings of the brain was triggered by an event in which he seemed to be in telepathic communication with his sister. He pioneered work on recording the electrical activity of the brain by placing electrodes directly onto the brain surface of a patient whose skull had been imperfectly formed at birth. Today these electrical 'brain waves' can be recorded by sensitive electrodes placed on the skull itself, then fed to a pen which draws a trace of the electrical signal being picked up. The result is an electroencephalograph, or EEG. In Haber's words: 'When you see another ... dream ... recorded in black and white on the electroencephalograph, ... you don't speak of dreams as "unreal". They exist; they are events; they leave a mark behind them'.

As a research student, Eugene Aserinsky studied the cycle of sleep and wakefulness in infants, and recorded EEGs. He noticed that the eyes of the infant continued to move underneath the closed lids. Aserinsky showed that these eye movements related better to patterns of brain activity than did the gross movements of the infant's limbs. This interesting observation led Aserinsky and Kleitman to study patterns of eye movement in sleeping adults too. As in the case of infants, the periods of rapid eye movements (REM) were associated with particular patterns of brain wave activity. The spectacular finding, though, was that on about 80 per cent of the occasions when people were wakened during REM sleep they reported dreams; outside the REM period – in NREM sleep – they reported dreams only about 10 to 15 per cent of the time.

Why isn't the relationship between REM sleep and dreaming perfect? Dement and Kleitman, in a follow-up study reported in 1957, used stricter criteria of 'dreaming', so that subjects were judged to have been dreaming 'only if they could relate a coherent, fairly detailed description of dream content' and vague assertions that they had dreamed, without recall of content, were considered negative. The proportion of dreams reported in REM stayed at over 80 per cent of awakenings but the proportion reported in NREM sleep fell to 7 per cent. They argued that many NREM dreams could actually have taken place during REM sleep which the recording machine failed to detect because it noted side-to-side eye movements only and failed to record up-and-down movements (for example, watching somebody on a trampoline). It is also possible to have visual dreams that involve few scanning patterns, for example looking at different points on a distant horizon. Kleitman reports that the presence of REMs seem to relate to the degree to which the dreamer is involved in the events of the dream. So in a passive dream REMs are less likely to be observed than in a dream in which the sleeper plays an active part.

Early workers in the field were convinced that there was a strong association between REM sleep and dreaming – and even that the two were identical. Dr William Haber used a phrase to Orr which sums it up – 'the very specific state that occurs during sleep, the dreaming state, REM sleep, the d-state.'

This view has been modified a good deal since the early sixties; NREM sleep isn't as devoid of mental activity as was originally thought – although reports of either visual or sensory imagery are fairly rare. When people are asked if anything was going through their minds when awoken from NREM sleep, they often report mental activities which resemble everyday thinking. When reports taken from REM and NREM sleep are compiled

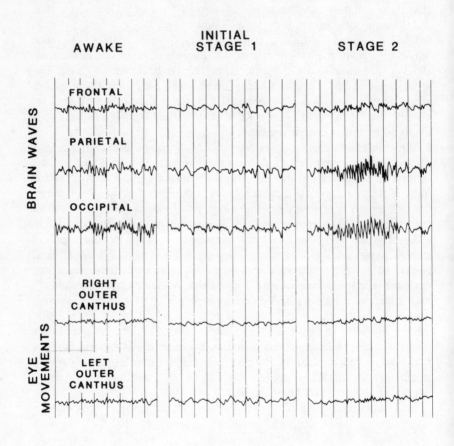

Figure 3.1. Electroencephalograms.

STAGE 3   STAGE 4   EMERGENT STAGE 1 (DREAMING)

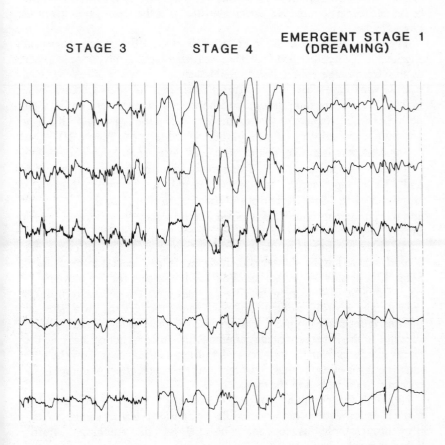

Reprinted with permission from Nathaniel Kleitman (1960) Patterns of dreaming. *Scientific American*, *203(5)*, 82–88. ©1960 Scientific American Inc.

and given to judges to classify as being extracts from REM or NREM sleep, judges can usually classify them correctly about 80% of the time. The features that seem to distinguish REM from NREM mental activities are that REM activities are primarily visual in nature, and are longer than reports obtained from NREM periods, and are less connected. (We'll see some examples later.)

Let's trace through the electrical activities that can be recorded from the brain and eye as people fall asleep starting with the description given in *Orr's Dreams*.

Try to relate the description on page 65 to the EEG records shown in Figure 3.1. Remember that Dr Haber was using the Augmentor to help Orr to skip from Stage 2 directly into REM sleep.

EEG waves are classified in terms of their most obvious features; how high the waves are (amplitude), and how many waves there are in a set period of time (frequency). For example, a *delta* wave is a wave with a very low frequency and very large amplitude. (See Stage 4 in Figure 3.1.)

Someone who is awake, resting with eyes closed shows an alpha rhythm ('frontal awake' in Figure 3.1). These are waves with a frequency between 8 and 13 cycles per second and modest amplitude. As we fall asleep the amplitude of the wave decreases and the rhythm slows down to between 4 and 6 cycles per second. This is called Stage 1 sleep. As the sleeper enters Stage 2 sleep so-called 'sleep spindles' appear ('occipital stage 2' in Figure 3.1). These are bursts of waves of high frequency (14 to 16 cycles per second) whose amplitude waxes then wanes. In the deepest level of sleep, Stage 4, large slow waves appear. You will notice that the eye movements recorded in Stage 4 sleep are moving in synchrony. These trace recordings are *not* trace recordings of true eye movements, they are merely a sign that the electrodes placed at the side of the eyes are picking up spreading brain activity. In the Emergent Stage genuine REMs occur – notice that now the trace recordings from the two electrodes placed by the eyes are now showing mirror images of each other showing a push and pull effect of complimentary muscles attached to the eyes.

Although we talk about 'Stages', the traces of these 'typical examples' make it clear that our brain waves shift their pattern steadily and imperceptibly through these 'Stages' – analysing EEGs isn't like watching the traffic lights change!

We have talked about measuring brain activity on an EEG and recording REM. What other sorts of physiological measures might we take? Obvious contenders are the electrical activity of muscles in different parts of the body; the sleeper's breathing patterns; heart rate; and even the activity of their sexual organs! We can then look at the pattern across all these different measures.

What do we find? In NREM sleep things stay pretty constant. Recordings of muscles that move the eye show little activity (hardly surprising).

The heart rate is maintained at around 60 beats per minute and respiration is also steady. But REM sleep is characterized by changes in variability in almost all the measures we have mentioned. Obviously recording the eye muscles shows significant activity. Heart beat is irregular – as slow as 45 beats per minute or as high as 100 beats per minute; respiration rate is also irregular and genital changes occur regularly too. For example, in males penile erection occurs 90 per cent of the time during REM sleep; in females corresponding changes like increases to the vaginal blood supply also occur. These genital changes are *not* responses to erotic dreams; they simply reflect general changes in arousal across a wide range of bodily functions.

So much for patterns of physical and electrical activity as we drift from being awake through to REM sleep. When does REM activity occur at night? For how long? Back to our resident oneirologist, Dr Haber.

'Normally you only enter d-stage (REM sleep) four or five times a night, every hour or two, only for a quarter of an hour at a time. The rest of the time you are in one stage or another of normal sleep.'

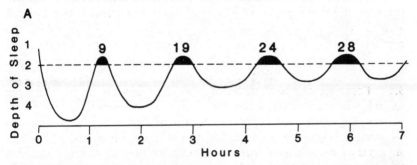

Figure 3.2. Episodes of dreaming.
Reprinted with permission from Nathaniel Kleitman (1960) Patterns of dreaming. *Scientific American*, 203(5), 82–88. ©1960 Scientific American Inc.

The cycle of movements through the various stages of sleep is shown in Figure 3.2. Notice that REM occurs at different stages in the night, and that the period of time spent in REM sleep steadily increases as the sleep continues. Although the pattern of brain activity in dreaming and wakefulness is similar, it is actually harder to awaken somebody from dreaming state than from any of the other levels we have described. This accounts for the name given to REM sleep by some researchers as 'paradoxical sleep'.

A simple but important fact emerges from this dream research. REM sleep is something inherent in the nature of sleeping. It occurs regularly throughout sleep, and for a predictable length of time. If we believe that REM sleep and dreaming are the same thing, this has profound implications for theories about *why* we dream.

Are there any differences in either the quality or the quantity of dreams reported in these different periods of REM sleep?

If people are awoken during their first REM period they report dreams about 60 per cent of the time; if they are woken up during their second REM period they report dreams about 70 per cent of the time and for later periods of REM the rate of reporting of dreams rises to about 85 per cent. As sleep progresses the dreams become longer, more vivid and more emotional. If we ask people about the content of dreams, little continuity is found between dream periods – the same theme doesn't recur through each of the separate phases of dreaming during the night. Of course, a measure like REM or any of the other physiological measures can tell us nothing about the *content* of the dream. By analogy standing outside a football ground and listening to the crowd noises will give clues about whether the game is exciting or not, but can give no description of the exact play which is taking place.

STUDYING DREAMS IN THE LABORATORY

These findings hold the promise of a research tool which can let us examine subjective events like dreams fairly directly. We can answer some of the questions about dreaming which people have puzzled over for centuries by doing experiments in the laboratory. We can examine dream content almost immediately after the dream has occurred. If we wait until morning (or even ask for anecdotes long after the dream has passed) we are likely to suffer from a wide range of losses and corruption in memory. For example, we can wake the dreamer at any stage in the dreaming process – just after the onset of dreaming; after 5 minutes; or after 30 minutes; and ask for dream reports.

How else might we find out about dreams? Before we step into Dr Haber's dream laboratory, we can simply ask people what they dream about.

Asking about Dreams

The obvious way to find out about the characteristics of 'normal' dreaming is to ask a large number of people about their dreams. Let's do it before we talk about it.

THE DREAM QUIZ

1. How often do you dream? (Several times a night? never?)

2. Do you dream in colour? (Always? never?)

3. Can you say what your dreams are like? (Visual? auditory? tactile?)

4. What sort of story lines do your dreams contain?

5. Are your dreams emotionally charged? How? (Anger? happiness? sadness?)

6. Are characters in dreams pleasant or unpleasant?

7. Where are your dreams set? (At home? in the street? nowhere you know?)

8. Do you ever have dreams of falling? being chased? being naked in public? finding money? finding a corpse? seeing yourself dead?

9. Can you control the images you see?

10. Can you change the course of a dream deliberately to make it better?

11. Have you ever had the experience of an outside event affecting your dream? For example 'hearing' the alarm clock as a firebell? Jot down the circumstances.

12. How do you feel in the morning after nights when you don't remember dreaming?

13. Can you plan to have a dream of a particular type before you go to sleep?

14. How often do you have nightmares?

15. Do you often have *recurrent* nightmares – that is, the same theme occurring in successive dreams on different occasions?

16. Have you ever had dreams which seem to predict the future?

17. Do you ever have dreams which seem to give you information about things that are happening in other parts of the world when you are dreaming?

Surveys using questionnaires of this kind can give us general descriptions of the content and pattern of dreaming.

The most obvious characteristic of dreams for most people is that they have a vivid visual quality. Other kinds of imagery occur too, for example images of sound, of touch, sometimes of smell and taste. These images are experienced as if they have been perceived rather than as if they have been remembered. Another major characteristic of dreams is their bizarreness. Dream stories are disconnected. The dreamer can shift from scene to scene and move about in time, without any apparent reason. Dead people can appear and can be responded to as if they were alive. Despite all these peculiarities the dream's lack of continuity holds no surprises for the dreamer during the dream experience. Generally, ill fortune is commoner in dreams than good fortune. Indeed good fortune is remarkably rare. Falling and being attacked, arriving late, finding someone dead, and being nude in public are all quite commonly reported. Pleasant events like finding money, enjoying a party and the like occur relatively infrequently. Calvin Hall collected and analysed 10 000 dreams. Hall found that of over 600 dream episodes roughly two-thirds were hostile in nature. Feelings of happiness appear in less than 20 per cent of dreams; whereas feelings of apprehension and anger together acount for nearly 60 per cent of emotions in dreams! Despite this, dreamers reported that about 40 per cent of dreams were pleasant in nature compared to only 25 per cent that were related as being unpleasant in nature.

An analysis based on about 1800 dreams from people in the age range from 18 to 28 years revealed the mundane nature of dreams; roughly 40 per cent of dreams involve the dreamer interacting with a stranger; in the bulk of dreams the dreamer was interacting with friends, acquaintances or relatives; famous people appeared in only 1 per cent of dreams.

Exotic or bizarre locations are almost never mentioned. Despite this the dream settings are *not* completely typical of everyday life. Locations related to place of work are rather under-represented whereas dwellings, places of recreation and methods of travel are rather over-represented.

The dominant feature of the survey data is that in about a third of the dreams the dreamer was engaged in some form of vigorous movement – for example walking, running or riding. Common domestic activities such as cleaning and cooking were hardly ever mentioned whereas strenuous recreational activities such as swimming, playing games or dancing were mentioned quite frequently. Again dreams appear to be focused on recreational activities rather than representing aspects of everyday life equally.

Sigmund Freud placed great emphasis on the importance of sexual dreams. In a study by Hall and Van de Castle about one in ten dreams reported by young adult males contained some sexual imagery; the corresponding figure for females was one in thirty dreams. These figures might be underestimates, given the Freudian claims that sexual dreams are often disguised by elaborate symbolism!

The major fault with this method of finding out about dreams via surveys is that the reports of dreams are not fresh. We know that people have problems remembering everyday events and actions – let alone things as disconnected as dreams. Freud reminded us about the way that 'dreams melt away in the morning'. People are likely to dream far more than they are able to recall the next day – let alone at some arbitrary point in time chosen by the experimenter.

If Freud is also right in saying that important elements in dreams are disguised from the dreamer, then the experimenter has yet another problem. Important elements may be repressed – for example particularly threatening episodes in dreams, or dreams that arouse anxiety because of their overtly sexual nature may simply not be available to dreamers' conscious thought. Of course the highly emotional aspects of the dream may also inhibit the dreamer from reporting them.

Another problem we all face when we try to describe our dreams is that dreams are primarily visual in character, and coding pictures into words is no easy process! Imagine trying to describe a sunset to someone who wasn't there.

Let us ask some more specific questions about dreaming. Try asking a few friends whether they dream or not. Some people claim they never dream. Are they correct? Goodenough and his co-workers conducted a laboratory study on people who said they dreamt less than once a month and compared them with a group who said they dreamt every night. In the laboratory the 'non-dreamers' recalled dreaming 53 per cent and the 'dreamers' recalled dreaming 93 per cent of the times they were awakened from REM sleep. Both groups had the same number of REM sleeps during the night; however, the REM periods of non-dreamers were shorter on average than those of dreamers, and the dreams they reported were less dramatic in quality. So we can say as a broad statement that everyone dreams.

Why don't people remember their dreams? One possible reason is that the content of the dream is threatening, and that this results in repression. So the dream isn't stored in memory in a way which permits recall when the sleeper is awake. But surveys of what people actually say they dream about show that the largest number of dreams are not particularly threatening. Another explanation might simply be that dreams are hard to remember. Bartlett has argued that we possess mental schema which make things easier or harder to remember depending on whether the incoming material fits existing knowledge structures or not. Dreams obviously have a disconnected quality and are therefore hard to relate to organised knowledge structures. Also, remembering often depends on deliberate effort to remember at the time when the event occurred. There seems little point in remembering dreams, unless one takes the view that the dreams have something informative to tell the dreamer, once awake.

Dreaming in colour? Day-time reports of dreaming in colour vary a good deal. A study involving Dement and his co-workers suggests that all dreams are in colour. As before, the experimenters wait until people are in REM sleep and then awaken them to ask about the nature of their dreams. Everyone in their studies reported dreaming in colour. This suggests that it is the inability to remember, rather than the original experience, that affects our reports of what we dream about.

Do animals dream? Both Lucretius and Aristotle noted that animals' legs twitch while they are asleep, and, for example, sleeping dogs may whine. Both concluded from these observations that animals dream. Animals also show rapid eye movements when asleep. Can we conclude that they dream?

Vaughan carried out an interesting experiment to investigate this. Monkeys were shown pictures that were flashed up on to a screen. When each picture was shown they received an electric shock. They were able to avoid the electric shock by pressing a lever. After a few trials the monkeys were reliably able to avoid being shocked by pressing the lever. When these animals were asleep they attempted to press the lever during REM sleep but not during NREM sleep! This strongly suggests that monkeys experience visual images during REM sleep in just the same way that humans do – suggesting that they dream too.

The perfect research tool? When we looked at other methods of investigating dreaming we offered some criticisms. What about studies done in the laboratory, where sleepers are awoken in REM sleep? Surely there are no problems here? Such sleepers often report dreams connected with their experiences immediately before taking part in the sleep experiment. Dream content may show elements to do with preparation for electrodes being stuck onto the skull or may contain elements connected with the laboratory setting itself. In short, the process of collecting the dream experiences immediately after they have happened can in itself colour the *content* of the dreams.

Affecting Dream Content

Dr Haber was quite confident that he could determine the content of Orr's dreams. He used a trancap to make Orr dream, and post-hypnotic suggestion to affect the actual subject of the dream. Is this possible? From Haber's description of the Augmentor, it sounds like a distant relative of bio-feedback machines which are now quite readily available. In the case of the Augmentor, however, electrical activity from deep in the brain is somehow detected and analysed, and fed back to the subject. In ordinary bio-feedback people are awake and deliberately try to control some physiological measure such as skin resistance or alpha wave activity (people find it almost impossible to describe the mental events associated with controlling such low level processes). Haber's Augmentor is quite a technological triumph! Not only does it detect a very small, specific set of signals in a large background of noise, it also succeeds in changing the electrical activity of the cells that produce these signals.

Sigmund Freud noted that post-hypnotic suggestion could be effective, too. But is there any laboratory- based evidence that it can affect dream content? Yes. Both Stoyva (1965) and Tart (1969) have shown that it *can* work. Both authors remark on the big differences in susceptibility of different people to the suggestions. Here is an extract from Stoyva's paper:

Dream Suggestion: You will dream in every dream tonight that you fall from a horse.
Subject 3: Awakened after 9.0 minutes in REM period 2.

I was, it was in this field in the dark; it was at night. There was this horse, and I had a huge knife and I was chopping at it, and I was chopping at it, and I was chopping at it, attacking me (sic) and it wouldn't go away; cut it and chop at it, its sumpin' awful! It wouldn't fall off, and, a, a, attacked the horse and it wouldn't go, just wouldn't go! I hated it! I don't know why, why I dream about horses, anyway. I hate horses! I don't dare get near a horse!

An interesting feature of many of Stoyva's other reports, too, is that although the topic named in the post hypnotic suggestion is present in many of the dreams, the context in which it is embedded is quite unpredictable. This is quite consistent with Orr's dream; Haber suggested that he should dream about a horse, but he had no idea about the context.

What happens when people are stimulated when they are dreaming? Have you ever absorbed some physical event into a dream – say the absence of bedcovers as a trip in the Arctic; or too many covers as a dream of fever? There are many such anecdotes. People have speculated about these things for a long time. Two obvious questions are: does it really happen at all (or are the anecdotes based on chance coincidences of dream and stimulation)?; are external and internal (hunger, thirst, etc.) events the major causes of dreams?

Maury was a noted philosopher who wrote about dreaming in the nineteenth century. Freud discussed his work. Maury arranged for experiments to be carried out on him while he slept. Some of them had no effect on his dreams, some did. Here are the successful ones:

- When given eau de cologne to smell he subsequently reported a dream in Cairo in Johann Maria Farina's shop.
- When pinched lightly on the neck he dreamt that he was being given a mustard plaster, and thought about the doctor who had treated him when he was a child.
- When a drop of water was dropped onto his forehead he reported a dream set in Italy in which he was sweating violently and drinking white wine.
- When light from a candle was repeatedly shone upon him through a sheet of red paper he reported dreams of the weather and of heat and was once again in a storm in the English Channel.

Tart (1969) summarized many of the early anecdotal reports of attempts to affect dream content. He remarked, 'There seems to be a general concensus in these studies that tactile stimuli are more effective in affecting dream content than stimuli in other sensory modalities'. Does this anecdotal evidence stand up to experimental investigation in the laboratory?

Dement and Wolpert (1958) tried out different ways of stimulating sleepers, to look at the effect on dream content. Many of the dreams recalled reflected these outside sensations. The best results were obtained using drops of water falling on the skin. Of 33 sleepers who suffered the water, 14 reported dreams which contained water; of 15 sleepers who were actually awoken by the water, six reported dreams containing water as an element. Using an electric bell to awaken sleepers resulted in a bell scene in only 20 out of over 200 dreams – most commonly appearing as a telephone or a door bell. Dement and Wolpert persuaded three people to go without fluid for 24 hours on five different occasions. Five of the reported 15 dreams could be related to thirst.

Berger (1963) presented first names to sleepers during Stage 1 dreaming. Some of the names were emotionally significant to the dreamer, and some had no significance. Subsequently subjects were woken and asked to recall their dreams. Later each subject and an independent judge tried to match dream content with the names spoken. Both subject and judge were able to relate the name to the dream content far more often than if the two had been prepared at random. The effect of the name itself – whether it was emotionally significant or not - - had no effect on the chance of the name being incorporated into the dream.

So evidence from dream reports and from laboratory studies gives the same answer to our first question – outside stimulation *can* affect dream content, and the proportion of dreams affected is quite high.

What about our second question – are *most* dreams *caused* by internal or external stimulation? How would you find out? Dement and Wolpert (1958) decided to test the 'stimulation causes dreaming' idea by stimulating people during NREM sleep. If the stimulation theory is correct the sleepers should switch to REM sleep rapidly, or report dreams in NREM sleep. Neither of these things happened. So we can rule out the idea that stimulation is a major cause of dreaming. What other evidence have we seen in this chapter which makes stimulation a poor bet as a major cause of dreams?

Haber caused Orr to have a dream which lasted for about 6 minutes, whose content was triggered by a post- hypnotic suggestion. Do dreams *always* take up measurable time in the non-dream world? Freud describes Maury's most famous dream, set during the French Revolution.

He was ill and lying in his room in bed, with his mother sitting beside him, and dreamt that it was during the Reign of Terror. After witnessing a number of frightful scenes of murder, he was finally himself brought before the revolutionary tribunal. There he saw Robespierre, Marat, Fouquier-Tinville and the rest of the grim heroes of those terrible days. He was questioned by them, and after a number of incidents which were not retained in his memory, was condemned, and led to the place of execution surrounded by an immense mob. He climbed onto the scaffold and was bound to the plank by the executioner. It was tipped up. The blade of the guillotine fell. He felt his head being separated from his body, woke up in

extreme anxiety – and found that the top of the bed had fallen down and struck his cervical vertebrae just in the way in which the blade of the guillotine would actually have struck him.
Sigmund Freud, *The Interpretation of Dreams*.

In its day this dream stimulated a good deal of argument and discussion. It strongly suggests that 'instantaneous' dreams are possible – that is to say an event in the dreamer's external world can stimulate a dream which occupies a long period of time, while the actual time between the stimulus and the sleeper awaking is extremely short (in this case, the time it took the blow from the top of the bed to wake Maury).

If we accept this view we are immediately faced with a paradox. We know that thinking when awake takes measureable amounts of time; we now need to claim that thinking while asleep need not! What other explanation might we put forward for Maury's dream? We might suggest that Maury was mistaken in some of the details that he reports – although this is a rather uncharitable view to take. Or we might use the defence that Freud put forward.

Maury's dream represents a fantasy which had been stored up ready-made in his memory for many years and which was aroused – or I would rather say 'alluded to' –at the moment at which he became aware of the stimulus which awoke him.

Freud goes on to suggest that the story was a fantasy from Maury's younger days, which had lain dormant in his memory for a considerable time. Go back to the story and see if you can find the elements used to defend Freud's idea about a young man's fantasy! According to Freud the impact of the wood on Maury's neck served to gain access to the guillotine fantasy. The fantasy itself was not gone through during the dream – rather it was revisited by the awakened sleeper once its location in memory had been retrieved.

What do you think of Freud's account? Does Maury's dream have the characteristics of incoherence, irrationality and disconnectedness that one often associates with dreams, or does it flow in a continuous story? Well, how are *you* going to account for it?

Maury's dream, of course, highlights the problems that dream analysts face. It is a particularly interesting dream, with a very strong central theme. Is this typical of dreams in general? How long was it after the dream that Maury attempted to recall it in detail? Could Maury have been mistaken about the time when the revolution story was created? We know from laboratory studies that people are well able to remember images such as faces – but have great difficulty remembering where it was that these faces were seen. Do you think that this will be true of other memories we have, too? Let's go into the dream laboratory again, and see what we can discover.

Kleitman found *no* evidence for instantaneous dreams. When subjects were awakened and asked for a narrative of their dreams, the time span implied by the narrative always corresponded to the time span estimated by looking at the length of time the person spend in REM dreaming. (Kleitman didn't try to create Maury-like dreams, though, by waking people up with good dream triggers. No one else has either, to our knowledge.) This suggests that reports of seemingly instantaneous dreams are either best accounted for in terms of our difficulties in remembering durations of time accurately, or are confusions of memory, or are extremely rare events which have not yet been captured in the laboratory.

But let us return to the story – what happens when people are deprived of REM sleep?

REM DEPRIVATION

William Haber made strong assertions about the ill- effects of REM deprivation. He likened our need for REM sleep to our needs for food, water and air, and argued that total deprivation would result in death. Before that, though, 'it will make you irritable, hungry, unable to concentrate ... Liable to daydreams, uneven as to reaction times, forgetful, irresponsible, and prone to paranoid fantasies'. Strong stuff – but is the good doctor correct?

What happens if we stop people dreaming? For the time being we will agree with Dr Haber that REM sleep and dreaming are the same thing. Orr chose to use a mixture of drugs to do this – scientists in sleep laboratories have much more direct methods of achieving the same ends! Given that dreaming is associated with REM, perhaps all we need to do to prevent dreams is to wake people up as soon as REM is observed! What happens? First of all we should note that this method isn't perfect for removing all REM activity since REM activity has to be recognized before the sleeper can be woken. Nevertheless REM time can be reduced to about 75 per cent to 80 per cent of its normal level. Dement began by finding out how long normal subjects slept and dreamed. The average for his eight male subjects was 82 minutes in about seven hours of sleep. For a sequence of nights Dement woke each subject as soon as REM activity was observed. Successive nights required increasing numbers of awakenings. Subjects deprived of sleep were anxious, irritable, ate more and put on weight, in comparison to six other subjects who were simply awoken in NREM sleep. Dement planned to deprive these eight people of REM sleep for five consecutive nights. One of these subjects dropped out after three nights, two more refused to tolerate REM deprivation after four nights.

Dement was interested in seeing the pattern of sleep and dreaming when the sleep deprivation study had finished. Again both dream-deprived and non-dream deprived subjects spent their nights in the laboratory. Now, however, Dement stopped waking them up, and simply observed how long they dreamt for. During this 'recovery' period the dreaming time of five of the eight dream-deprived subjects went up by about 30 per cent and gradually went back to normal levels over successive nights. Control subjects awakened at times randomly distributed through their sleep showed none of these effects.

Why do these results come about? Let's look again at the context in which the experiments were conducted. We saw earlier that REM sleep occurs regularly in everyone's dreaming. Verbal reports from people who claim not to dream were disconfirmed – what they *couldn't* do was remember their dreams. So everyone dreams, every night (if they sleep every night, that is). Why? Well, because we need to dream. But just because something happens, we *can't* conclude either that 'nature made it that way' or that it *ought* to happen. So let's look for other reasons which will convince us about the need to dream. Psychoanalytic ideas suggest that an essential function of dreaming is to discharge some sort of psychic energy. This pressure model predicts that if the night release valve didn't work, then the 'psychic energy' would pour out whenever it could (including during daytime activities), a point made very strongly by Dr Haber in our story. Kleitman quotes Charles Fisher, a New York psychiatrist, as follows: 'The dream is the normal psychosis and dreaming permits each and every one of us to be quietly and safely insane every night of our lives'. Or in Dement's words, 'it is possible that if the dream suppession were carried out long enough, a serious disruption of the personality would result'.

We don't have to believe a psychoanalytic account, of course. We might take refuge in a more conservative biological-style explanation, and argue that we dream not because of the benefits of dreams themselves, but because dreaming just happens to be the psychological manifestation of a physical (i.e. physiological) mechanism which is essential to our well-being.

Dement's first report attracted a lot of scientific interest. Since this early study a large number of deprivation studies have been carried out. In general, careful attempts to demonstrate the dramatic effects that Dement found initially were quite unsuccessful! Dement himself has carried out many studies which disconfirm his initial data. For example, in two papers in the *American Journal of Psychiatry* in 1965 he wrote, 'clear-cut evidence that such deprivation (i.e. REM deprivation) is harmful has not been forthcoming'. 'It seems likely that the psychological changes observed in the earlier studies were an artifact of the experimental procedures and the expectations of the experimenters' (quoted by Vogel).

Let's see what Dement meant by his 'artifact of the experimental procedures and the expectations of the experimenters'.

The early studies were flawed in a number of ways. Researchers often failed to compare REM deprivation with NREM deprivation; subjects were often aware of the experimental and control conditions in the studies in which they were taking part; the evaluators of the dream reports were also often aware of the group membership – experimental or control – of the person whose dreams they were evaluating; reliable measures of psychological change were often not used – or where they were used showed no harm resulting from the procedure. Such 'artifacts' are a common problem in psychological research. Try and say how each one could give rise to false conclusions.

As well as these experimental errors there are a number of other over-simplifications made in the original research.

Take the distinction between REM and NREM reports. David Foulkes found that subjects produced reports of mental phenomena from NREM sleep about as often as they did from REM sleep. He comments, 'Apparently no point of absolute dream onset exists, in the sense that there is no point in the sleep cycle at which consciousness suddenly appears. It seems to be there all along'. The differences seem to be that REM reports are more likely to be labelled as 'dreams' whereas NREM reports are more likely to be called 'thoughts'.

Foulkes quotes some examples from an undergraduate student of English Literature.

1. He pictures Anna Karenina. She is sitting at a table, then gets up, turns to the left, and walks away (NREM).

2. He is in a sleep laboratory, filling out a pencil- and-paper form. Someone passes by, commenting that the task is a stupid one (NREM).

3. In the second scene, he is in a doctor's study with two women and the doctor. They are discussing two books. The heroine in the first book was a striptease dancer, but is no longer this, but a nurse. The women are discussing how much hardship she has as a nurse. A discussion than ensues of a second book, by John Steinbeck, in which the main character, also a nurse, did not, apparently, endure a similar hardship. The women discuss this avidly, as if they were going to go into 'this sort of thing' (REM).

The NREM reports here are tied quite closely to the things that the subject has been doing recently, while awake. The themes are also quite coherent. In the REM report the theme is more confused. Similar differences between REM and NREM reports have been found by other researchers.

Why didn't Dement and Kleitman notice mental activity during NREM states in their germinal studies? Foulkes argues that this is 'attributable to their very stringent criterion of recall, ... and to several features of their awakening procedure which probably served to depress recall outside REM periods'.

So we have to forget the nice neat story that REM sleep is associated with dreaming, and that NREM sleep is associated with mental blankness. If we want to deprive people of conscious mental activity at night, we have to totally deprive them of sleep too. Will REM deprivation remove visual experiences? I am afraid not. The hypnagogic imagery which occurs at the onset of sleep does not involve REM activity but shares with REM activity reports of dramatic sensory images. Judges find it rather difficult to discriminate between descriptions of dream-like experiences obtained from REM reports and from hypnagogic image reports.

So if we want to deprive subjects of dreams, it really is necessary to totally deprive them of sleep also. But is even this extreme measure enough to deprive people of dreams? Foulkes has shown that during periods of relaxed wakefulness without drugs and without prior sleep deprivation, subjects frequently report imaginary sensory experiences similar to dreams!

Vogel summarizes this as follows:

> In short, *dreaming, similar to and often indistinguishable from REM reports, occurs in all the other conventional natural states of consciousness* that sleep researchers recognize in wakefulness, sleep onset, and NREM sleep. Thus, REM sleep deprivation cannot be dream elimination.

Two major issues remain for discussion: why do we dream and how can we use dreams to change our lives?

WHY DO WE DREAM?

Freud argued that dreams represent the emergence of unconscious wishes and desires into consciousness in a disguised form; unconscious processes shape both the organization and the content of dreams. In everyday life we employ strong barriers to stop the emergence of the products of these processes into our conscious thoughts; in dreams the censors work inefficiently. The censors can no longer stop the emergence of emotionally toned materials into consciousness; however, they can distort the expression of drives, for example by symbolization. (For example sexual drives might be portrayed as a figure riding a horse rather than a couple having intercourse.) So dreams represent a compromise between an inefficient censor and unconscious drives and instincts, and therefore serve a useful function in allowing the expression of these drives without exposing the person to their own 'inner nature'. Obviously, then, to understand this inner nature it is necessary to have some knowledge of unconscious motivations and drives which human beings share, and to understand the symbolization process which the inefficient censor applies.

So the motivation for dreaming comes from instinctual drives and energies. This lets us predict that people should dream far more at times when they are experiencing periods of emotional frustration; and that people whose lifestyles are more emotionally frustrated should dream more; and that once dreaming has begun – that is to say once the unconscious processes have access to conscious thought – it should continue until the psychic energy of the unconscious has all been dissipated.

How does the evidence relate to Freud's theory? The most striking feature of electro-physiological studies is the cyclic nature of REM sleep. Nothing in Freud's theory accounts for this. Omissions are hardly damaging, though. More damaging is the fact that most adult subjects spend about 20 per cent of their time in REM sleep; there is not much individual variation, and little evidence that this figure of 20 per cent is changed much by the emotional state of the dreamer, as Freud would predict. So three predictions from Freud's theory fail. Can you think of ways that these criticisms can be deflected? (Think about quality of dreams, rather than quantity.)

Freud has also drawn attention to other functions of dreaming. He pointed out that many minor disturbances at night become incorporated into dreams, thus enabling the sleeper to continue sleeping. Although some dreams do wake us up if, for example, they are very frightening, Freud argues that such dreams are rare in comparison with dreams which maintain us in states of sleep. A second major use of dreams, for Freud, is to satisfy wishes. So students may dream of passing examinations; somebody short of money may have dreams about finding money; unsatisfied sexual urges might be fulfilled by erotic dreams; a hungry person might dream of food. But most dream surveys show that unpleasant dreams are far more common than pleasant ones. Freud has two defences to this argument: first, that such dreams give the dreamer a masochistic pleasure – that is a pleasure in being punished; second, that the part of the personality which is responsible for conscience (superego) produces anxiety dreams. So the superego in such a dream is punishing the dreamer for, say, having aggressive thoughts by sending dreams in which the sleeper is the victim of aggression.

Carl Jung's theory of dreaming has some similarities with Freud's wish fulfilment theory. He argues that people make up for things that they are missing in their everyday lives via their dream activities. Jung believed that the personality consists of a number of different parts. The goal of each of us, according to Jung, is to develop these parts to their full, and to weave them into a coherent whole. Any part of the personality which is ignored in the everyday life of the person will be expressed in that person's dreams. Unlike the Freudian account which suggests that dream images have been disguised and masked from conscious thought, for Jung they are deliberately drawn to the dreamer's attention so that these undeveloped aspects can be developed, then integrated into the whole personality. Jung argues that if our animal instincts are not developed and channelled into constructive tasks and purposes they will result in primitive and infantile sexual and aggressive dreams. So for Jung dreams can be warnings about undeveloped parts of our personality to which attention should be paid in everyday life! As with Freud, symbols can still need interpretation, although the reasons are quite different. For Freud they are masks and veils, for Jung they are mysterious because they are pointers to the way the person ought to behave in their everyday lives and to areas of personality which they have not yet developed.

Let's look at the evidence about the use of symbols in dreams which is independent of the psychoanalytical account. Bertini and his co-workers have produced clear evidence of the use of symbols and metaphor in a state related to dreaming, called hypnagogic imagery. Subjects in the laboratory are asked to lie down, while noise (a hissing sound, like steam escaping from a kettle) is played, and half ping-pong balls are placed over the subject's eyes. This creates a uniform input both to ears and eyes, rather like the input enjoyed by people in sensory deprivation experiments. Subjects are asked to talk continuously, describing thoughts, feelings or images that they have in this situation. These researchers also investigated the effects of stimulation prior to taking part in the sensory deprivation aspect of the study. Subjects were usually shown a film with a strong emotional content, for example a mother monkey hauling her dead baby about, an initiation rite which involved cutting a penis with a sharp stone, or childbirth.

Bertini and his co-workers found that the reports of their subjects during their period of imagery were often heavily influenced by the films they had seen. Material in the film was often transformed in the ways that Freud and Jung describe in their own studies of dreaming. For example after the childbirth film two subjects reported the following hypnagogic imagery:

See a volcano ... or a Polynesian island ... erupting and the black smoke is billowing up from the mouth of the volcano and the red lava is pouring down the side of it, steaming and thick and jelly like. And it's just pouring down the sides.

See a lot of tourists leaving the country and the customs inspector wants to see this lady's suitcase. So he is suspicious and she is taking some jewellery or diamonds or liquor or perfume out of the country and she goes to open up the suitcase and the whole bag opens up. And the contents fall out all over the floor.

The symbolism in the first image is clear; and is a classical transformation of the scene into a 'naturalistic' setting. About the second one, the observers comment, 'Here we have a classic representation of the vagina as a "suitcase" and its precious contents, all opening out onto the floor, in other words delivering the baby'.

So we do have some evidence that symbolization *does* occur (and, incidentally, more evidence that imagery can be affected by recent experience).

Nevertheless the psychoanalytic views of Freud and Jung require us to take a whole set of assumptions about our 'essential nature' on trust. Surely there must be simpler theories?

Perhaps the simplest view is that dreaming serves no useful function. Dreaming is thinking while asleep; mental activities like remembering, interpreting and the like carry on in almost the same way that they do in the waking state – however the things they work upon in everyday life, namely sensations and events in the real world, are no longer present. Instead there are chance patterns of electrical activity from sense organs, which are subject to the same sort of analysis that is applied to ordinary perception during wakefulness. A useful analogy is to think about watching the clouds or looking deep into a fire; it is easy to see faces, figures, animals and the like even though the perceptual evidence for these things is missing. Similarly, in dreams irrelevant internal events are richly interpreted. With this kind of explanation, symbolization occurs simply because the majority of dreams are experienced visually, so abstract ideas have to be somehow represented by images. The apparently disguised, veiled nature of these images arises as a result of the inability to express abstract ideas in pictures.

So why sleep at all? The reasons why we sleep are as mysterious as the reasons for dreaming. People have been found who live quite ordinary lives, but who require only a few hours' sleep per week – and who can easily skip these few hours, too. So sleep doesn't seem to serve any essential biological functions, any more than REM dreaming does. We can invent plausible tales about the biological advantages to an omnivorous animal of being turned off at night! Food sources are hard to find in the dark; the dangers of being caught by predators are greater, as are the dangers of self-damage. Less energy is consumed when asleep, too, than when awake. However, we should be aware that this biological 'explanation' is merely a fairy tale invented after the evidence has been collected, to explain 'facts'.

But why do we dream? Here are two more fairy tales with some explanatory power, but which predict nothing. The first is a 'maintenance' model. In sleep, it is important for the body to be both exercised and rested, so there is a cycle of arousal and rest. The areas of the brain responsible for higher cognitive functions are no exception – they are subject to cycles of arousal too. Our experiences in sleep derive from this brain activity. The second tale is a computer analogy. Suppose you have a computer program that controls a robot, and that, as a result of each day's activity, this program needs to be modified. If you try to modify it while the robot is running, the effect on the robot's behaviour will be quite unpredictable! So you shut down most of the robot's functions, modify the program and make sure that it works, then return the robot to normal functioning. In this analogy the role of dreaming is to update memory (in all aspects); the role of sleep is to allow this to occur safely. Can you think up a couple of similar 'explanations'?

HOW TO INTERPRET YOUR DREAMS

Analysing Individual Dreams

One of the characteristics of dreams that Freud noted is that dream activity is not under the control of direct logical thought. In dreams, hopes and fears, worries and anxiety flow across the dreamer unhampered. The investigation of dreams, then, offers a view of a person from the inside! Each individual's mental associations, desires and attitudes can be reflected in their dream material, which can be reported to a second party (or to themselves) who can then gain access to the dreamer's mental world in a unique unedited way. This offers two prospects: the dream itself might be interpreted in sensible ways for the dreamer; and looking at the kinds of metaphors we each use might give us some idea about internal desires and wishes we might not be able to find out about by other means.

We have two tasks to perform; one is to find out what you dream about, and the second is to discover what some of the meanings might be. Both are going to take quite a lot of effort on your part!

Let's think about meanings first. Suppose you have had a dream which you think is 'significant' in some way, but don't really know why. What can you do with it? The first thing to do is to write it down as soon after dreaming it as possible. Don't edit the dream in any way – in particular, don't cut out any 'irrelevant' elements, and don't add in connecting sequences to 'make sense' of the dream. Now what?

Jung offers this advice to his pupils: 'Learn as much as you can about symbolism; then forget it all when you are analyzing a dream. I have made it a rule to remind myself that I can never understand somebody else's dream well enough to interpret it correctly.'

In everyday speech a symbol is anything that stands for anything else. So a number such as 'eight' stands for the concept of eightness. The word 'cat' stands for the object that is small, furry, and purrs. Both of these symbols are quite arbitrary – that is to say there is nothing about the number 'eight' which gives clues to the nature of eightness, and there is nothing about the word 'cat' which gives clues about the nature of the cat. This, of course, *isn't* true of the way the word 'symbol' is used when talking about dreams. A symbol in a dream is much more like a metaphor. In dreams the symbols stand for things in the dreamer's experience that they share common features with. For example in Orr's dream about his aunt she was seen as a cat. Because symbols in dreams are *not* arbitrary, it becomes sensible to talk about the elements of the symbols that have significance to the dreamer.

To understand dreams, according to most psychoanalysts, it is necessary to distinguish between the content of the dream, and what the dream actually means. To get from the surface content to the meaning of the dreams Freud used his method of *free association*. This method is simple enough, but needs practice. With each element in the dream – say a house or a tree or a horse, simply say each word that comes into your head in association with the element, and follow these associations along. For example:

HORSE – stable – baby – mother – father – death ...

DOCTOR – medicine – spoon – feed – baby ...

Speak the chains of words into a tape recorder, and write them out later. Take each symbol in turn and simply talk out loud about the things it reminds you of. Do this for each symbol in the dream and then put them all together and see the ways in which they can be related together.

Jung's method of uncovering the meaning of dream symbols for the dreamer is his method of *amplification*. The purpose of amplification is to produce a cluster of associations around each symbol. To use this method, simply say the word over and over again, and note down all your associations with it. In Freud's method, the associative process can lead the association further and further away from the symbol. In Jung's amplification, the point of the activity is to explore the net of associations immediately around the symbol. An outside person can help the dreamer to do this. Jung believed that human beings at all times and in all locations have access to the same set of associations; his evidence is the production in societies remote in space and time of the same symbols for similar activities; the same themes recur in folk stories, mythologies and the like. So an outsider can help the dreamer to understand their own dreams because the outsider has access to the *collective unconscious* shared by all human beings. Let's return to Orr's cat. The Norse goddess Freyja was more concerned with fertility than with propriety. Her residence was referred to as the 'hall of many couches', and her chariot was drawn by – cats.

Jung's method might produce a network around CAT like this:

mother   promiscuous

     CAT   Freyja

pussy   fur

Both free association and amplification allow you to map out a network of words and their associations. Try it yourself and see what it shows you. Try and relate the key elements in your dream using these two methods. Perhaps it makes sense of the dream, and perhaps it doesn't.

What is the next treat in our Dream Book? How would you like to explore part of your mental life that you might even not know exists?

Exploring Hypnagogic Imagery

As we drop off to sleep there is a period of time when we are neither fully awake nor fully asleep. This no man's land is called the hypnagogic period. Some people have no conscious memory of this period at all; for others it can be a period in which they experience a whole range of sensations, for example visual or auditory imagery. As in the case of investigating dreams, there are problems in remembering experiences in this state. Let's start out by looking at a way to explore your own hypnagogic imagery! As you go to sleep lie flat on your back but hold your arm vertically upwards balanced on the elbow. You will find that you can get quite well into the hypnagogic state in this position, but as you slip into Stage one of sleeping you will find that your muscle tone suddenly decreases and your arm falls! So you will suddenly awake and have a chance to recall and explain this imagery. Different people report different amounts of control over their hypnagogic imagery; do practice controlling your own.

Dream Surveys

What do *you* dream about? Memory for dreams is often quite vague or even absent in the morning. One way round this problem is to keep a dream notebook. This can be either a tape recorder or a book which you keep by the side of the bed. Whenever you wake up jot down the things you have just been thinking about. Try not to edit it in any way but write it out exactly the way it occurred in your sleep. This technique, as well as being interesting in its own right, might also be useful to you in other ways. Many people report using images they see in dreams as part of their creative work. Some examples are Robert Louis Stephenson, Franz Kafka and Lewis Carroll in literature; Richard Wagner and George Frederick Handel in music; Salvador Dali and Paul Klee in painting.

The last part of the Dream Book is going to take a lot of effort! You need between 50 and 100 dreams from your dream notebook. We will use a technique called *content analysis* – which is not a dream symbol notebook allowing you to code things like 'horse = sexual experience' but rather a recipe for uncovering the things which preoccupy your sleep thinking. First decide on some sensible categories for the images that occur. A possible starting point is to categorize the human subjects as old/young, male/female, etc. You might choose a division of friends/strangers/relatives, too. For your classification of actions you may have simple categories such as pleasant/unpleasant or headings like: aggressive actions, chasing, sexual experiences, being locked up, finding things and so on. Your object group could include cars, motorbikes, surfboards, etc., and may again include people. It is important that you choose categories that are obviously present in your dreams. Just as we have argued that it isn't sensible to have a single system for decoding everyone's dream symbols into their 'absolute meaning', neither is it sensible to apply the same system of content analysis to everyone's dreams. So you must make up your own.

Now go through each dream and use a checklist to discover the frequency of occurrence of all the themes in the categories you have decided to use. You may decide that you need to add or remove categories during this process. At the end you will have a rough list of the people, themes and objects that most commonly occur in your dreams. Can you use this list to discover anything about the way you think about the most frequently occurring elements in your dreams? You may find it useful to adopt a 'consultant' role. Imagine that your dream diary was actually produced by someone else. What sort of story would you tell a third party about this dream notebook that you have come across? This has the advantage of allowing you to suspend your emotional reactions to the material as you go along. Only when you have engaged in the intellectual activity of analysing this person's dream notebook do you have the luxury of analysing its relevance to yourself. If you have the patience and energy to complete this task you may well agree with Dr Haber that dreams not only have reality but can also change the world.

You are the only person who can make judgements about how satisfactory any interpretation of a dream or a set of dreams is. There can be no 'correct' interpretation in the sense that there is a correct interpretation of the mystical symbols on the weather forecaster's board. The reward for this activity isn't to be found in the answer, but in the process of looking.

4

THEY

Robert A. Heinlein

They would not let him alone.

They never would let him alone. He realized that that was part of the plot against him – never to leave him in peace, never to give him a chance to mull over the lies they had told him, time enough to pick out the flaws, and to figure out the truth for himself.

That damned attendant this morning! He had come busting in with his breakfast tray, waking him, and causing him to forget his dream. If only he could remember that dream –

Someone was unlocking the door. He ignored it.

'Howdy, old boy. They tell me you refused your breakfast?' Dr. Hayward's professionally kindly mask hung over his bed.

'I wasn't hungry.'

'But we can't have that. You'll get weak, and then I won't be able to get you well completely. Now get up and get your clothes on and I'll order an eggnog for you. Come on, that's a good fellow!'

Unwilling, but still less willing at that moment to enter into any conflict of wills, he got out of bed and slipped on his bathrobe. 'That's better,' Hayward approved. 'Have a cigarette?'

'No, thank you.'

The doctor shook his head in a puzzled fashion. 'Darned if I can figure you out. Loss of interest in physical pleasures does not fit your type of case.'

'What is my type of case?' he inquired in flat tones.

'Tut! Tut!' Hayward tried to appear roguish. 'If medicos told their professional secrets, they might have to work for a living.'

'What is my type of case?'   'Well – the label doesn't matter, does it? Suppose *you* tell me. I really know nothing about your case as yet. Don't you think it is about time you talked?'

'I'll play chess with you.'

'All right, all right.' Hayward made a gesture of impatient concession. 'We've played chess every day for a week. If you will talk, I'll play chess.'

What could it matter? If he was right, they already understood perfectly that he had discovered their plot; there was nothing to be gained by concealing the

93

obvious. Let them try to argue him out of it. Let the tail go with the hide! To hell with it!

He got out the chessmen and commenced setting them up. 'What do you know of my case so far?'

'Very little. Physical examination, negative. Past history, negative. High intelligence, as shown by your record in school and your success in your profession. Occasional fits of moodiness, but nothing exceptional. The only positive information was the incident that caused you to come here for treatment.'

'To be brought here, you mean. Why should it cause comment?'

'Well, good gracious, man – if you barricade yourself in your room and insist that your wife is plotting against you, don't you expect people to notice?'

'But she *was* plotting against me – and so are you. White, or black?'

'Black – it's your turn to attack. Why do you think we are "plotting against you"?'

'It's an involved story, and goes way back into my early childhood. There was an immediate incident, however – ' He opened by advancing the white king's knight to KB3. Hayward's eyebrows raised.

'You make a piano attack?'

'Why not? You know that it is not safe for me to risk a gambit with you.'

The doctor shrugged his shoulders and answered the opening. 'Suppose we start with your early childhood. It may shed more light than more recent incidents. Did you feel that you were persecuted as a child?'

'No!' He half rose from his chair. 'When I was a child I was sure of myself. I knew then. I tell you; I knew! Life was worth while, and I knew it. I was at peace with myself and my surroundings. Life was good and I was good, and I assumed that the creatures around me were like myself.'

'And weren't they?'

'Not at all! Particularly the children. I didn't know what viciousness was until I was turned loose with other "children". The little devils! And I was expected to be like them and play with them.'

The doctor nodded. 'I know. The herd compulsion. Children can be pretty savage at times.'

'You've missed the point. This wasn't any healthy roughness; these creatures were *different* – not like myself at all. They *looked* like me, but they were *not* like me. If I tried to say anything to one of them about anything that mattered to me, all I could get was a stare and a scornful laugh. Then they would find some way to punish me for having said it.'

Hayward nodded. 'I see what you mean. How about grownups?'

'That is something different. Adults don't matter to children at first – or rather, they did not matter to me. They were too big, and they did not bother me, and they were busy with things that did not enter into my considerations. It was only when I noticed that my presence affected them that I began to wonder about them.'

'How do you mean?'

'Well, they never did the things when I was around that they did when I was not around.'

Hayward looked at him carefully. 'Won't that statement take quite a lot of justifying? How do you know what they did when you weren't around?'

He acknowledged the point. 'But I used to catch them just stopping. If I came into a room, the conversation would stop suddenly, and then it would pick up about the weather or something equally inane. Then I took to hiding and listening and looking. Adults did not behave the same way in my presence as out of it.'

'Your move, I believe. But see here, old man – that was when you were a child. Every child passes through that phase. Now that you are a man, you must see the adult point of view. Children are strange creatures and have to be protected – at least, we do protect them – from many adult interests. There is a whole code of conventions in the matter that – '

'Yes, yes,' he interrupted impatiently, 'I know all that. Nevertheless, I noticed enough and remembered enough that was never clear to me later. And it put me on my guard to notice the next thing.'

'Which was?' He noticed that the doctor's eyes were averted as he adjusted a castle's position.

'The things I saw people doing and heard them talking about were never of any importance. They *must* be doing something else.'

'I don't follow you.'

'You don't choose to follow me. I'm telling this to you in exchange for a game of chess.'

'Why do you like to play chess so well?'

'Because it is the only thing in the world where I can see all the factors and understand all the rules. Never mind – I saw all around me this enormous plant, cities, farms, factories, churches, schools, homes, railroads, luggage, roller coasters, trees, saxophones, libraries, people and animals. People that looked like me and who should have felt very much like me, if what I was told was the truth. But what did they appear to be doing? "They went to work to earn the money to buy the food to get the strength to go to work to get the strength to buy the food to earn the money to go to – " until they fell over dead. Any slight variation in the basic pattern did not matter, for they always fell over dead. And everybody tried to tell me that I should be doing the same thing. I knew better!'

The doctor gave him a look apparently intended to denote helpless surrender and laughed. 'I can't argue with you. Life does look like that, and maybe it is just that futile. But it is the only life we have. Why not make up your mind to enjoy it as much as possible?'

'Oh, no!' He looked both sulky and stubborn. 'You can't peddle nonsense to me by claiming to be fresh out of sense. How do I know? Because all this complex stage setting, all these swarms of actors, could not have been put here just to make idiot noises at each other. Some other explanation but not that one. An insanity as enormous, as complex, as the one around me had to be planned. I've found the plan!'

'Which is?'

He noticed that the doctor's eyes were again averted.

'It is a play intended to divert me, to occupy my mind and confuse me, to keep me so busy with details that I will not have time to think about the meaning. You are all in it, every one of you.' He shook his finger in the doctor's face. 'Most of them may be helpless automatons, but you're not. You are one of the conspirators. You've been sent in as a troubleshooter to try to force me to go back to playing the role assigned to me!'

He saw that the doctor was waiting for him to quiet down.

'Take it easy,' Hayward finally managed to say. 'Maybe it is all a conspiracy, but why do you think that you have been singled out for special attention? Maybe it is a joke on all of us. Why couldn't I be one of the victims as well as yourself?'

'Got you!' He pointed a long finger at Hayward. 'That is the essence of the plot. All of these creatures have been set up to look like me in order to prevent me from realizing that I was the center of the arrangements. But I have noticed the key fact, the mathematically inescapable fact, that I am unique. Here am I, sitting on the inside. The world extends outward from me. I am the center – '

'Easy, man, easy! Don't you realize that the world looks that way to me, too? We are each the center of the universe – '

'Not so! That is what you have tried to make me believe, that I am just one of millions more just like me. Wrong! If they were like me, then I could get into communication with them. I can't. I have tried and tried and I can't. I've sent out my inner thoughts, seeking some one other being who has them, too. What have I gotten back? Wrong answers, jarring incongruities, meaningless obscenity. I've tried, I tell you. God! – how I've tried! But there is nothing out there to speak to me – nothing but emptiness and otherness!'

'Wait a minute. Do you mean to say that you think there is nobody home at my end of the line? Don't you believe that I am alive and conscious?'

He regarded the doctor soberly. 'Yes, I think you are probably alive, but you are one of the others – my antagonists. But you have set thousands of others around me whose faces are blank, not *lived in,* and whose speech is a meaningless reflex of noise.'

'Well, then, if you concede that I am an ego, why do you insist that I am so very different from yourself?'

'Why? Wait!' He pushed back from the chess table and strode over to the wardrobe, from which he took out a violin case.

While he was playing, the lines of suffering smoothed out of his face and his expression took on a relaxed beatitude. For a while he recaptured the emotions, but not the knowledge, which he had possessed in dreams. The melody proceeded easily from proposition to proposition with inescapable, unforced logic. He finished with a triumphant statement of the essential thesis and turned to the doctor. 'Well?'

'Hm-m-m.' He seemed to detect an even greater degree of caution in the doctor's manner. 'It's an odd bit, but remarkable. 'S pity you didn't take up the violin seriously. You could have made quite a reputation. You could even now. Why don't you do it? You could afford to, I believe.'

He stood and stared at the doctor for a long moment, then shook his head as if trying to clear it. 'It's no use,' he said slowly, 'no use at all. There is no possibility of communication. I am alone.' He replaced the instrument in its case and returned to the chess table. 'My move, I believe?'

'Yes. Guard your queen.'

He studied the board. 'Not necessary. I no longer need my queen. Check.'

The doctor interposed a pawn to parry the attack.

He nodded. 'You use your pawns well, but I have learned to anticipate your play. Check again – and mate, I think.'

The doctor examined the new situation. 'No,' he decided, 'no – not quite.' He retreated from the square under attack. 'Not checkmate – stalemate at the worst. Yes, another stalemate.'

He was upset by the doctor's visit. He *couldn't* be wrong, basically, yet the doctor had certainly pointed out logical holes in his position. From a logical standpoint the whole world might be a fraud perpetrated on everybody. But logic means nothing – logic itself was a fraud, starting with unproved assumptions and capable of proving anything. The world is what it is! – and carries its own evidence of trickery.

But does it? What did he have to go on? Could he lay down a line between known facts and everything else and then make a reasonable interpretation of the world, based on facts alone – an interpretation free from complexities of logic and no hidden assumptions of points not certain? Very well –

First fact, himself. He knew himself directly. He existed.

Second facts, the evidence of his 'five senses', everything that he himself saw and heard and smelled and tasted with his physical senses. Subject to their limitations, he must believe his senses. Without them he was entirely solitary, shut up in a locker of bone, blind, deaf, cut off, the only being in the world.

And that was not the case. He knew that he did not invent the information brought to him by his senses. There had to be something else out there. Some *otherness* that produced the things his senses recorded. All philosophies that claimed that the physical world around him did not exist except in his imagination were sheer nonsense.

But beyond that, what? Were there any third facts on which he could rely? No, not at this point. He could not afford to believe anything that he was told, or that he read, or that was implicitly assumed to be true about the world around him. No, he could not believe any of it, for the sum total of what he had been told and read and been taught in school was contradictory, so senseless, so wildly insane that none of it could be believed unless he personally confirmed it.

Wait a minute – The very telling of these lies, these senseless contradictions, was a fact in itself, known to him directly. To that extent they were data, probably very important data.

The world as it had been shown to him was a piece of unreason, an idiot's dream. Yet it was on too mammoth a scale to be without some reason. He came wearily back to his original point: Since the world could not be as crazy as it appeared to be, it must necessarily have been arranged to appear crazy in order to deceive him as to the truth.

Why had they done it to him? And what was the truth behind the sham? There must be some clue in the deception itself. What thread ran through it all? Well, in the first place he had been given a superabundance of explanations of the world around him, philosophies, religions, 'common sense' explanations. Most of them were so clumsy, so obviously inadequate, or meaningless, that they could hardly have expected him to take them seriously. They must have intended them simply as misdirection.

But there were certain basic assumptions running through all the hundreds of explanations of the craziness around him. It must be these basic assumptions that he was expected to believe. For example, there was the deep-seated assumption that he was a 'human being', essentially like millions of others around him and billions more in the past and the future.

That was nonsense! He had never once managed to get into real communication with all those *things* that looked so much like him but were so different. In the agony of his loneliness, he had deceived himself that Alice understood him and was a being like him. He knew now that he had suppressed and refused to examine thousands of little discrepancies because he could not bear the thought of returning to complete loneliness. He had needed to believe that his wife was a living, breathing being of his own kind who understood his inner thoughts. He had refused to consider the possibility that she was simply a mirror, an echo – or something unthinkably worse.

He had found a mate, and the world was tolerable, even though dull, stupid, and full of petty annoyance. He was moderately happy and had put away his suspicions. He had accepted, quite docilely, the treadmill he was expected to use, until a slight mischance had momentarily cut through the fraud - then his suspicions had returned with impounded force; the bitter knowledge of his childhood had been confirmed.

He supposed that he had been a fool to make a fuss about it. If he had kept his mouth shut they would not have locked him up. He should have been as subtle and as shrewd as they, kept his eyes and ears open and learned the details of and the reasons for the plot against him. He might have learned how to circumvent it.

But what if they had locked him up – the whole world was an asylum and all of them his keepers.

A key scraped in the lock, and he looked up to see an attendant entering with a tray. 'Here's your dinner, sir.'

'Thanks, Joe,' he said gently. 'Just put it down.'

'Movies tonight, sir,' the attendant went on. 'Wouldn't you like to go? Dr. Hayward said you could – '

'No, thank you. I prefer not to.'

'I wish you would, sir.' He noticed with amusement the persuasive intentness of the attendant's manner. 'I think the doctor wants you to. It's a good movie. There's a Mickey Mouse cartoon – '

'You almost persuade me, Joe,' he answered with passive agreeableness. 'Mickey's trouble is the same as mine, essentially. However, I'm not going. They need not bother to hold movies tonight.'

'Oh, there will be movies in any case, sir. Lots of our other guests will attend.'

'Really? Is that an example of thoroughness, or are you simply keeping up the pretence in talking to me? It isn't necessary, Joe, if it's any strain on you. I *know* the game. If I don't attend, there is no point in holding movies.'

He liked the grin with which the attendant answered this thrust. Was it possible that this being was created just as he appeared to be – big muscles, phlegmatic disposition, tolerant, dog-like? Or was there nothing going on behind those kind eyes, nothing but robot reflex? No, it was more likely that he was one of them, since he was so closely in attendance on him.

The attendant left and he busied himself at his supper tray, scooping up the already-cut bits of meat with a spoon, the only implement provided. He smiled again at their caution and thoroughness. No danger of that – he would not destroy this body as long as it served him in investigating the truth of the matter. There were still many different avenues of research available before taking that possibly irrevocable step.

After supper he decided to put his thoughts in better order by writing them; he obtained paper. He should start with a general statement of some underlying postulates of the credos that had been drummed into him all his 'life'. Life? Yes, that was a good one. He wrote:

'I am told that I was born a certain number of years ago and that I will die a similar number of years hence. Various clumsy stories have been offered me to explain to me where I was before birth and what becomes of me after death, but they are rough lies, not intended to deceive, except as misdirection. In every other possible way the world around me assures me that I am mortal, here but a few years, and a few years hence gone completely – non-existent.

'WRONG – I am immortal. I transcend this little time axis; a seventy- year span on it is but a casual phase in my experience. Second only to the prime datum of my own existence is the emotionally convincing certainty of my own continuity. I may be a closed curve, but closed or open, I neither have a beginning nor an end. Self-awareness is not relational; it is absolute, and cannot be reached to be destroyed or created. Memory, however, being a relational aspect of consciousness, may be tampered with and possibly destroyed.

'It is true that most religions which have been offered me teach immortality, but note the fashion in which they teach it. The surest way to lie convincingly is to tell the truth unconvincingly. They did not wish me to believe.

'Caution: Why have they tried so hard to convince me that I am going to "die" in a few years? There must be a very important reason. I infer that they are preparing me for some sort of a major change. It may be crucially important for me to figure out their intentions about this – probably I have several years in which to reach a decision. Note: Avoid using the types of reasoning they have taught me.'

The attendant was back. 'Your wife is here, sir.'

'Tell her to go away.'

'Please, sir – Dr. Hayward is most anxious that you should see her.'

'Tell Dr. Hayward that I said that he is an excellent chess player.'

'Yes, sir.' The attendant waited for a moment. 'Then you won't see her, sir?'

'No, I won't see her.'

He wandered around the room for some minutes after the attendant had left, too distrait to return to his recapitulation. By and large, they had played very decently with him since they had brought him here. He was glad that they had allowed him to have a room alone, and he certainly had more time free for contemplation than had ever been possible on the outside. To be sure, continuous effort to keep him busy and to distract him was made, but, by being stubborn, he was able to circumvent the rules and gain some hours each day for introspection.

But, damnation! – he did wish they would not persist in using Alice in their attempts to divert his thoughts. Although the intense terror and revulsion which she had inspired in him when he had first rediscovered the truth had now aged into a simple feeling of repugnance and distaste for her company, nevertheless it was emotionally upsetting to be reminded of her, to be forced into making decisions about her.

After all, she *had* been his wife for many years. Wife? What was a wife? Another soul like one's own, a complement, the other necessary pole to the couple, a sanctuary of understanding and sympathy in the boundless depths of aloneness. *That* was what he thought, what he had needed to believe and had believed fiercely for years. The yearning need for companionship of his own kind had caused him to see himself reflected in those beautiful eyes and had made him quite uncritical of occasional incongruities in her responses.

He sighed. He felt that he had sloughed off most of the typed emotional reactions which they had taught him by precept and example, but Alice had gotten under his skin, way under, and it still hurt. He had been happy – what if

99

it had been a dope dream? They had given him an excellent, a beautiful mirror to play with – the more fool he to have looked behind it!

Wearily he turned back to his summing up.

'The world is explained in either one of two ways: the common-sense way which says that the world is pretty much as it appears to be and that ordinary human conduct and motivations are reasonable, and the religio- mystic solution which states that the world is dream stuff, unreal, insubstantial, with reality somewhere beyond.

'WRONG – both of them. The common-sense scheme has no sense to it of any sort. "Life is short and full of trouble. Man born of woman is born to trouble as the sparks fly upward. His days are few and they are numbered. All is vanity and vexation." Those quotations may be jumbled and incorrect, but that is a fair statement of the common-sense world-is-as-it-seems in its only possible evaluation. In such a world, human striving is about as rational as the blind dartings of a moth against a light bulb. The "common- sense world" is a blind insanity, out of nowhere, going nowhere, to no purpose.

'As for the other solution, it appears more rational on the surface, in that it rejects the utterly irrational world of common sense. But it is not a rational solution, it is simply a flight from reality of any sort, for it refuses to believe the results of the only available direct communication between the ego and the Outside. Certainly the "five senses" are poor enough channels of communication, but they are the only channels.'

He crumpled up the paper and flung himself from the chair. Order and logic were no good – his answer was right because it smelled right. But he still did not know all the answers. Why the grand scale of the deception, countless creatures, whole continents, an enormously involved and minutely detailed matrix of insane history, insane tradition, insane culture? Why bother with more than a cell and a strait jacket?

It must be, it had to be, because it was supremely important to deceive him completely, because a lesser deception would not do. Could it be that they dare not let him suspect his real identity no matter how difficult and involved the fraud?

He had to know. In some fashion he must get behind the deception and see what went on when he was not looking. He had had one glimpse; this time he must see the actual workings, catch the puppet masters in their manipulations.

Obviously the first step must be to escape from this asylum, but to do it so craftily they would never see him, never catch up with him, not have a chance to set the stage before him. That would be hard to do. He must excel them in shrewdness and subtlety.

Once decided, he spent the rest of the evening in considering the means by which he might accomplish his purpose. It seemed almost impossible – he must get away without once being seen and remain in strict hiding. They must lose track of him completely in order that they would not know where to center their deceptions. That would mean going without food for several days. Very well – he could do it. He must not give them any warning by unusual action or manner.

The lights blinked twice. Docilely he got up and commenced preparations for bed. When the attendant looked through the peephole he was already in bed, with his face turned to the wall.

Gladness! Gladness everywhere! It was good to be with his own kind, to hear the music swelling out of every living thing, as it always had and always would –

good to know that everything was living and aware of him, participating in him, as he participated in them. It was good to be, good to know the unity of many and the diversity of one. There had been one bad thought – the details escaped him – but it was gone – it had never *been;* there was no place for it.

The early-morning sounds from the adjacent ward penetrated the sleep- laden body which served him here and gradually recalled him to awareness of the hospital room. The transition was so gentle that he carried over full recollection of what he had been doing and why. He lay still, a gentle smile on his face, and savored the uncouth, but not unpleasant, languor of the body he wore. Strange that he had ever forgotten despite their tricks and stratagems. Well, now that he had recalled the key, he would quickly set things right in this odd place. He would call them in at once and announce the new order. It would be amusing to see old Glaroon's expression when he realized that the cycle had ended –

The click of the peephole and the rasp of the door being unlocked guillotined his line of thought. The morning attendant pushed briskly in with the breakfast tray and placed it on the tip table. 'Morning, sir. Nice, bright day – want it in bed, or will you get up?'

Don't answer! Don't listen! Suppress this distraction! This is part of their plan – But it was too late, too late. He felt himself slipping, falling, wrenched from reality back into the fraud world in which they had kept him. It was gone, gone completely, with no single association around him to which to anchor memory. There was nothing left but the sense of heartbreaking loss and the acute ache of unsatisfied catharsis.

'Leave it where it is. I'll take care of it.'

'Okey-doke.' The attendant bustled out, slamming the door, and noisily locked it.

He lay quite still for a long time, every nerve end in his body screaming for relief.

At last he got out of bed, still miserably unhappy, and attempted to concentrate on his plans for escape. But the psychic wrench he had received in being recalled so suddenly from his plane of reality had left him bruised and emotionally disturbed. His mind insisted on rechewing its doubts, rather than engage in constructive thought. Was it possible that the doctor was right, that he was not alone in his miserable dilemma? Was he really simply suffering from paranoia, delusions of self-importance?

Could it be that each unit in this yeasty swarm around him was the prison of another lonely ego - helpless, blind, and speechless, condemned to an eternity of miserable loneliness? Was the look of suffering which he had brought to Alice's face a true reflection of inner torment and not simply a piece of play-acting intended to maneuver him into compliance with their plans?

A knock sounded at the door. He said, 'Come in,' without looking up. Their comings and goings did not matter to him.

'Dearest – ' A well-known voice spoke slowly and hesitantly.

'Alice!' He was on his feet at once, and facing her. 'Who let you in here?'

'Please, dear, please – I had to see you.'

'It isn't fair. It isn't fair.' He spoke more to himself than to her. Then: 'Why did you come?'

She stood up to him with a dignity he had hardly expected. The beauty of her childlike face had been marred by line and shadow, but it shone with an unexpected courage. 'I love you,' she answered quietly. 'You can tell me to go

101

away, but you can't make me stop loving you and trying to help you.'

He turned away from her in an agony of indecision. Could it be possible that he had misjudged her? Was there, behind that barrier of flesh and sound symbols, a spirit that truly yearned toward his? Lovers whispering in the dark – 'You *do* understand, don't you?'

'Yes, dear heart, I understand.'

'Then nothing that happens to us can matter, as long as we are together and understand – ' Words, words, rebounding hollowly from an unbroken wall –

No, he *couldn't* be wrong! Test her again – 'Why did you keep me on that job in Omaha?'

'But I didn't make you keep that job. I simply pointed out that we should think twice before – '

'Never mind. Never mind.' Soft hands and a sweet face preventing him with mild stubbornness from ever doing the thing that his heart told him to do. Always with the best of intentions, the best of intentions, but always so that he had never quite managed to do the silly, unreasonable things, that *he* knew were worth while. Hurry, hurry, hurry, and strive, with an angel- faced jockey to see that you don't stop long enough to think for yourself –

'Why did you try to stop me from going back upstairs that day?'

She managed to smile although her eyes were already spilling over with tears. 'I didn't know it really mattered to you. I didn't want us to miss the train.'

It had been a small thing, an unimportant thing. For some reason not clear even to him he had insisted on going back upstairs to his study when they were about to leave the house for a short vacation. It was raining, and she had pointed out that there was barely enough time to get to the station. He had surprised himself and her, too, by insisting on his own way in circumstances in which he had never been known to be stubborn.

He had actually pushed her to one side and forced his way up the stairs. Even then nothing might have come of it had he not – quite unnecessarily – raised the shade of the window that faced toward the rear of the house.

It was a very small matter. It had been raining, hard, out in front. From this window the weather was clear and sunny, with no sign of rain.

He had stood there quite a long while, gazing out at the impossible sunshine and rearranging his cosmos in his mind. He re-examined long- suppressed doubts in the light of this small but totally unexplained discrepancy. Then he had turned and had found that she was standing behind him.

He had been trying ever since to forget the expression that he had surprised on her face.

'What about the rain?'

'The rain?' she repeated in a small, puzzled voice. 'Why, it was raining of course. What about it?'

'But it was *not* raining out my study window.'

'What? But of course it was. I did notice the sun break through the clouds for a moment, but that was all.'

'Nonsense!'

'But darling, what has the weather to do with you and me? What difference does it make whether it rains or not – to us?' She approached him timidly and slid a small hand between his arm and side. 'Am I responsible for the weather?'

'I think you are. Now please go.'

She withdrew from him, brushed blindly at her eyes, gulped once, then said in a voice held steady: 'All right, I'll go. But remember – you *can* come home if you want to. And I'll be there if you want me.' She waited a moment, then added hesitantly: 'Would you ... would you kiss me goodby?'

He made no answer of any sort, neither with voice nor eyes. She looked at him, then turned, fumbled blindly for the door, and rushed through it.

The creature he knew as Alice went to the place of assembly without stopping to change form. 'It is necessary to adjourn this sequence. I am no longer able to influence his decisions.'

They had expected it, nevertheless they stirred with dismay.

The Glaroon addressed the First for Manipulation. 'Prepare to graft the selected memory track at once.'

Then, turning to the First for Operations, the Glaroon said: 'The extrapolation shows that he will tend to escape within two of his days. This sequence degenerated primarily through your failure to extend that rainfall all around him. Be advised.'

'It would be simpler if we understood his motives.'

'In my capacity as Dr. Hayward, I have often thought so,' commented the Glaroon acidly, 'but if we understood his motives, we would be part of *him*. Bear in mind the Treaty! He almost remembered.'

The creature known as Alice spoke up. 'Could he not have the Taj Mahal next sequence? For some reason he values it.'

'You are becoming assimilated!'

'Perhaps. I am not in fear. Will he receive it?'

'It will be considered.'

The Glaroon continued with orders. 'Leave structures standing until adjournment. New York City and Harvard University are now dismantled. Divert him from those sectors. Move!'

Social reality ... in this distinctively human world, is not a hard immutable thing but is fragile and adjudicated – a thing to be debated, compromised and legislated. Those who most succeed in this world are those who are most persuasive and effective in having their interpretations ratified as the true reality. Those who do not are relegated to the fringes of the human world – are executed as heretics or traitors, ridiculed as crackpots, or locked up as lunatics.

G. McCall and J.L. Simmons, 1966, *Identity and Interaction*. New York: Free Press.

They concentrates our attention on everything that passes as knowledge of the world, from sensory experiences like touch, taste, sight and hearing, through memories and knowledge about social realities.

DESCRIBING AND EXPLAINING PEOPLE AND EVENTS

All of our experiences are open to a great many different interpretations. Different observers of the same events are likely to produce different descriptions of, and explanations for, the events witnessed. George Kelly has developed a theory in which he tries to take account of these alternative views. Kelly argues that we do not respond to events in our lives in a passive way. Rather, we try to predict events and to control them. To this end, we form theories about many aspects of our lives. Our theories serve to guide the way in which new events are interpreted, and they guide responses to these events and shape our future plans. We each interpret the world in ways which are personal to ourselves. For us to understand human behaviour, we must understand the *personal constructions* which each individual makes to interpret the world they find themselves in. The term 'construct' covers anything which relates to our ideas about the world, or plans for action – 'hypotheses', 'rules of thumb', 'heuristics', for example, are all *constructs*.

Individuals are said to 'construe' whenever they make interpretations about something. We have constructs, for example, which allow us to judge things to be like each other or unlike each other. Each of these constructs is an invention of our own, which does not reside in the object itself. So constructs might be descriptions such as 'hard–soft'; 'introverted–extraverted'; 'happy– sad'; 'powerful–weak'; – in short, anything that we use to describe events or objects in the world around us.

We can deduce from the story that one of His constructs about individuals classifies them as 'other' or 'empty' depending on whether he judges them to be creatures plotting against Him, or merely automata. The constructs we have are not necessarily applicable to the whole range of objects, events and experiences which we have. Different constructs will differ in what they can be applied to. For example a psychological construct like 'intelligent–dull' is unlikely to be applied to furniture; a construct like 'tall–short' is unlikely to be applied to the weather.

We come to these constructs via a mixture of conscious and unconscious thinking. Constructs are invented to explain the world as we see it, and to be the basis for predicting events so that we can act to control them. Constructs which we find useful in explaining, controlling, and predicting our world we retain, while the ones which we find useless for these purposes we reject, and then start to seek for new ones. Kelly draws an analogy between the processes engaged in by scientists and the processes engaged in by all of us in our attempts to understand the world. The scientific community spells out these activities far more clearly than the rest of us do. For example, a scientist might place importance on the need to identify the issues to be explained; to generate possible explanations for these events; to collect evidence relevant to the events; and to try to decide which explanations the evidence favours; to modify hypotheses in the light of evidence collected; and to repeat this cycle of events. Of course, when people engage in this sort of scientific activity, we make mistakes at all sorts of levels: for example we may fail to define the events we are interested in; we may make observations we cannot interpret; we may generate hypotheses that we couldn't dismiss on the basis of *any* data that we could possibly collect; we might not be able to generate hypotheses at all; we may draw unwarranted conclusions; and the like.

For the scientific community any scientific statements can only be viewed as the current 'best bet'. There is no such thing as 'the truth'. We might make observations that we find we can replicate quite reliably, and we might have explanations for these events. However, it is always logically possible that future events will show us that our understanding of earlier events was only partially correct, or perhaps wrong. Newton's laws of motion provide an illustration of this. They went unchallenged for about 350 years, until Einstein's relativity theory showed them to be only partially correct.

Kelly, too, argues that no construction about the world can ever be judged to be the right one. As well as the obvious problems of 'correctness' just outlined, the 'human as scientist' has other problems too. The social world in which we move is in a constant state of change, and so too must be our views about this social world.

Kelly argues that individuals continually learn from their experiences, and can always revise their ideas about their experiences either in the light of new experiences, or by reflecting on past experiences.

Kelly's fundamental postulate is that 'a person's processes are psychologically channelised by the ways in which he (*sic*) anticipates events'. Experience allows us to elaborate our system of constructs. We develop constructs to handle unfamiliar events; we develop constructs and elaborate constructs we already have to explain events which are familiar to us.

What happens when our constructs fail to allow us to predict the world? We modify our constructs, perhaps invent new ones, and perhaps reject old ones. From time to time we change our views about the relationship between our constructs. All this emphasizes the idea of people as active problem solvers trying to understand the world in which they live and to predict future events. It also portrays our mental life as being an active process in which we engage in a good deal of searching out of patterns. Of course our past experiences shape the sort of constructs we have. However, this shaping process should not be viewed as being excessively restrictive on the ways we construe the world, and about the sort of predictions we make. In Kelly's words no one need be 'a victim of ... biography'. We escape being victims because we modify and review our constructs, and use the revised constructs to re-interpret our past experiences. This is illustrated by the way in which He changed His whole view of the world after the incident with the sunshine at the back of the house. We need not be surprised that people differ a good deal in their willingness and their ability to change their views of the world.

How can we compare individuals? It is important to distinguish between the observation that two individuals have experienced the 'same' events and the assertion that their constructions of these events are similar. In our story both He and Alice have shared a great many events together; at the end of the story it is quite clear that neither of them construe these events in the same way. Is it possible to find out about people's constructions about the world? A useful tool that Kelly has developed for this is his Role Construct Repertory Test, or Repertory Grid Test. Perhaps you would like to have a go at this activity for yourself.

An Activity

We are going to explore some of the ways that you think about people. For this exercise you should choose individuals that you know quite well. Friends form an obvious group, so too do family. Write down the names of six people in the spaces below. If you are spoilt for choice write down the names of: best friends of the same and opposite sex; two people of different sexes that you like least well; the most interesting person you know, and the most successful person you know. To look at the way you see your family, simply write down the names of the six people who are most significant to you.

1

2

3

4

5

6

Now think about these people in groups of three. Think about people in slots 1, 2 and 3. In what *important* way are two of those people similar to each other, and different to the third?

On the fill-in chart labelled 'Construct–Contrast' write down this important difference in A1, and the opposite of A1 in A2.

Now please repeat this exercise for people in slots:

4, 5, 6 (construct and contrast go in B1 and B2)

1, 5, 6 (construct and contrast go in C1 and C2)

2, 3, 4 (construct and contrast go in D1 and D2)

Next you need to transfer all this information to the larger chart. The names of your construct and their contrasts go into the rows; the names of persons go in the columns. Put your own name in Column 7.

Now you should rate each person on every construct/contrast on a scale from +3 to -3. If a construct is highly relevant to a person, write a 3 in the appropriate cell in the table; if the contrast is highly relevant, write -3; if it cannot be applied, write '?'. Fill in your ratings for every space.

What can you learn from this process? The constructs and contrasts show the ways you think about people. Have you ever tried to spell this out before? You might find that when you try this exercise for the first time the labels you produce don't capture your intentions at all. Don't worry! This is a tool to help you to clarify your thoughts, not a test – so you can repeat the exercise as many times as you like, until you are satisfied with the results. If a construct and contrast pair seem to be considering different dimensions, don't worry. Put each one into the table as a construct, and use NOT (construct) as its contrast.

Compare the numbers in all pairs of *rows* in turn. If you find identical rows, or rows with very similar entries, this suggests that the construct/contrasts identified in the two rows are very similar. You should decide if they really are the same – if so, change one, and repeat the exercise. If not, think of a person who highlights the difference, and add them onto the list of people. Compare this new person with pairs of people already there and add new constructs to the list of constructs.

Compare the numbers in all the pairs of *columns* in turn. If you find identical columns, or columns with very similar entries, this suggests that you see the two people being rated as having similar characteristics. Do you really think of them as being alike? If not, think of a way in which they are different, and add this difference to the construct/contrast list, then rate *all* the people on this new construct.

Look closely at the ways you have rated yourself. What do your ratings tell you? Rate the constructs as being desirable or undesirable. Do you score highly on desirable ones? What can you do to make your view of yourself more positive? Compare the way that you rate yourself with your ratings of everyone else in the table by comparing your column with theirs. Who are you most like? Who are you least like? Does this surprise you at all?

This activity began by comparing just a few people in just a few constructs to illustrate Repertory Grid test technique. By now you have probably added more people and more constructs, and have done a good deal of hard thinking! At any point you are free to go back and change the people you want to think about or the constructs you use. The purpose of the activity is to get to a description of a set of people that reflects the ways that *you* think about them.

Anything can be the focus of the Repertory Grid technique – it need not

Robert A. Heinlein: They

CONSTRUCT		CONTRAST
A1		A2
B1		B2
C1		C2
D1		D2

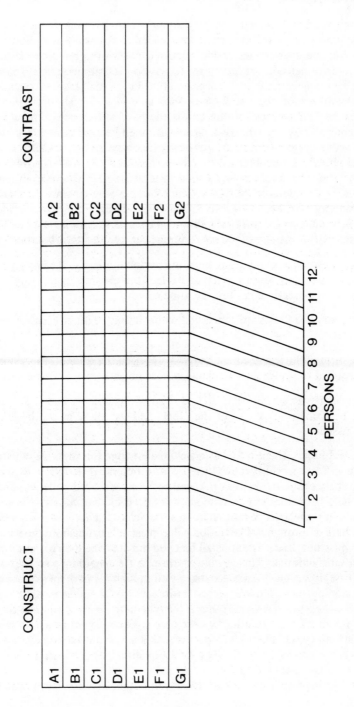

be people you know. You might think about famous politicians, if you want to reflect on your political views; experiences, if you want to explore the things you enjoy; countries, if you want to expose your prejudices; books, to see your dimensions of literature; television programmes; films; motor cars; trees; cameras; holiday resorts; and the like. In each case you compare some members of the set with others, and look for similarities and differences. The nature of the similarities and differences which you describe, and the way that you group the members of the set together reveals your personal constructions about that aspect of the world.

There are a number of forms of the Repertory Grid test; the main purpose of each form is to elicit a person's constructs so that they can be examined. This allows us to look at the way in which another person views the world. The Repertory Grid test allows us to examine both the content of a person's constructs and also the inter-relations of constructs within the system. The Repertory Grid test technique has a number of interesting properties:

It is concerned with revealing the way a person thinks about some aspects of their world; it does *not* try and relate this pattern to the way that 'people in general' engage in the same activity.

Repertory Grid tests are concerned with eliciting relationships between constructs.

The form of the test need not be fixed, nor need the content, the test can be applied to pretty well any collection of objects.

Once constructs have been elicited from two people we can show each one the construal system of the other, and use these as the basis for discussion.

The technique, then, offers us a way of allowing Him to judge whether His view of the world is indeed shared with others. If there is a genuine attempt between partners to work together for more shared understanding. It can help here, too. One way to get to understand someone else's viewpoint about some topic of mutual interest (say close friends and relatives) is to ask them to tutor you! The tuition will consist of learning both the nature of the constructs in sufficient detail that you can describe then to your tutor to their satisfaction, and in learning where each element of interest (person, in this case) is located on each construct well enough to put them in the same places as your tutor. If there is a real desire for mutual understanding, then a process of each tutoring the other is likely to help a great deal. The act of each understanding the other's viewpoint is likely to bring about some shifts in both views. The social aspect where each person takes on the role of both teacher and pupil establishes some equality, rather than a view that one person is 'right' and the other 'wrong'.

By repeating the Repertory Grid test technique on successive occasions, it can give some idea about the changes in construals about the world which each partner undergoes as a course of their joint efforts towards mutual understanding.

In this form, the Repertory Grid test doesn't allow us to express our views about *causality* very easily. A central theme for Him is the origin, purpose and control of the world. To examine these sorts of mental theory, we need to turn to different sorts of representations. We might stick with words as He does, and try to find a way of expressing our theories clearly; we might try to draw some diagrams; we might use techniques like the Repertory Grid test to help us with each of these approaches. We have had enough experience by now, though, of exploring our own views about the world. Let's return to *They* and examine His attempts to explain the world he finds himself in.

Logic and Understanding

His supposition that the world has been set up with the sole purpose of deceiving Him is the same as that adopted by the French philosopher and mathematician, René Descartes. Descartes proved his existence by arguing, 'I think therefore I am' (*Cogito ergo sum*). Does this follow logically? I'm afraid it doesn't. By saying 'I think', you are assuming an 'I'. Part of the definition of 'thinking' is someone doing it. He could just as well have argued, 'I know I exist, therefore I know I exist'. Hidden assumptions leading to circular arguments are but one of the traps of logic. We will agree happily with him that logic is quite unsuitable as a tool for analysing philosophical questions about the meaning of life and the nature of the world. We will also agree that the evidence of our senses is a good starting point to discuss the nature of knowledge.

In *Burden of Proof* we saw that perception and remembering are both affected by our pre-existing knowledge about the physical world, by our purposes and actions at the time of seeing and recall, and by our expectations about what is likely to happen. As well as our knowledge of the physical world, we also have knowledge of ideas, people and events which comes to us via perceptual experience, but which cannot be tested directly in the way that direct perceptions can. Such knowledge is acquired on the basis of the events that we experience, and is shaped by our reflections about these events. In turn, the knowledge structures which we develop concerning ideas, people and events serve to direct our attention to particular aspects of the world. In the short term, our knowledge and expectations about a particular person direct us to behave towards them in particular ways, and to interpret their behaviour towards us in a way which is consistent with the beliefs and values we have built up where they are concerned. These global frameworks colour the things we choose to attend to (for instance the newspapers we read) and colour the way we interpret the things we see. So that at all levels of our intellectual, social and emotional

111

functioning we develop extensive 'knowledge' about domains of interest. This knowledge affects the sources of information we choose to expose ourselves to. This in turn determines the sorts of events we perceive. Of course we are often made aware of events and circumstances which occur that we have not set out deliberately to sample, and we perceive these through the knowledge structures which we have developed. People with different viewpoints – for example supporters of different political parties, supporters of different football teams – will interpret the 'same' events quite differently in terms of the conceptual structures which they have built up.

Events can change conceptual structures. This is indeed the whole basis of learning. We are motivated to actively clarify inconsistencies and 'blind spots' in our views of particular classes of events by finding out more information, or simply by reasoning through the inconsistencies. So we see a pattern of interdependence between the events which we experience and our conceptual structures. Our conceptual structures are derived from our life experiences; they guide us in our analyses of these life experiences. Events which we experience determine our knowledge and conceptual structures about these events and the ways we choose to act. Events lead to learning; learning leads to the rich interpretation of events. We will return to this theme several times during the discussion which follows.

Knowing about Ourselves

How do we form views about ourselves? How do we decide what we are like, why we do things, how important we are, what our place is in the world? We all take on a variety of social roles: pupil, customer, client, voter, and so on. Sometimes we feel like actors. Remember being in a new situation for the first time? Did you feel as if you were play acting, with everyone around you feeding you prompts about your lines? Of course, the social conventions and routines that we learn and use are often useful. Routine saves a great deal of mental effort when we do everyday things: we don't have to relearn and reinvent patterns of communication each time. The social pressures on behaviour are really pretty powerful and make it hard to change one's 'image'. It is a truism that prophets don't do well in their home town. Their own socialization, and all the expectations of the people they know, go against them presenting themselves in a completely new, elevated role.

Charles H. Cooley argued that other people provide the most important source of information about ourselves, and describes the 'looking-glass self'. He draws an analogy between our views of ourselves as people and our views of our appearance. When we look in a mirror we see our face and figure and clothing, and take interest in them because they are our own. We judge our physical features on the basis of how well they match up to our expectations. Similarly our self-image is reflected in our social dealings with other people.

There are three aspects of this idea of self: the way we think the other person sees us; the way we think the other person judges us; and our own evaluation of this other person's judgement – whether it gives us pleasure or discomfort. George Mead offered a similar view. He asserted that the ability to view ourselves as objects in relation to other social objects is essential for rational behaviour. When we reflect about social behaviour and we think about what other people think about us, we have no direct insight into their thoughts – rather we are making informed guesses. This process of trying to see ourselves through the eyes of others helps shape our social identities, i.e. our social selves. Mead believed that the most important quality of the self is that the self can be an object to itself. That is to say, 'I' can think about 'me'. Socialization is an essential part of this ability to see oneself as 'me'. Language provides the tool for reflection, the process of acquiring language involves interacting with others, and in taking the view that each of us is but one element in a social environment. Before this view is reached, each individual can believe themselves to be the centre of the universe, perhaps its only inhabitant. Interactions with other people are essential if we are to develop as we do.

From His point of view the idea that we believe and treat as real those experiences we share with others and doubt those we cannot share, is rather bad news. His inner self which He experiences when asleep cannot be easily expressed – even if it were, the Glaroon and Alice would most certainly deny that these experiences had any 'reality'. The world which has been created around Him is the one which they insist is 'real'. If Cooley is correct then He will be unable to free himself.

William James, writing before the turn of this century, had a more optimistic view. He describes three features of our self conceptions each with its own sources of information. The first feature is a material 'me' which includes our personal possessions, the second is a social 'me' which consists of our reputation and the way we are seen by others; and the third is a spiritual 'me' which refers to our inner life.

So James, in contrast to Mead and Cooley, places importance on our inner lives (as He does in the story). The views which 'I' form when reflecting on different aspects of 'me' can actively reshape the 'me' in a way that the 'looking-glass self' cannot be reshaped. This difference of opinion between theorists can probably be found among individuals too, in the importance they assign to information from outside themselves compared to information within. For example, a mystic is unlikely to scan the *Financial Times*, and a banker is unlikely to meditate about the sound of one hand clapping. Different individuals deliberately focus attention onto different aspects of the experiences which are potentially available, and choices of quite different kinds of action result. Can we demonstrate experimentally rather than anecdotally that changing the focus of attention can lead to different judgements?

In an interesting study by Duval and Wicklund, subjects were given a series of stories to read, and asked to imagine that they themselves had been involved in the situations described in the stories. They were then asked to make judgements about how much they would be to blame for the consequences of the events described. One group read the stories in a room which also contained a piece of psychological apparatus. They were asked to ignore the apparatus and simply to report their judgements. The second group, which read the same stories, were asked to operate the machinery which involved pressing their finger on a turntable to keep it spinning as well as reading the stories and making their judgements about blame. Girls in the second group attributed 20 per cent more blame to causes outside themselves for the events in the stories than girls in the first group.

In a second experiment students in one group were seated in front of a mirror and students in another group were not. In this experiment judgements had to be made in terms of the 'responsibility to oneself'. For the group seated in front of the mirror their judgements were 20 per cent higher than for the group who were not. Both these studies led to the surprising conclusion that manipulating attention either towards or away from oneself can make the self more or less salient; this salience then affects the person's judgement about things which on a logical basis should be quite unaffected.

Explaining Actions and Events

In the last 10 years or so social psychologists have become increasingly interested in the way in which we perceive and explain both our own actions and the actions of others. When we ask friends why they think that, say, Alice acted the way she did, we are asking them for their opinions and theories about what was happening. People's explanations are called their *attributions*. Not surprisingly, psychologists' accounts of these explanations are referred to as 'attribution theories'. Of course, the whole of psychology involves the development of attribution theories of one sort or another.

Attribution theory, started by Heider in the late 1950s, is based on the assumption that people make causal attributions in order to help them control their social environments as well as to understand them. Most of the time we feel we know why we do things, but from time to time we are often puzzled at our own behaviour and ask ourselves *why* we behaved as we did. The way we see ourselves is quite important to the way we behave. How do we come about our impressions of ourselves? Suppose we see ourselves as being 'cheerful' how do we judge this? Perhaps the most obvious explanation is that we *feel* cheerful; we assess our internal mood and label it the way we do. Notice that even judgements about feelings are made with respect to other people. We are unlikely to label ourselves as having noses or ears because all other humans have these too. When we choose a label like 'cheerful' there is an implicit judgement which compares us to others. The second source of ideas about ourselves, as well as information we get from our internal states, is information about the way we behave. There is evidence to suggest we observe the way we behave, and use this to make judgements about ourselves.

An interesting study was conducted by Storms and Nisbett in 1970 on insomniacs, showing that attributions can be based on both internal evidence and knowledge of outside events. In insomnia people report breathing difficulties, feeling too warm, being alert, and experiencing an increased heart rate. Storms and Nisbett argued that if they could persuade their patients to attribute these symptoms to some cause outside themselves, then they could relieve some of the symptoms of insomnia. Three groups of insomniacs were used in the study; all subjects reported the time it took them to get to sleep on two consecutive nights before the study began. For the next two nights the three groups received different treatments. All subjects were given a pill to take before they went to sleep; the pill had no pharmacological effects whatsoever. One group was told that the pill would produce rapid heart rate, increased mental alertness, etc.: in short, all the symptoms of insomnia. The second group was told that the pill would have the effect of reducing all these symptoms, that is to say it would relax them. The third group was given the pill and was not informed about any possible effects.

Storms and Nisbett predicted that the first group would be able to get to sleep faster with the pill than without it because they would attribute their symptoms to the pill; and the second group would take longer to get to sleep because they would judge their symptoms to be particularly bad, given that they believed the pill would alleviate symptoms like these. The third group was a control group against which these first two effects could be judged. The experiment asked the subjects how long it took them to get to sleep on each night and why. Reports of how well subjects had slept showed that the subjects who had been told that the pill would act like a stimulant slept significantly better than the control group, and that subjects who were expecting sedative effects reported sleeping significantly worse. These results are quite consistent with the hypotheses put forward by Storms and Nisbett. Interestingly the attributions of the subjects about their sleeping patterns were quite different to the experimenters' attributions. Both experimental groups attributed changes in sleeping patterns to events which occurred during the day – for example, arguments with people, or the completion of some task successfully. People maintained their beliefs even when they were told about the different conditions used in the experiment. We can conclude that we do not always have insight into the things which control our behaviour. It is also worth noting that we usually provide explanations for our own behaviour even when these explanations do not match up with 'external' explanations.

Review
Our views about ourselves and our behaviour are built up by the way we

interpret a whole range of ambiguous information. Some of this ambiguous information is presented from within, and relates to physiological and emotional state, moods, emotions and the like; some of the ambiguous information arises from the things we perceive in the world (including the way we see ourselves behave) the way people treat us, the way we treat them, and the way we interpret these interactions.

It is probably as well to spell out the limits of the extent to which our worlds are knowable to each individual and the extent to which we need consensual validation to be sure about 'reality'. Suppose you are thinking of going ice skating on the pond but are doubtful about the thickness of the ice. You take a stone and throw it to the middle of the ice sheet; the stone passes straight through and splashes water around. The evidence of your senses is likely to convince you that the ice is not safe for skating on. Conversations with others – however prestigious or important – are unlikely to convince you of the solidity of the ice and persuade you to skate on it. Let's take the opposite end of the spectrum where the topic at issue cannot be observed directly. If the topic is 'the country would be in a much better state if the losers had won the last election' or 'Rocky Marciano was a better boxer than Mohammed Ali' the only way in which 'reality' can be established is by consensus and discussion with other people. We might all have our own individual views about any such topic but the only way we can validate these views is by discussion with other people. Our views about ourselves lie somewhere between these extremes. Some aspects of ourselves can be validated against external reality; some must be negotiated with others.

THE GLAROON'S APPROACH TO MIND CONTROL

Karl Marx argues (as have many people) that human thoughts arise both from the things we do, like playing, working and making love, and from our social relationships. Our 'consciousness', or experience of our thoughts, depends very heavily on our social activities. Marx has two key concepts that He ought to be aware of. The first is the concept of 'ideology': the notion that ideas serve as weapons for social interests.

If you can control the explanation that people have for the way society is organized and for each person's place in society, you are well on the way to controlling the society itself. If people believe that they exist to serve the state, or that God will reward them in heaven, no matter what they have to put up with on Earth, they will be quiescent and easy to rule. This is His problem. He can't see through the social pressures that are constraining Him from 'announcing the new order' as being an ideological weapon. Marx's second key concept is that of 'false consciousness'. This is the idea that a person may look at the world in a way that is quite inappropriate to someone in his or her social situation. For example, if teachers can be persuaded that wage inflation will cause economic disaster, they are likely to be far more modest in their wage demands than if they believe that the education system must attract able graduates via large salaries, if the long-term future of society is to be protected. Notice that Marx *isn't* saying that there is a 'true consciousness' that everyone should aspire to: for instance, a better deal for workers, or even anarchy and revolution. He is arguing that people who have power in a society, and people who are subject to this power, *should* have different views of society. If the powerful can persuade the powerless that their view is correct, then control becomes relatively easy. You don't have to be a Marxist to see the usefulness of this insight. In our story, He is struggling to overcome the 'false consciousness' that the Glaroon has constructed so carefully. The Glaroon himself, as we have seen, is fully aware of the power of ideology, and the need to instil a false consciousness in Him. The Glaroon warns his fellow conspirators of the dangers of viewing things from His point of view: 'If we understood His motives, we would be part of Him'. So the Glaroon has deliberately set out to control His consciousness by controlling His whole world, and all the knowledge He has.

The Glaroon, using both the First for Manipulation and the First for Operations, has created His whole world, both physically and socially. The Glaroon has subtly built in a particular approach to existence built on a society which demands work from its members in return for physical comforts, which is futile in the extreme. People (especially Him) are the raw materials which society consumes; when their working life is over they rest a while, then die. The Glaroon hoped that He would be unable to free Himself from the intellectual bondage of the society created for Him; the Glaroon also hopes that He will be too busy with the trivial details of living to reach out for important questions. He didn't get it quite right, though, did he?

The Glaroon's Failure

Why did the Glaroon fail? Because he was unable to control His mental reflections about events which He had experienced. Kelly's theory of personal constructs about the world argues that our views do not depend entirely on our past experiences, but can be changed by both conscious and unconscious thought – we know from the story what the trigger for this re-evaluation was. Remember Marx's 'ideology' which can be used as a tool by particular groups in society to achieve their aims? Karl Mannheim placed a lot of emphasis on Utopian thought. Utopian thought is produced by someone's own thinking, and is not simply learned from someone else. This Utopian thought can then become a plan for social action. The individual starts off with Utopian thought then tries to act on people around so that the social reality copies the thought. In *They* He made several attempts at Utopian thought during his life with Alice, but she succeeded in suppressing them all, until the incident over the rain. A similar view has been put forward by William James, who emphasizes the importance of our internal experiences such as aesthetic joy and spiritual feelings in shaping our views about ourselves. The Glaroon is going to have trouble with this kind of thinking too, as we know from 'Gladness! Gladness everywhere!' just before He was awoken by Joe from His dreams. Let's see why the Glaroon had Him locked up.

Misuse of Institutions for Social Control

His view of the world was no longer the one that suited the Glaroon, and so He was moved to the clinic. What is so special about clinics?

Well, the clinic differs from the world outside in a number of important ways. Outside, people work, sleep and play in different environments; inside, the whole day's activities are scheduled, there are well-defined rules which people must conform to and people are split into a 'managed' group and a 'managing' group.

People come to mental hospitals with their own world view which they have built up at home and at work. This view has to be adapted considerably, if they are to cope in their new circumstances. Of course if their stay in the institution is prolonged, readjustment back to the outside world may prove to be very difficult. One of the first things that happens to new patients is that the props to their old social identity are removed. New clothes may be provided; contact with friends and relatives is reduced; old roles can no longer be played. Their legal rights may also be removed.

It is hard for patients to hold anything privately: their clothes, possessions and living space are controlled by the institution. The daily routine, like rising, going to bed, and meal times are all outside the patients' control. Remember His flashing light signal for bed time? How would *you* respond to being placed in an institution like this? One of the first casualties would probably be your view of yourself as an efficient person who can make up their own mind and act responsibly and effectively.

The Glaroon is hoping to bring His mind in check again. How might this be brought about? Well, He has to be convinced that His old way of looking at the world was quite inappropriate, and that a new view, supplied by the Glaroon, is better. The whole system of beliefs which underlies mental hospitals gives patients the view that there is something wrong with *them*. It apportions responsibility for whatever brought the patient to the clinic to the patient. What about treatment? One view of personality that is often put forward in psychiatry and sometimes in psychology too, is that the person consists of a series of layers; on the surface are the observable behaviours which are open to all; next are layers which correspond to the person's own mental states which they have access to by introspection; and lowest down are unconscious wishes and desires. It is also asserted that one can never understand one's own unconscious wishes and desires without recourse to an 'expert'. If we can never really know who we are, and we agree that somebody else can, we are immediately in a very weak negotiating position. We come readily under the control of the other.

A recurrent theme in this chapter is that we all have a strong tendency to make sense of the circumstances we find ourselves in, and to make the best of them. At any point in our lives we look back and systematically select different pieces of evidence, distorting the things we remember, so as to make sense of our current situation. In unfavourable circumstances we can blame bad luck, but our image of ourself suffers too. Institutionalization sounds like just the treatment He needs to bring Him back under control.

Let's explore the Glaroon's abuse of psychiatry. One of the great virtues of the medical model of mental illness from the Glaroon's standpoint is that He can only get out of the institution by accepting Hayward's description of Himself, and the things that have happened to Him. He must appear to see Himself as being ill, and to want treatment; he must report His symptoms clearly. These actions confirm Hayward's role as a skilled medical practitioner. If He makes the error of just seeing the psychiatrist as a person of great power, He might respond quite inappropriately, say, like a prisoner asking for release from a jailer. If He responds by refusing to talk to someone who obviously thinks that He is crazy, this just confirms the psychiatrist's view that He is ill, far too ill to be released. So, before He can be released, He has got to agree that He is mad, and accept any treatment that Hayward deals out. Remember the Glaroon's order to the First for Manipulation? 'Prepare to graft the selected memory trace at once.' Sounds pretty horrible.

ALL THE ANSWERS?

So far we have talked about His situation in terms of His view of the world, and in terms of the ways that the Glaroon has set about controlling His consciousness. We haven't offered any answers to His problems about why the world exists, and what His place in it might be.

You shouldn't be too surprised to learn that psychology hasn't got answers to these fundamental questions. Most psychologists set out to explain human motives, desires and search for knowledge in terms of processes within ourselves, rather than in terms of outside agencies like gods or aliens. Psychological research has focused more on *how* we acquire knowledge and why we behave as we do rather than on asking *why* things are as they are. Philosophers have devoted a good deal of time these much larger issues with about as much success as He had.

Postscript. Our discussion of the Glaroon's abuse of psychiatry has shown us that mental hospitals can be used for the purposes of social control. Mental hospitals exist because distressed and mentally disturbed people exist. There is a good deal of debate among psychologists and psychiatrists about how such people can best be helped, but few people would doubt the commitment to patients' well-being of almost all who work in the area of mental health, both inside and outside hospitals. We would need another chapter to be able to discuss rival approaches to the treatment of mental illness.

5

THE QUESTION OF SEX

Ursula Le Guin

From field notes of Ong Tot Oppong, Investigator, of the first Ekumenical landing party on Gethen/Winter, Cycle 93 E.Y. 1448.

1448 day 81 . It seems likely that they were an experiment. The thought is unpleasant. But now that there is evidence to indicate that the Terran Colony was an experiment, the planting of one Hainish Normal group on a world with its own proto-hominid autochthones, the possibility cannot be ignored. Human genetic manipulation was certainly practiced by the Colonizers; nothing else explains the hilfs of S or the degenerate winged hominids of Rokanan; will anything else explain Gethenian sexual physiology? Accident, possibly; natural selection, hardly. Their ambisexuality has little or no adaptive value.

Why pick so harsh a world for an experiment? No answer. Tinibossol thinks the Colony was introduced during a major Interglacial. Conditions may have been fairly mild for their first 40 or 50,000 years here. By the time the ice was advancing again, the Hainish Withdrawal was complete and the Colonists were on their own, an experiment abandoned.

I theorize about the origins of Gethenian sexual physiology. What do I actually know about it? Otie Nim's communication from the Orgoreyn region has cleared up some of my earlier misconceptions. Let me set down all I know, and after that my theories; first things first.

The sexual cycle averages 26 to 28 days (they tend to speak of it as 26 days, approximating it to the lunar cycle). For 21 or 22 days the individual is *somer*, sexually inactive, latent. On about the 18th day hormonal changes are initiated by the pituitary control and on the 22nd or 23rd day the individual enters *kemmer*, estrus. In this first phase of kemmer (Karh. *secher*) he remains completely androgynous. Gender, and potency, are not attained in isolation. A Gethenian in first-phase kemmer, if kept alone or with others not in kemmer, remains incapable of coitus. Yet the sexual impulse is tremendously strong in this phase, controlling the entire personality, subjecting all other drives to its imperative. When the individual finds a partner in kemmer, hormonal secretion is further stimulated (most importantly by touch – secretion? scent?) until in one partner either a male or female hormonal dominance is established. The genitals engorge or shrink accordingly, foreplay intensifies, and the partner, triggered by the change, takes on the other sexual role (? without exception? If there are exceptions, resulting in kemmer-partners of the same sex, they are so rare as to be ignored). This second phase of kemmer (Karh. *thorharmen*), the mutual

121

process of establishing sexuality and potency, apparently occurs within a time-span of two to twenty hours. If one of the partners is already in full kemmer, the phase for the newer partner is liable to be quite short; if the two are entering kemmer together, it is likely to take longer. Normal individuals have no predisposition to either sexual role in kemmer; they do not know whether they will be the male or the female, and have no choice in the matter. (Otie Nim wrote that in the Orgoreyn region the use of hormone derivatives to establish a preferred sexuality is quite common; I haven't seen this done in rural Karhide.) Once the sex is determined it cannot change during the kemmer-period. The culminant phase of kemmer (Karh. *thokemmer*) lasts from two to five days, during which sexual drive and capacity are at maximum. It ends fairly abruptly, and if conception has not taken place, the individual returns to the somer phase within a few hours (note: Otie Nim thinks this 'fourth phase' is the equivalent of the menstrual cycle) and the cycle begins anew. If the individual was in the female role and was impregnated, hormonal activity of course continues, and for the 8.4-month gestation period and the 6- to 8-month lactation period this individual remains female. The male sexual organs remain retracted (as they are in somer), the breasts enlarge somewhat, and the pelvic girdle widens. With the cessation of lactation the female re-enters somer and becomes once more a perfect androgyne. No physiological habit is established, and the mother of several children may be the father of several more.

Social observations : very superficial as yet; I have been moving about too much to make coherent social observations.

Kemmer is not always played by pairs. Pairing seems to be the commonest custom, but in the kemmerhouses of towns and cities groups may form and intercourse take place promiscuously among the males and females of the group. The furthest extreme from this practice is the custom of *vowing kemmering* (Karh. *oskyommer*), which is to all intents and purposes monogamous marriage. It has no legal status, but socially and ethically is an ancient and vigorous institution. The whole structure of the Karhidish Clan-Hearths and Domains is indubitably based upon the institution of monogamous marriage. I am not sure of divorce rules in general; here in Osnoriner there is divorce, but no remarriage after either divorce or the partner's death: one can only vow kemmering once.

Descent of course is reckoned, all over Gethen, from the mother, the 'parent in the flesh' (Karh. *amha*).

Incest is permitted, with various restrictions, between siblings, even the full siblings of a vowed-kemmering pair. Siblings are not however allowed to vow kemmering, nor keep kemmering after the birth of a child to one of the pair. Incest between generations is strictly forbidden (in Karhide/Orgoreyn; but is said to be permitted among the tribesmen of Perunter, the Antarctic Continent. This may be slander.)

What else have I learned for certain? That seems to sum it up.

There is one feature of this anomalous arrangement that might have adaptive value. Since coitus takes place only during the period of fertility, the chance of conception is high, as with all mammals that have an estrus cycle. In harsh conditions where infant mortality is great, a race survival value may be indicated. At present neither infant mortality nor the birthrate runs high in the civilized areas of Gethen. Tinibossol estimates a population of not over 100 million on the three continents, and considers it to have been stable for at least a millenium. Ritual and ethical abstention and the use of contraceptive drugs seem to have played the major part in maintaining the stability.

There are aspects of ambisexuality which we have only glimpsed or guessed at, and which we may never grasp entirely. The kemmer phenomenon fascinates all of us Investigators, of course. It fascinates us, but it rules the Gethenians, dominates them. The structure of their societies, the management of their industry, agriculture, commerce, the size of their settlements, the subjects of their stories, everything is shaped to fit the somer-kemmer cycle. Everybody has his holiday once a month; no one, whatever his position, is obliged or forced to work when in kemmer. No one is barred from the kemmerhouse, however poor or strange. Everything gives way before the recurring torment and festivity of passion. This is easy for us to understand. What is very hard for us to understand is that, four-fifths of the time, these people are not sexually motivated at all. Room is made for sex, plenty of room; but a room, as it were, apart. The society of Gethen, in its daily functioning and in its continuity, is without sex.

Consider: Anyone can turn his hand to anything. This sounds very simple, but its psychological effects are incalculable. The fact that everyone between seventeen and thirty-five or so is liable to be (as Nim put it) 'tied down to childbearing', implies that no one is quite so thoroughly 'tied down' here as women, elsewhere, are likely to be – psychologically or physically. Burden and privilege are shared out pretty equally; everybody has the same risk to run or choice to make. Therefore nobody here is quite so free as a free male anywhere else.

Consider: A child has no psycho-sexual relationship to his mother and father. There is no myth of Oedipus on Winter.

Consider: There is no unconsenting sex, no rape. As with most mammals other than man, coitus can be performed only by mutual invitation and consent; otherwise it is not possible. Seduction certainly is possible, but it must have to be awfully well timed.

Consider: There is no division of humanity into strong and weak halves, protective/protected, dominant/submissive, owner/chattel, active/passive. In fact the whole tendency to dualism that pervades human thinking may be found to be lessened, or changed, on Winter.

The following must go into my finished Directives: When you meet a Gethenian you cannot and must not do what a bisexual naturally does, which is to cast him in the role of Man or Woman, while adopting towards him a corresponding role dependent on your expectations of the patterned or possible interactions between persons of the same or opposite sex. Our entire pattern of socio-sexual interaction is nonexistent here. They cannot play the game. They do not see one another as men or women. This is almost impossible for our imagination to accept. What is the first question we ask about a newborn baby?

Yet you cannot think of a Gethenian as 'it'. They are not neuters. They are potentials, or integrals. Lacking the Karhidish 'human pronoun' used for persons in somer, I must say 'he', for the same reasons as we used the masculine pronoun in referring to a transcendent god: it is less defined, less specific, than the neuter or the feminine. But the very use of the pronoun in my thoughts leads me continually to forget that the Karhider I am with is not a man, but a manwoman.

The First Mobile, if one is sent, must be warned that unless he is very self-assured, or senile, his pride will suffer. A man wants his virility regarded, a woman wants her femininity appreciated, however indirect and subtle the indications of regard and appreciation. On Winter they will not exist. One is respected and judged only as a human being. It is an appalling experience.

Back to my theory. Contemplating the motives for such an experiment, if such it was, and trying perhaps to exculpate our Hainish ancestors from the guilt of barbarism, of treating lives as things, I have made some guesses as to what they might have been after.

The somer-kemmer cycle strikes us as degrading, a return to the estrus cycle of the lower mammals, a subjection of human beings to the mechanical imperative of rut. It is possible that the experimenters wished to see whether human beings lacking continuous sexual potentiality would remain intelligent and capable of culture.

On the other hand, the limitation of the sexual drive to a discontinuous time-segment, and the 'equalizing' of it in androgyny, must prevent, to a large extent, both the exploitation and the frustration of the drive. There must be sexual frustration (though society provides as well as it can against it; so long as the social unit is large enough that more than one person will be in kemmer at one time, sexual fulfilment is fairly certain), but at least it cannot build up; it is over when kemmer is over. Fine; thus they are spared much waste and madness; but what is left, in somer? What is there to sublimate? What would a society of eunuchs achieve? – But of course they are not eunuchs, in somer, but rather more comparable to pre-adolescents: not castrate, but latent.

Another guess concerning the hypothetical experiment's object: The elimination of war. Did the Ancient Hainish postulate that continuous sexual capacity and organized social aggression, neither of which are attributes of any mammal but man, are cause and effect? Or, like Tumass Song Angot, did they consider war to be a purely masculine displacement-activity, a vast Rape, and therefore in their experiment eliminate the masculinity that rapes and the femininity that is raped? God knows. The fact is that Gethenians, though highly competitive (as proved by the elaborate social channels provided for competition for prestige, etc.), seem not to be very aggressive; at least they apparently have never yet had what one could call a war. They kill one another readily by ones and twos; seldom by tens or twenties; never by hundreds or thousands. Why?

It may turn out to have nothing to do with their androgyne psychology. There are not very many of them, after all. And there is the climate. The weather of Winter is so relentless, so near the limit of tolerability even to them with all their cold-adaptations, that perhaps they use up their fighting spirit fighting the cold. The marginal people, the races that just get by, are rarely the warriors. And in the end, the dominant factor in Gethenian life is not sex or any other human thing: it is their environment, their cold world. Here man has a crueler enemy even than himself.

I am a woman of peaceful Chiffewar, and no expert on the attractions of violence or the nature of war. Someone else will have to think this out. But I really don't see how anyone could put much stock in victory or glory after he had spent a winter on Winter, and seen the face of the Ice.

What, in unenlightened societies, colour, race, religion or, in the case of a conquered country, nationality, are to some men, sex is to all women; a peremptory exclusion from almost all honourable occupations. John Stuart Mill, 1869.

Feminism is not concerned with *a group of people it wants to benefit* , but with *a type of injustice it wants to eliminate*. Richards, 1980.

The topic of sex differences evokes strong emotions. This makes it hard to discuss rationally because the discussion reflects directly on our self-images and on our world views. Perhaps the best place to start thinking about the issues involved, then, is to invite you to examine your own attitudes towards the roles of women in society. Here is a questionnaire produced by Spence, Helmreich and Stapp – do fill it in!

Measuring Attitudes towards Women

Instructions. The statements below describe attitudes toward the role of women in society. There are no right or wrong answers, only opinions. Please express your feeling about each statement by indicating whether you (A) agree strongly, (B) agree mildly, (C) disagree mildly, or (D) disagree strongly. Please indicate your opinion by entering A, B, C or D in the space next to each item.

1. Swearing and obscenity are more repulsive in the speech of a woman than of a man.
2. Women should take increasing responsibility for leadership in solving the intellectual and social problems of the day.
3. Both husband and wife should be allowed the same grounds for divorce.
4. Telling dirty jokes should be mostly a masculine prerogative.
5. Intoxication among women is worse than intoxication among men.
6. Under modern economic conditions with women being active outside the home, men should share in household tasks such as washing dishes and doing the laundry.
7. It is insulting to women to have the 'obey' clause remain in the marriage service.
8. There should be a strict merit system in job appointment and promotion without regard to sex.
9. A woman should be as free as a man to propose marriage.
10. Women should worry less about their rights and more about becoming good wives and mothers.
11. Women earning as much as their dates should bear equally the expense when they go out together.
12. Women should assume their rightful place in business and all the professions along with men.
13. A woman should not expect to go to exactly the same places or to have quite the same freedom of action as a man.

125

14. Sons in a family should be given more encouragement to go to college than daughters.

15. It is ridiculous for a woman to run a locomotive and for a man to darn socks.

16. In general, the father should have greater authority than the mother in the bringing up of children.

17. Women should be encouraged not to become sexually intimate with anyone before marriage, even their fiancés.

18. The husband should not be favored by law over the wife in the disposal of family property or income.

19. Women should be concerned with their duties of childbearing and house tending, rather than with desires for professional and business careers.

20. The intellectual leadership of a community should be largely in the hands of men.

21. Economic and social freedom are worth far more to women than acceptance of the ideal of femininity which has been set up by men.

22. On the average, women should be regarded as less capable of contributing to economic production than are men.

23. There are many jobs in which men should be given preference over women in being hired or promoted.

24. Women should be given equal opportunity with men for apprenticeship in the various trades.

25. The modern girl is entitled to the same freedom from regulation and control that is given to the modern boy.

Reprinted with permission of the authors and the Psychonomic Society from J.T. Spence, R. Helmreich and J. Stapp (1973) A short version of the Attitudes Toward Women Scale (AWS). *Bulletin of the Psychonomic Society, 2,* 219–220.

Scoring is quite straightforward. For questions 1, 4, 5, 10, 13, 14, 15, 16, 17, 19, 20, 22, and 23:

$$\text{Score A} = 0; \text{B} = 1; \text{C} = 2; \text{D} = 3$$

For questions 2, 3, 6, 7, 8, 9, 11, 12, 18, 21, 24, and 25:

$$\text{Score A} = 3; \text{B} = 2, \text{C} = 1, \text{D} = 0$$

Baron and Byrne (1981) report that 'when the Attitudes towards Women scale was given to a large group of college students (241 females and 286 males), the average scores were as follows: males = 44.80; females = 50.26. Thus, not surprisingly, the females were more liberal in their attitudes than the males. When the scale was given to 292 mothers and 232 fathers, the average scores were: fathers = 39.22; mothers = 41.86. Thus, mothers were more liberal than fathers, but both sets of parents were more traditional in their beliefs than college students.'

How did you score? If you reread all the items, it is clear that they are asking about your attitudes to women and men, not about your knowledge about sex differences. We have started off with attitudes, because attitude and belief can easily colour the 'information' you consider reliable, and the kind of conclusions you are prepared to accept.

Another way of looking at people's stereotypes of men and women is to ask a variety of people to describe 'typical males' and 'typical females'. Table 5.1 shows the results that Frieze and co-workers got when they did just this.

Table 5.1. Stereotypes of men and women

Women are:	Men are:
Submissive	Blunt
Dependent	Rough
Tactful	Not aware of the feelings
Gentle	of others
Talkative	Aggressive
Passive	Ambitious
Followers, not leaders	Leaders
Lacking in self-confidence	Self-confident
Lacking in ambition	Adventurous
Sensitive to the feelings	Logical
of others	Competitive
Overly emotional	Decisive
	Dominant

Based on information presented by Frieze *et al.*, 1979; ex Baron and Byrne.

Are your stereotypes similar to the ones in the list? If we want to look at the *status* of men and women in society, we can ask people to rate each of these traits as to how desirable they are without telling them about our interest in sex roles. When this was done in America and Britain the results were what you would expect; traits which 'typify' women are less desirable than those which 'typify' men. Perhaps women are not as good as men?

Before we go much further, we must make a distinction between a person's *sex*, determined by their chromosomes and their genitalia, and a person's *gender*, determined by their behaviour. We will refer to male and female sex, and masculine and feminine gender. If we cross cultures and time, we will still find agreement about the essence of 'male' and 'female'. We won't find complete agreement about the roles played by males and females, though – that is, the behaviours that are thought to be typically 'masculine' and 'feminine'.

Most of us have strong beliefs about the nature of masculinity and femininity (i.e. about gender roles) and about the nature of males and females (i.e. about sex differences) which are central to our views about ourselves. In this chapter we will be reviewing a good deal of evidence about sex differences. Some of it will probably go against your current views; don't just ignore it! If you don't like the evidence, study it carefully and look for further explanations, or for other sources of evidence which we haven't considered. If you don't like the arguments, try to pick holes in them, or put forward your own, which are consistent with the available evidence.

What sources of evidence can we explore which will provide information about differences between the sexes? Assertions about differences are often based on stories about the way that the evolution of mankind has specialized males and females for different roles – so we must examine these evolutionary arguments. We must also inquire in detail about the nature of the differences between males and females that we are trying to account for – there isn't much point in developing a theory to account for differences in, say, verbal skills between the sexes, unless we are sure that these differences exist! Most of the studies of sex differences which we will report have been carried out in Britain and North America; so we must be careful not to assume that the differences discovered will be universally true (or that other cultures won't show sex differences which ours don't). Once we have identified differences we can look for the sources of these differences – are girls *taught* to be feminine, and boys *taught* to be masculine? We can also examine the rapid and radical changes which have taken place in our conceptions of 'masculine' and 'feminine' over relatively short periods of time.

Looking at cultures other than our own, offers the promise of useful information about sex differences, too. If the same patterns of behaviour distinguish males from females everywhere, we might want to talk about 'biological differences' or at least about 'stable dispositions'. If, on the other hand, we discover no similarities in sex roles between cultures, we will need to discuss gender differences as having social rather than biological roots. Attributing causation in human affairs rarely results in a straightforward choice between two alternatives – in this case 'biological differences' or 'patterns of socialization'. So we will spend some time discussing the relationship between our genetic make-up, and the environment which we are brought up in, in determining the kind of people we become. These notions about causes of sex roles sound rather deterministic, don't they? We must not forget that it is people who bring up children, and it is people who determine the nature of the societies we live in. Even if we are able to discover large 'biologically determined' differences between the sexes, it does not follow that we should accept these differences passively, and institutionalize them in our societies. An essential feature of humanity is the freedom to choose between alternative courses of action, and to set down equitable rules for the regulation of society. We will not ignore the moral and philosophical aspects of discussions about sex differences.

What do we know about sexual behaviour on Gethen? The Gethenian cycle is a little shorter than that of the human female cycle (26–28 days compared to 28–30 days); humans are potentially active almost all the time, whereas Gethenians are potentially active for only four to seven days of their cycle. In this respect Gethenians resemble female, non-human primates, which also have relatively short periods of sexual receptivity and little or no menstruation. In both cases, the cycle relating to childbearing is directed by hormones released by the pituitary gland.

Is Gethenian sexuality strange or is it an interesting variant on the normal development of human sexuality? Let's start off just after conception. Male and female children (judged by their chromosomes) have identical sexual organs until the second to third month of pregnancy. Internally, both have structures which could produce male or female sex organs, if stimulated appropriately. The so-called Wolffian structure contributes just to male sexuality; the Mullerian structure contributes just to female sexuality. 'Normal' sexual development produces a female; the Mullerian structure develops into the uterus, the sex gland becomes an ovary and the genital tubercle becomes a clitoris; the Wolffian structure atrophies. External genitalia become developed. In the case of a child with a Y chromosome, a hormone produced by the gonads triggers the development of male sexuality. The Wolffian structure becomes the Vas, the sex gland becomes a testis, and the genital tubercle becomes a penis; the Mullerian structure atrophies. The skin on each side of the opening, which in the female forms the labia, unites to form the scrotum (hence the visible seam). So males and females are conceived with the same apparatus for the development of genitals; it is the presence or otherwise of the male hormone that determines sex. Presumably, on Gethen one or other of these changes occurs during kemmer and has temporary, not permanent, effects.

Hormones are produced by a number of glands both in the brain and body. Normal males and females produce identical hormones, but in different amounts. Females produce more oestrogen and progesterone, and males produce more androgens. These hormones are referred to (a bit misleadingly) as 'female' and 'male' sex hormones.

Up to about eight years of age only small amounts of sex hormone are produced. Then the production of male sex hormones in *both* girls and boys increases steadily, with boys, on average, producing more than girls. This reaches a peak between the ages of 20 and 40. At about age 10, the level of female hormone rises dramatically in girls, and hardly at all in boys. The production of female hormone is cyclic in girls and controls the menstrual cycle.

There are great differences between the amounts of different hormones which are produced by different people. You can't even classify people as being male or female with much reliability, if all you know is how much of different hormones they are producing!

The account that we have offered here of a basic human form which can be triggered into either maleness or femaleness depending on the presence or absence of particular hormones doesn't sound like the basis for large qualitative sex differences, does it? Perhaps an evolutionary perspective will give us more clues. Before we begin to cloud our emotions with evidence, though, we should get the views of a few great men that we can trust, to guide us along the right pathways.

> It is generally admitted that with women the powers of intuition, of rapid perception, and perhaps of imitation, are more strongly marked than in man: but some, at least, of these faculties are characteristic of the lower races, and therefore of a past and lower state of civilization.
> Charles Darwin, 1896.

Stanley Hall was a major figure in the foundation of psychology as an academic discipline in America. From him we learn that

> Over-activity of the brain during the critical period of the middle and late teens will interfere with the full development of mammary power and of the functions essential for the full transmission of life generally.
> Stanley Hall, 1905.

These experts offer a description of the differences between males and females in terms of biological differences between the sexes which have arisen as a result of the evolutionary pressures which have shaped humans to be as we are. Gethen provides a stark reminder that our biological inheritance might play a large part in shaping the lives we lead. Has evolution produced qualitative differences between males and females?

EVOLUTION AND MANKIND

Before we can talk about human evolution, we need to do some groundwork on the theory of evolution itself. In every species the range in genetic make-up of individuals is maintained and extended by chance mutation; novel combinations of genes are ensured by sexual reproduction, where each offspring receives genetic material from both parents. Different environments favour some genetic compositions more than others – that is, certain individuals are likely to be better suited to their environment than others, and are more likely to produce more offspring which survive to reproduce.

Terms like 'struggle for life' and 'survival of the fittest' should be seen as metaphors: it is quite wrong to equate 'struggle' with physical violence and personal competitiveness or 'fitness' with Superman-like qualities. The terms indicate the ability of an individual to produce offspring which grow to a fertile adulthood. Think about Superman again!

Let's take an obvious example of *unnatural* selection. Humans have been engaged in genetic engineering for thousands of years: breeding animals for particular purposes; deliberately cultivating certain kinds of cereals, fruit and vegetables. Darwin got some of his inspiration by spending time in the communities concerned with the breeding of racing pigeons. The processes of selection are clear. Pigeons are reared to maturity; only the pigeons who are most successful at racing are allowed to breed (or at least, whose offspring survive to breed themselves). Over several generations faster and more enduring pigeons have been produced. The same process has been used with other sporting animals like racehorses and greyhounds, as well as with domestic animals. So, species evolve because of the effects of selection on genetic diversity. Of course evolution works *after* the fact of genetic diversity; there is no ideal creature that we are evolving towards, by some providential design.

If we want to talk about the genetic inheritance of humans we have to look at the evolutionary pressures which have shaped us, and the adaptations we have made to these pressures as a species.

Humans have only been around in their present form for about 50 000 years, say 2000 generations. The great apes, like the orangutan, gorilla and chimpanzee, are our closest living relatives. We have to go back about 15 million years – long before the emergence of either apes or humans – to find a common ancestor in *Ramipithecus*. It was about another 10 million years before a distinct man-ape, *Australopithecus*, appeared. From fossil remains found in Africa it is now clear that *Australopithecus* was about five feet tall, could walk on two legs with an upright posture and had a skull balanced on its backbone, as humans do. Most significantly, stone tools have been found alongside bones from *Australopithecus* in a number of sites in Africa.

Charles Darwin's early conjecture about the relationship between tool use and upright stance does seem to be borne out by the fossil evidence. An upright stance frees the hands for tool use. Tool use conveys many advantages, notably by increasing the range of foods that can be obtained (e.g. larger animals) and by decreasing the risks posed by predators, thus applying selection pressure in favour of an upright stance. This sort of inter-relationship is easily shown as a diagram but is hard to describe in terms of simple cause and effect.

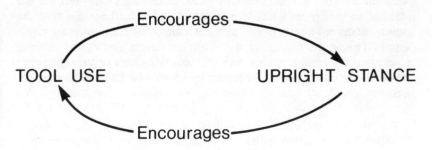

Tool use and upright stance in turn put evolutionary pressure on other parts of the body, notably the pelvis, hands and brain. Brain size developed rapidly, roughly trebling in size in the few hundred thousand years between man-ape and Neanderthal man (who had about the same brain volume as *homo sapiens*). Volume is a pretty crude indicator of what can be done with a brain – it is its function which is important.

The top part of the brain is called the *cortex*. Different parts of the cortex are specialized for different functions. When we look at the cortexes of humans and apes, it is clear that the human cortex is not just an enlarged ape cortex – it is specialized for different sorts of activity. The *sensory-motor cortex* is the part of the brain that registers sensations and directs the activities of our body. As a rough rule the larger the area of cortex that is devoted to a particular part of the body, the better able that part of the body is to feel sensations, and to discriminate between sensations and to make carefully controlled movement. So the lips have more sensory-motor cortex devoted to their control than does the trunk. One difference between the human and ape sensory-motor cortex is the area devoted to the hand and thumb, which is very much greater in humans, allowing far more skilful use to be made of our hands than can be made by monkeys. The thumb is essential for fine control of tools. Try writing with a pencil without using your thumb. Of course you can do it, but the results are slow and rather crude. The evolutionary pressures which lead to the development of a large thumb also lead to the development of the cortex to control it accurately. The same is true for other areas of the cortex. Perhaps the best example is the presence in humans of a part of the brain which is specialized for language use. Again, we can imagine tremendous evolutionary advantages in favour of even primitive language users in occupations like hunting, and food gathering in general.

But now we come to the crunch. We are trapped by two competing evolutionary pressures. Upright stance leads to evolutionary pressures for a modified pelvis design in the direction of reduction in the size of the birth canal. The larger brain needs a wider birth canal, if the infant is to get out at all! The partial reconciliation of these contradictory demands has led to a biological adaptation with profound social implications – the birth of the infant at an earlier stage of development. The result has been that the human infant needs attention and sustenance from adults during this period. The adults providing the attention cannot easily also be food gatherers at the same time, and so some adaptations are necessary ...

And this is where the stories about the nature of the male and female begin to be told.

The societies in which the available males undertake the harder labours, and so, relieving the females from undue physical tax, enable them to produce more and better offspring, will, other things being

equal, gain in the struggle for existence with societies in which the women are not thus relieved.
Spencer, 1898.

In Desmond Morris' book *The Naked Ape*, we learn that:

Behind the facade of modern city life there is the same old naked ape. Only the names have been changed: for 'hunting' read 'working', for 'hunting ground' read 'place of business', for 'home base' read 'house', for 'pair bond' read 'marriage', for 'mate' read 'wife' and so on.
Morris, 1967.

This view, at least, chooses to ignore the 12 million years of evolutionary change which has led to the differences between the great apes and humans. Washburn argues it is this period of our evolution which is critical to our understanding of our biological inheritance.

He points out that hunting does not necessarily lead to increased aggressiveness; it is more likely to provide evolutionary pressures for co-operation, mutual trust and language development.

It is clear that all these authors agree that we can learn about how we came to be as we are by tracing back to our evolutionary heritage. The trouble is, there is no easy way to find out what this heritage might be, and they differ widely in the story they tell. Biological explanations are often used to argue that current social structures reflect inevitable evolutionary pressures. The argument runs thus: Aboriginals, Africans, Asians (essentially every human who isn't a white Westerner) are genetically inferior because only the whites have experienced genetic selection for intelligence, adaptability and the like. Within this white master race, there are social divisions. Why is it that the rich are cultured and educated, whereas the poor are relatively ignorant and boorish? Well, it's genetic selection again. Naturally talented people rise to the top of any society they happen to be in; the less talented drift downwards. Talented people have talented children; so each society naturally partitions itself into strata, with the most able group enjoying positions of power and prestige.

And then there are females. Females have children; children need constant supervision and care and affection. The children most likely to survive are those with caring, affectionate mothers. Children need to be provided for and so need parents who can obtain resources for their families, so there are clear biological advantages in specializing the sexes for different functions. Men have been selected to be competitive 'bread winners' for their families: special attributes like aggression, intelligence, persistence, physical strength, etc., are the result of these pressures. Women have been selected for kindness and domesticity, even if this has resulted in a certain lack of general physical and intellectual competence.

If we take this line of argument, though, we should also be happy with its reflection – that there are some jobs which ought to be performed exclusively by women, because of their biological heritage. For example, jobs in health, social services and education are all the 'natural' responsibility of women. Any male doctors, social workers or teachers should be persuaded to join the armed services, commerce or agriculture instead, so that they can act their biological inheritance, and not suffer sterility and early death! Are you still happy with an evolutionary argument? Arguments based on biology and evolution can suddenly lose their appeal when they no longer support the *status quo* ! Let us review the argument: the current social and sexual divisions that we see in society give us evidence about our genetic make-up; this genetic make-up then explains why society is as it is. When society changes, the story about the 'essential nature of mankind' changes too!

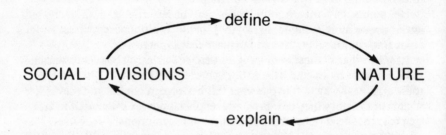

It is an easy defence to say that things are as they are because that is their 'true nature'. However, it isn't any sort of explanation at all, unless there is a coherent story, with good supporting evidence gathered outside the range of facts now being explained, which back up the 'true nature' explanation. This coherent story, as we have seen, is sadly lacking in evolutionary accounts.

Do we have to *deduce* what men and women are like on the basis of evolutionary fairy tales, or can we actually find out directly? Are men and women fundamentally different from each other, or does basic humanness dominate sex differences?

DISCOVERING AND MEASURING SEX DIFFERENCES

1. School and Careers

In Western societies a common stereotype is that men and women differ fundamentally, and that most of the differences reflect female deficiencies. Men dominate science, technology and mathematics, and women are more prevalent in languages, arts and biology. We can see these differences quite clearly by looking at the take- up of different courses in school, and the pass rates for girls and boys.

In England and Wales education is compulsory up to the age of 16. At age 16 most pupils sit examinations which are set and marked by nationally organized examination boards. Most pupils take a core of English, Mathematics, a foreign language, and a science, together with other subjects. Roughly one third of these pupils sit Ordinary Level examinations; a further third take Certificate of Secondary Education exams (soon to be merged into GCSE). Of the Ordinary Level candidates, about two-thirds of the candidates pass each exam. One way to look for differences between the sexes is to look at differences in the subjects taken, and in the relative performances of girls and boys.

Table 5.2 (a) shows the percentage of males and females who took different examinations, and the pass rate of each group. The most striking differences are in the relative take-up rates, and examination success in Home Economics versus the 'Practical Technology' group, which are completely dominated by females and males respectively. Languages, Biology and History are female dominated; Physics, Computer Studies, Chemistry and Geography are male dominated. In Mathematics the take-up rate is about the same for males and females but males get better results.

Table 5.2 (a). Sex differences in examination success at Ordinary Level

	Female candidates		Male candidates		Total candidates
	Percentage of entry	Percentage pass	Percentage of entry	Percentage pass	
Home economics	96	48	4	18	21 970
French	62	57	38	54	47 931
Biology	62	50	38	62	58 271
English literature	60	64	40	55	71 065
History	56	59	45	56	52 882
English language	54	56	46	47	152 810
Mathematics	49	53	51	63	85 253
Geography	45	56	55	60	58 782
Chemistry	42	58	58	61	54 416
Computer studies	32	60	68	69	12 697
Physics	29	59	71	57	60 686
Woodwork Metalwork Engineering workshop Geometric and engineering design	3	35	97	50	27 101

From Joint Matriculation Board Annual Report 1981—82.
Joint Matriculation Board, Manchester, 1983.

After passing Ordinary Level examinations, pupils may choose to study three or four subjects to Advanced Level, and take examinations typically after a further two years' study. Table 5.2 (b) shows the take-up rate and relative successes of males and females at Advanced Level. A similar pattern emerges to the pattern at Ordinary Level; now, however, mathematics has become predominantly a male subject.

Table 5.2 (b). Sex differences in examination success at Advanced Level

	Female candidates		Male candidates		Total candidates
	Percentage of entry	Percentage pass	Percentage of entry	Percentage pass	
Home economics	99	51	1	17	1228
English literature	75	70	25	66	15 605
Biology	58	70	42	73	12 923
Mathematics	24	68	76	68	13 347
Physics	22	71	78	71	15 896
Woodwork					
Metalwork					
Geometry and engineering drawing	2	56	98	47	722

How would you account for these differences between the sexes? Try out some of these explanations, which all have a biological flavour. Do you agree with any of them?

• Male (Female) hormones facilitate thinking about metalwork (home economics), but inhibit thinking about literature (physics).
• The X (Y) chromosome plays an important part in woodwork (home economics) but retards the development of aptitude to study biology (physics).

Before we decide, we should consider another piece of evidence. In 1968, only 37 per cent of the Mathematics O- level entry was from girls (in 1982 it was 49 per cent), and only 17 per cent of the A-level entry (in 1982 it was 24 per cent). If you believe fundamental, biologically based sex differences to be the major explanation of different take-up rates in different school subjects, you need a story about a rapid shift in these biological bases, too!

2. Specific Abilities
Can we find out about the 'true' nature of males and females directly? We have already seen that distinguished scientists of the past have been happy to describe sex differences in terms of qualities like 'passive/active'; 'conservative'; 'sluggish'; 'stable'; 'intuitive'; 'intelligent'; 'perceptual speed'. Large numbers of studies of all sorts of skills, dispositions and attitudes have been carried out by psychologists – surely they must contain a good deal of evidence about sex differences? But beware: there is a real danger

that when you set out to find sex differences, you will find more than are really there! The temptation is to consider studies which actually find differences, and ignore ones which do not – a danger enhanced by the practice in scientific journals of publishing results which show that something interesting has happened, while publishing very few studies which show no effects. This is rather like the rarity of a newsflash such as, 'Today no one was killed by a falling tree, or lightning, or sharks'. Maccoby and Jacklin made a special effort to locate studies which might have been expected to show sex differences but which did not. Many of the common stereotypes about sex differences were found to be false; at the same time they *did* find a few interesting sex differences, as Table 5.3 shows.

Table 5.3. Sex differences and similarities

Abilities

General intelligence	No difference on most tests.
Verbal ability	Females excel after age 10 or 11.
Quantitative ability	Males excel from the start of adolescence.
Creativity	Females excel on verbal creativity tests; otherwise no difference.
Cognitive style	No general difference.
Visual-spatial ability	Males excel from adolescence on.
Physical abilities	Males more muscular, males more vulnerable to illness, disease; females excel on manual dexterity tests when speed important, but findings ambiguous.

Personality characteristics

Sociability and love	No overall difference; at some ages boys play in larger groups; some evidence that young men fall in love more easily; out of love with more difficulty.
Empathy	Conflicting evidence.
Emotionality	Self-reports and observations conflict.
Dependence	Conflicting findings; dependence probably not a unitary concept.
Nurturance	Little evidence available on adult male reactions to infants; issue of maternal vs. paternal behaviour remains open; no overall difference in altruism.
Aggressiveness	More males aggressive from pre-school age on.

Reprinted with permission from C. Tavris and C. Offir (1977) *The Longest War: Sex Differences in Perspective*. Orlando, Fl.: Harcourt Brace Jovanovich.

Before we look at some of these headings in more detail, we should say what we mean by 'sex difference' or 'significantly greater'. Both these phrases conjure up an image of a yawning gap in ability, where, for example, nearly all of the females are superior to nearly all of the males. Let us look at the largest difference we can find, to see how big it really is. One of the largest and most reliable sex differences is found in 'spatial ability', shown in

Figure 5.1. 'Spatial ability' refers to the ability to do a range of tasks which involve diagrams, mental rotation, geometry, and the like.

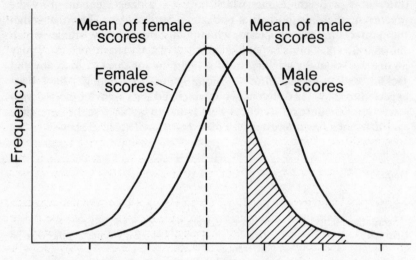

Figure 5.1. Spatial performance scores. (The shaded area represents 25 per cent of female scores which are above the mean of male scores.)

Figure 5.1 shows that about 25 per cent of women score better than half of men. So if you were selecting people to perform a job which required 'spatial ability' of the sort measured by these tests, it would be a great mistake to ignore women (as well as a flaunting of anti- discrimination legislation), since you would miss the chance of selecting all the women with high spatial ability. But if you were using 'spatial ability' to choose your future employees, and if a representative sample of both men and women applied for the job, you would finish up choosing more men than women. Now back to the headings in Table 5.3.

What about *intelligence* ? Unfortunately for our purposes, tests of intelligence are usually designed so that they do not discriminate between males and females – so they are unsuitable for discovering differences between the sexes.

Males are usually significantly better at tasks which require spatial skills (as we have just seen) and females are usually significantly better at tasks requiring verbal skills. We don't really know if girls talk younger or more in the first four years of life – psychologists' studies so far have not produced clear- cut results. The differences become apparent at age 10 or 11, and the superiority of girls increases slightly as they get older (both at low level skills like defining words, and at higher level tasks like verbal reasoning). No differences in quantitative ability emerge until puberty, then males outper- form females, even when different amounts of mathematics training are taken into account.

Men on average are *larger* and *stronger* than women; they can carry more oxygen in their blood, and can deal better with the waste products of physical exertion. Ashley Montagu lists 62 specific disorders found almost exclusively in males, including haemophilia, some forms of mental deficiency and colour blindness. In Western societies females live longer than males (for example in Britain life expectancy at birth is 74.8 years for females and 68.1 for males). Females are less prone to death from infectious disease in the first few weeks of life, survive harsh conditions better, for the same level of smoking are half as likely to contract lung cancer.

In the Maccoby and Jacklin review, in every society where men and women differ in *aggressiveness* , it is the males who are more aggressive. Males engage in more physical aggression, play aggression and fantasy aggression than do females. These differences appear as soon as children begin to play together, and last into adulthood.

Most violent *crime* is committed by men. Groups committed to organized violence on behalf of individual states, such as the army, or the police, consist mainly of men. Ong Tot Oppong, of course, has speculated that Gethenian sexuality was designed by Hainish genetic engineers with the explicit purpose of finding out *why* this sex difference is found so often.

Review

Do you remember Sherlock Holmes' case, in which the family dog did not bark? The absence of something expected gave the clue to the mystery. The most striking features of Maccoby and Jacklin's review aren't really to do with the few interesting sex differences that they have found, but rather, with the scarcity and smallness of differences that they were able to find consistently. Baron and Byrne have reviewed Maccoby and Jacklin's work as well as a good number of studies conducted since 1974. They conclude that 'stereotypes concerning differences between the sexes are only partly true at best. While the behaviour of males and females does indeed differ in certain respects, these differences are smaller, both in degree and number, than has often been assumed. In short, there seems to be a bit more "myth" than "reality" to cultural stereotypes concerning sex differences in behaviour'.

Nevertheless, there are differences to explain. What causes them? Do we learn how to be masculine or feminine? Or what?

Learning Sex Roles?

Let's go back to educational achievement by boys and girls in different school subjects. It is clear that boys achieve far better results overall in mathematics, science and technology. Reviews of differences in ability between males and females show fairly small differences compared to the huge sex differences in A- level results.

We also saw that in mathematics the imbalance between boys and girls was appreciably worse in 1968 than in 1982. Both findings suggest that the reasons for the differences in examination success lie in social factors within our society, rather than in the essential nature of males and females. One way to test this idea is to look at patterns of achievement in different societies – the greater the difference we find between cultures, the more confident we can be that social factors play an important part in achievement.

The International Study of Achievement in Mathematics looked at mathematical performance in a number of countries, and found, in general, the same pattern of boys performing better than girls overall, but especially in geometry. However there were considerable differences between countries, the smallest differences being in Sweden and the USA and the largest being in Japan and Belgium. These differences, as we have said, offer direct evidence about the importance of cultural influences on the kinds of skills which we all develop.

How could we identify the mechanisms of social and cultural effects on performance?

- We could look at the way young children are treated – for example at the presents they receive. (Boys are given more 'scientific' toys and girls more dolls, according to Maccoby and Jacklin's review).
- We could ask parents about their hopes for their children. 'Parents still often hold lower educational aspirations for girls than boys, and it has been found in the USA that low levels of mathematical achievement are more easily accepted by parents of girls than by parents of boys ...'(Para. B 32 of the Cockcroft Report on Mathematical Education, 1982.)
- We could look at the content of magazines and television programmes intended for young people. (Teenage magazines offer stereotypes of the image of girls as 'marriage fodder', focusing on relationships with boys, engagement, marriage and the like, according to a survey conducted by Weiner.)
- We could look at the way that children view achievement in different areas. (Girls who are mathematically gifted are likely to fear that their achievement in mathematics will put off potential boyfriends, according to Fox.)

Studies which have watched mathematics being taught, recording which pupils the teacher speaks to, show clearly that teachers of both sexes treat boys and girls differently.

In mixed schools, in which boys and girls are following the same course, ... teachers have been shown to interact more with boys than they do with girls ... and to give more serious consideration to boys' ideas ...; they also give boys more opportunity to respond to higher cognitive level questions. High achieving girls have been found to receive significantly less attention in mathematics classes than do high achieving boys.

Para. B 25 of the Cockcroft Report on Mathematical Education, 1982.

So girls and boys are treated rather differently in school, in mathematics lessons. Surely, though, no one could claim that differences between males and females in things such as aggression or job success can arise because of the way that young males and young females are socialized?

Adults' responses are affected by a child's sex before they reach the classroom. In England, it is common for infant boys to be dressed in blue, and infant girls to be dressed in pink! Will and co-workers introduced mothers to an infant that they had never met before; some mothers were told that the baby was male, and some that the baby was female. Mothers presented a train more often to 'males' and a doll more often to 'females' – they also smiled more often at 'females'. Other researchers have found similar results for other adult groups (male, female, parent, non-parent), most commonly reporting that males behave in a more stereotyped way than females. According to Lewis (1972), who asked pregnant women about the behaviour of their growing foetuses, active kicking is usually interpreted as a sign that the foetus is male. So sex typing can begin before birth!

Weitzman and co-workers analysed prize-winning books for children for the cultural stereotypes that they contain. For each picture of a female, there were 11 of males (in the case of animals, this ratio rose to 1:95!). Males were shown as being active, as being leaders; females were passive, and followed. Other surveys report similar results. Your own television viewing will tell you how many female characters are portrayed as being independent, high status people, who routinely overcome difficult problems compared with the numbers portrayed as sex objects, and the proportion of commercials showing women in traditional, subservient roles.

It is pleasing to note that this wealth of anti- female propaganda doesn't seem to have much effect on the sorts of basic ability that Maccoby and Jacklin reviewed. It isn't too surprising, though, to see that boys and girls choose quite different school subjects, and that prospects for career success are so different for males and females.

Nothing that we have said so far denies the existence of consistent differences in the natural abilities and behaviours of males and females. It seems a perfectly reasonable proposition that differences *do* exist. Finding out what these differences are, though, is very hard to do, because of the different expectations that adults have of boys and girls, and the differences in socialization that they are each subjected to. The majority of the studies reported here were carried out in England and the USA. They show how the beliefs that our society has about the nature of masculinity and femininity is reflected in the experiences that males and females brought up in our society receive. This makes it extremely difficult to get any sort of idea about the 'essential' natures of males and females (supposing that this phrase has a real meaning at all) by looking at just one society. So how can we investigate the problem? The Hains resorted to experiments, like the one on Gethen, which we can't do, even if we wanted to, but we can compare masculinity and femininity in different societies. Presumably different cultures will have different approaches to child rearing, and will have different ideas about the roles which males and females should perform. If we find that there are consistent patterns in the behaviour of males and females that go across all the societies that we observe, this is good evidence about the nature of male and female. There *are* some consistencies in human behaviour that are found in all cultures in which they have been examined – for example the kinds of facial expression which humans use to express emotions such as pleasure, anger, disgust and surprise – so what about sex-linked behaviour?

MALES AND FEMALES AROUND THE WORLD

Anthropologists have studied literally thousands of different societies across the world in considerable detail and have shown the wide range of gender roles adopted by males and females. In some cultures, women do all the heavy work; in some, women initiate sexual contact; in others, women play a major political role; in some cultures it is the men who wear most adornment.

> Almost every trait that has been assigned to women in one society has been given to men in at least one other society. In fact, there seem to be only two true universals: the lower status of women and sexual dimorphism.
> Hoyenga and Hoyenga, 1979.

Every society divides tasks between the sexes and socializes children into appropriate gender roles. The performance of jobs by males and females differs a good deal from society to society. Roy D'Andrade summarized evidence from 224 societies: trapping, herding, fishing, the manufacture of weapons, boat building, musical instruments and working in wood and metal were most commonly performed by men; cooking, carrying water and grinding grain were commonly performed by women. In all cultures, housework is almost invariably performed by women.

Sexual Behaviour
The classical study in the area of sexual behaviour in different human

cultures was conducted in 1951 by Clellan Ford and Frank Beach. They compared sexual behaviour in 190 different cultures, most of which were pre-literate. In all cultures, heterosexual relations between adults was the most common sexual partnering. However, almost every kind of sexual activity with every kind of sexual partner was accepted in at least one of the societies studied. So great variety on Gethen shouldn't surprise us.

> In every known human society, the male's need for achievement can be recognized. Men may cook, or weave or dress dolls or hunt humming birds, but if such activities are appropriate occupations of men, then the whole society, men and women alike, votes them as important. When the same occupations are performed by women, they are regarded as less important.
> Margaret Mead, 1950.

Mead's last observation promises rather slow progress towards equality in our own society. If a high percentage of women become doctors or dentists or teachers, Mead would predict that the status of these jobs would decrease, rather than that the status of women would increase. This has been confirmed in Russia, where medicine has become a female dominated profession; in Denmark with dentistry, and in the USA with teaching.

Women have lower status in societies in which they are isolated from everyone but their own children, according to Rosaldo's work; and in societies with father-son property inheritance and descent of authority, from studies by Gouldner and Peterson. Women have higher status when they contribute about as much of the food as the men, and divide the labour roughly equally, according to Sanday. On Gethen, according to Ong Tot Oppong, there was no basis for any such status differences.

The most obvious conclusion we can draw from cross- cultural studies is that the sex roles adopted in our society are not predetermined – a wide range of sex roles can be found in other societies. Clearly we are not slaves to our biological inheritance.

If we are to make our own society fairer in the ways that males and females are treated, these cross-cultural studies offer some strong suggestions about how to proceed.

Anthropology and Western Society

We can ask if an anthropological approach really does help us to understand our society better. Where is the evidence within our society to support the cross-cultural findings? As an example let's look at sex roles in the two World Wars. Nowadays, historical accounts tend to play down the role of women in the 'War Effort'. Television images of effeminate women (now there is an insult to be proud of!) ineffectually waiting for their adored men to return, do considerable violence to the truth. As well as direct involvement in the war in 'female' jobs such as nursing, and quasi-female jobs in the support branches of the armed services, there was a major involvement of women in almost all branches of agriculture and industry, as women took over essential jobs once performed by men who had to be called up. Women were employed in heavy industries such as shipbuilding, armaments manufacture, and engineering in general, performing jobs which before the war they were considered quite unsuited for. During the war such women were viewed as fulfilling their patriotic duty, and were respected for it. The women weren't treated in exactly the same way as male workers, of course, for example they weren't usually paid as much for doing the same job, and their working conditions were often harsher.

When the war ended, female workers were no longer patriots – overnight they became hard, unfeminine people who were keeping war heroes out of their hard-earned jobs. The real role of women switched in the eyes of society to that of 'home-maker', or some other syrupy forties euphemism for 'unemployed female'. Role switches occurred in all the Western nations heavily involved in the war. The film *Rosie the Rivetter* provides a cutting chronicle of this cycle in the USA.

In summary, the evidence shows that males and females do not have many characteristics which are fixed by their biology. We need not be surprised to find differences between men and women, of course, but where we find large differences, these are usually much easier to explain in terms of society than in terms of biology.

There is great diversity in human societies. We can find many societies where women have lower status and fewer rights than they have in the United Kingdom and the United States, and a few societies where they have higher status and more rights. One of the few observations true of every society examined so far is that jobs *are* divided between men and women, and that the status of women everywhere is lower than the status of men.

If males are dominant everywhere, can we say that this is 'natural', and that male dominance is just what ought to happen? It is a great mistake to deduce ideas about what *ought to be* from observations of the way things *are*. Try this sentence: 'Males are violent everywhere, so this is natural, and ought to happen.' The argument has the same structure as before, but now I think we can agree that it doesn't really follow.

Nature and Nurture

Has the study of Gethen helped us to understand ourselves at all? One of the themes that has run right through this chapter is the relationship between human biology and the human environment in determining the sort of people we become. What *is* the relationship between biology and environment in determining gender differences? All we can really be sure of is that the relationship isn't simple. It is obvious that the environment affects the way we develop, for example an adequate diet is essential for normal development. But which factor plays the biggest role – biological inheritance or socialization? This question isn't easy to answer either. Suppose we look around for individuals who are genetically identical (as are identical twins); any differences between these individuals which we can find must be due to differences in their environments before or after birth. Similarly, if it were possible to provide exactly the same environment for a group of individuals, then any differences between them must have arisen because of genetic differences. But both of these assertions are too simple – the genetic endowment of the identical twins must interact with the environment for the twins to grow up at all. The environment will have different effects on the variety of genetic materials in our other group. So these studies could only show us the relative effects of genetic and environment for *particular* genes and for a *particular* environment, respectively. Let us take another extreme illustration. Suppose that the identical twins both suffered from some major genetic disease. Environmental differences would have little effect, and we would conclude that the effects of genetics far outweigh the effect of environment. Next, suppose that the environment were extreme: if it is extremely poor, then normal development is likely to be inhibited in all our varied sample – we will conclude that environmental effects are far more important than genetic ones. Paradoxically, if we can produce an environment which is ideal for fostering the full potential of each individual, then this will show us that genetic factors are far more important than environmental ones!

A useful analogy for understanding the relationship between environment and biology is Seligman's (1970) concept of *preparedness* . Let's start off with an example. Suppose you drive down to town with a friend to see a concert. Before the concert you have a drink together: after the concert you go for a meal. Back at home you feel ill, and become violently sick. Why? What parts of the evening are you unlikely to repeat? You are most likely to associate being sick with the meal (or perhaps with the drink); you are unlikely to avoid concerts or your friend in the future. This isn't necessarily the result of conscious thought – you can show analogous behaviour in rats. If a rat becomes sick after drinking water with a novel taste, it will avoid drinking water with this taste in the future. If a rat becomes sick after drinking water in the presence of flashing lights and noise, it *won't* avoid water presented to it with lights and noise in the future. So some learning associations are much easier to make than others. This isn't a subtle effect either – the rat had no problem detecting loud noises and flashing lights – the problem was making the link with being sick. If there are biologically primed sex differences in *any* aspect of behaviour then, given the same stimulation, sex differences will arise. Conversely, if the less prepared sex receives a good deal of experience of the situation, and the well prepared sex receives none, then the 'normal' sex difference will be reversed. If the well prepared sex receives far more experience in the situation, then the 'normal' sex difference will be magnified. If the situations which trigger particular behaviours are totally absent, then neither sex will show the behaviour; if the environment continually provides appropriate learning experiences, then both sexes will develop the behaviour.

Let's take differences in physical abilities as an example. We said earlier that males on average are larger and stronger than females, that they carry more oxygen in their blood, and are more efficient than females in removing the waste products of physical exertion in their muscles. All of these differences (apart from size) can be affected quite dramatically by physical exercise. Compare the differences between the abilities of 'ordinary' people who decide to take up marathon running with those who don't, for example. If males and females take about the same amount of exercise, then a sex difference will be observed between comparable people. If, however, it is 'unfeminine' to exercise, and 'masculine' to be fit and strong, then the sex difference will be magnified. If, on the other hand, it is 'feminine' to be physically fit, and 'masculine' to stay inside and drink beer all day, the sex difference will be reversed. In this last case, notice that males could still build up muscle far faster than females – showing that this story still makes sense, even when one sex are more 'prepared' to develop in particular ways in response to the environment than the other sex are.

If we relate this idea of 'preparedness' back to the anthropological evidence discussed earlier, we can tell a story about males and females which fits the wide range of roles deemed to be masculine and feminine. Likely contenders for 'biologically primed' behaviour are assertiveness and aggression in males, and the absence of these (or perhaps opposite traits) in females. Triggers for the emergence of these behaviours might be harsh child-rearing practices; social violence (e.g. from gangs, neighbouring groups, adjacent countries) or the threat of social violence; things often associated with violence such as a shortage of resources; and the like. In social conditions where these triggers are absent, pronounced gender differences are far less likely to emerge.

Sex Differences, Discrimination and Morality

The ebb and flow of the discussion about Gethenian sexuality tells us something about the relationship between science, politics and morality. We saw at the beginning of the chapter that eminent scientists are sometimes prepared to use the cloak of science quite improperly to justify existing social structures. The techniques of science, though, can be used to see how plausible some of these justifications actually are.

Another kind of justification of sexual discrimination which is often used is to appeal to economic arguments like 'efficiency' or 'cost effectiveness'. Traditionally, any aspect of human behaviour related to sex, like menstruation, having children and rearing them, have either been ignored, or have been used as a 'reason' to discriminate against females. For example pregnancy, childbirth and childcare reduce the period of economic activity of women, and therefore might make a female employee more of a financial risk than a male employee. Conversely, one might argue that discrimination leads to *less* efficient industry. For example since about half of women are all more intelligent than about half of men, they should be employed in jobs which require intellectual skills. If we believe in a free society in which people sell their labour for rewards, anything which interferes with free activities, like discrimination on the grounds of sex, colour or social class, smacks of feudalism, and operates against the interests of the free market (as does anything which allocates one's place in society to anything but ability). Both these arguments have an economic basis which can be quantified, in principle. If provision for women to have time off work for maternity leave will lead to a national economic disaster, we should know about it. If the children of working mothers are more disturbed, or achieve less at school than the children of comparable parents, we should count the social costs of the parents' employment.

However, what we do when we have counted the financial and social costs is an affair of morality and politics. Costs of hiring and training employees are employers' costs; we must be careful not to sweep away the rights of individuals to be treated fairly, under the banner of 'industrial efficiency'. Suppose that there are social costs associated with mothers working – again, society might make a decision to uphold the rights of both parents to seek employment, and look for ways to maximize the developmental achievement of each child via the provision of, say, well-equipped nursery schools run by caring, qualified staff.

An obvious missing theme here is that it is parents who have children, not women. (So why not discriminate against parents, instead of women?) One route to equality might be to share all the jobs to be performed in a household between parents – working for money, looking after children, and domestic duties. (A number of surveys have shown that the equal division of labour in the home hardly ever occurs.) A second route to social equality is to value child care at least as highly as working for money. Do you think that, say, manufacturing vehicles, making television programmes, or selling insurance is as important as bringing up children? Relatively recently, fertility control has become available which allows people to decide how many children to have, and when to have them. Bottle feeding of infants does not injure their health, in Western societies, as far as we know. These two technological advances offer scope for quite radical social change in the pattern of family structures and sex roles, if we make the political or moral decisions to use them. So decisions about what *ought* to happen are political ones, which each citizen should help to formulate. When we discuss the issues surrounding sex roles, we must take great care to separate statements that refer to 'facts' (or what we take to be facts) from our judgements about the implications that we draw from these facts. Anyone can join in either debate about 'what the facts are' or 'what ought to

147

be done about them'. Finding out about 'what is' requires a range of scientific and technical skills. Discussing 'what to do' requires statements about our moral principles, our views of the world, and our political opinions. We should strive to keep the two apart.

You and Your Gender

Does all this research have anything to offer each of us personally? By now we should all have had our prejudices exposed – but what do we do with them? Here are a few review paragraphs, by different authors, to ponder about.

> All human individuals, as a result of their bisexual disposition and of cross-inheritance, combine in themselves both masculine and feminine characteristics, so that pure masculinity and femininity remain theoretical constructions of uncertain content.
> Sigmund Freud, 1925.

> Masculine and feminine behaviours belong at different dimensions, not on opposite ends of a single dimension: and animal can be masculinized without being defeminized. So it seems quite possible for an organism to be both masculine and feminine, or to be neither.
> Hoyenga and Hoyenga, 1979.

> An increasing body of research findings suggests that persons show-ing ... a mixture of supposedly 'masculine' and 'feminine' traits ... are often happier and better adjusted than those who adhere rigidly to traditional sex roles and stereotypes ... In short, men who are capable of showing such traditionally 'feminine' traits as tenderness and women who can demonstrate such traditionally 'masculine' traits as competitiveness, often seem better adjusted than persons incapable of such flexibility.
> Baron and Byrne, 1981.

6

WHAT TO DO UNTIL THE ANALYST COMES

Frederik Pohl

I just sent my secretary out for a container of coffee and she brought me back a lemon Coke.

I can't even really blame her. Who in all the world do I have to blame, except myself? Hazel was a good secretary to me for fifteen years, fine at typing, terrific at brushing off people I didn't want to see, and the queen of them all at pumping office gossip out of the ladies' lounge. She's a little fuzzy-brained most of the time now, sure. But after all!

I can say this for myself, I didn't exactly know what I was getting into. No doubt you remember the – Well, let me start that sentence over again, because naturally there is a certain doubt. Perhaps, let's say, *perhaps* you remember the two doctors and their headline report about cigarettes and lung cancer. It hit us pretty hard at VandenBlumer & Silk, because we've been eating off the Mason-Dixon Tobacco account for twenty years. Just figure what our fifteen per cent amounted to on better than ten million dollars net billing a year, and you'll see that for yourself. What happened first was all to the good, because naturally the first thing that the client did was scream and reach for his chequebook and pour another couple million dollars into special promotions to counteract the bad press, but that couldn't last. And we knew it. V.B. & S. is noted in the trade as an advertising agency that takes the long view; we saw at once that if the client was in danger, no temporary spurt of advertising was going to pull him out of it, and it was time for us to climb up on top of the old mountain and take a good long look at the countryside ahead.

The Chief called a special Plans meeting that morning and laid it on the line for us. 'There goes the old fire bell, boys,' he said, 'and it's up to us to put the fire out. I'm listening, so start talking.'

Baggott cleared his throat and said glumly, 'It may only be the paper, Chief. Maybe if they make them without paper ...' He's the a.e. for Mason-Dixon, so you couldn't really blame him for taking the client's view.

The Chief twinkled: 'If they make them without paper they aren't cigarettes any more, are they? Let's not wander off into side issues, boys. I'm still

149

listening.'

None of us wanted to wander off into side issues, so we all looked patronizingly at Baggott for a minute. Finally Ellen Silk held up her hand. 'I don't want you to think,' she said, 'that just because Daddy left me a little stock I'm going to push my way into things, Mr VandenBlumer, but – well, did you have in mind finding some, uh, angle to play on that would take the public's mind off the report?'

You have to admire the Chief. 'Is that your recommendation, my dear?' he inquired fondly, bouncing the ball right back to her.

She said weakly, '*I* don't know. I'm confused.'

'Naturally, my dear,' he beamed. 'So are we all. Let's see if Charley here can straighten us out a little. Eh, Charley?'

He was looking at me. I said at once, 'I'm glad you asked me for an opinion, Chief. I've been doing a little thinking, and here's what I've come up with.' I ticked off the points on my fingers. 'One, tobacco makes you cough. Two, liquor gives you a hangover. Three, reefers and the other stuff — well, let's just say they're against the law.' I slapped the three fingers against the palm of my other hand. 'So what's left for us, Chief? That's my question. Can we come up with something new, something different, something that, one, is not injurious to the health, two, does not give you a hangover, three, is not habit-forming and therefore against the law?'

Mr VandenBlumer said approvingly, 'That's good thinking, Charley. When you hear that fire bell, you really jump, boy.'

Baggott's hand was up. He said, 'Let me get this straight, Chief. Is it Charley's idea that we recommend to Mason-Dixon that they go out of the tobacco business and start making something else?'

The old man looked at him blandly for a moment. 'Why should it be Mason-Dixon?' he asked softly, and left it at that while we all thought of the very good reasons why it *shouldn't* be Mason-Dixon. After all, loyalty to a client is one thing, but you've got an obligation to your own people too.

The old man let it sink in, then he turned back to me. 'Well, Charley?' he asked. 'We've heard you pinpoint what we need. Got any specific suggestions?'

They were all looking at me to see if I had anything concrete to offer. Unfortunately, I had.

*

I just asked Hazel to get me the folder on Leslie Clary Cloud, and she came in with a copy of my memo putting him on the payroll two years back. 'That's all there was in the file,' she said dreamily, her jaw muscles moving rhythmically. There wasn't any use arguing with her, so I handed her the container of lemon Coke and told her to ditch it and bring me back some *coffee*, C-O-F-F-E-E, coffee. I tried going through the files myself when she was gone, but *that* was a waste of time.

So I'll have to tell you about Leslie Clary Cloud from memory. He came into the office without an appointment and why Hazel ever let him in to see me I'll never know. But she did. He told me right away, 'I've been fired, Mr McGory. Canned. After eleven years with the Wyoming Bureau of Standards as a senior chemist.'

'That's too bad, Dr Cloud,' I said, shuffling the papers on my desk. 'I'm

150

afraid, though, that our organization doesn't –'

'No, no,' he said hastily. 'I don't know anything about advertising. Organic chemistry's my field. I have a, well, a suggestion for a process that might interest you. You have the Mason-Dixon Tobacco account, don't you? Well, in my work for my doctorate I –' He drifted off into a fog of long-chain molecules and short-chain molecules and pentose sugars and common garden herbs. It took me a little while, but I listened patiently and I began to see what he was driving at. There was, he was saying, a substance in a common plant which, by cauliflamming the whingdrop and di-tricolating the residual glom, or words something like that, you could convert into another substance which appeared to have many features in common with what is sometimes called hop, snow or joy-dust. In other words, dope.

I stared at him aghast. 'Dr Cloud,' I demanded, 'do you know what you're suggesting? If we added this stuff to our client's cigarettes we'd be flagrantly violating the law. That's the most unheard-of thing I ever heard of! Besides, we've already looked into this matter, and the cost estimates are –'

'No, no!' he said again. 'You don't understand, Mr McGory. This isn't any of the drugs currently available, it's something new and different.'

'Different?'

'Non-habit-forming, for instance.'

'Non-habit-forming?'

'Totally. Chemically it is entirely unrelated to any narcotic in the pharmacopeia. Legally – well, I'm no lawyer, but I swear, Mr McGory, this isn't covered by any regulation. No reason it should be. It doesn't hurt the user, it doesn't form a habit, it's cheap to manufacture, it – '

'Hold it,' I said, getting to my feet. 'Don't go away – I want to catch the boss before he goes to lunch.'

So I caught the boss, and he twinkled thoughtfully at me. No, he didn't want me to discuss it with Mason-Dixon just yet, and yes, it did seem to have some possibilities, and certainly, put this man on the payroll and see if he turns up with something.

So we did; and he did.

Auditing raised the roof when the vouchers began to come through, but I bucked them up to the Chief and he calmed them down. It took a lot of money, though, and it took nearly six months. But then Leslie Clary Cloud called up one morning and said, 'Come on down, Mr McGory. We're in.'

The place we'd fixed up for him was on the lower East Side and it reeked of rotten vegetables. I made a mental note to double-check all our added-chlorophyll copy and climbed up the two flights of stairs to Cloud's private room. He was sitting at a lab bench, beaming at a row of test tubes in front of him.

'This is it?' I asked, glancing at the test tubes.

'This is it.' He smiled dreamily at me and yawned. 'Excuse me,' he blinked amiably. 'I've been sampling the little old product.'

I looked him over very carefully. He had been sampling something or other, that was clear enough. But no whisky breath; no dilated pupils; no shakes; no nothing. He was relaxed and cheerful, and that was all you could say.

'Try a little old bit,' he invited, gesturing at the test tubes.

Well, there are times when you have to pay your dues in the club. V.B. & S.

had been mighty good to me, and if I had to swallow something unfamiliar to justify the confidence the Chief had in me, why I just had to go ahead and do it. Still, I hesitated for a moment.

'Aw,' said Leslie Clary Cloud, 'don't be scared. Look, I just had a shot but I'll take another one.' He fumbled one of the test tubes out of the rack and, humming to himself, slopped a little of the colourless stuff into a beaker of some other colourless stuff – water, I suppose. He drank it down and smacked his lips. 'Tastes awful,' he observed cheerfully, 'but we'll fix that. Whee!'

I looked him over again, and he looked back at me, giggling. 'Too strong,' he said happily. 'Got it too strong. We'll fix that too.' He rattled beakers and test tubes aimlessly while I took a deep breath and nerved myself up to it.

'All right,' I said, and took the fresh beaker out of his hand. I swallowed it down almost in one gulp. It tasted terrible, just as he said, tasted like the lower floors had smelled, but that was all I noticed right away. Nothing happened for a moment except that Cloud looked at me thoughtfully and frowned.

'Say,' he said, 'I guess I should have diluted that.'

I guess he should have. *Wham.*

But a couple of hours later I was all right again.

Cloud was plenty apologetic. 'Still,' he said consolingly, standing over me as I lay on the lab bench, 'it proves one thing. You had a dose about the equivalent of ten thousand normal shots, and you have to admit it hasn't hurt you.'

'I do?' I asked, and looked at the doctor. *He* swung his stethoscope by the earpieces and shrugged.

Nothing organically wrong with you, Mr McGory – not that I can find, anyway. Euphoria, yes. Temporarily high pulse, yes. Delirium there for a little while, yes – though it was pretty mild. But I don't think you even have a headache now.'

'I don't,' I admitted. I swung my feet down and sat up, apprehensively. But no hammers started in my head. I had to confess it: I felt wonderful.

Well, between us we tinkered it into what Cloud decided would be a 'normal' dosage – just enough to make you feel good – and he saturated some sort of powder and rolled it into pellets and clamped them in a press and came out with what looked as much like aspirins as anything else. 'They'd probably work that way too,' he said. 'A psychogenic headache would melt away in five minutes with one of those.'

'We'll bear that in mind,' I said.

What with one thing and another, I couldn't get to the old man that day before he left, and the next day was the weekend and you *don't* disturb the Chief's weekends, and it was Monday evening before I could get him alone for long enough to give him the whole pitch. He was delighted.

'Dear, dear,' he twinkled. 'So much out of so little. Why, they hardly look like anything at all.'

'Try one, Chief,' I suggested.

'Perhaps I will. You checked the legal angle?'

'On the quiet. It's absolutely clean.'

He nodded and poked at the little pills with his finger. I scratched the back of my neck, trying to be politely inconspicuous, but the Chief doesn't miss much. He looked at me inquiringly.

'Hives,' I explained, embarrassed, 'I, uh, got an overdose the first time, like I said. I don't know much about these things, but what they told me at the clinic was I set up an allergy.'

'Allergy?' Mr VandenBlumer looked at me thoughtfully. 'We don't want to spread allergies with this stuff, do we?'

'Oh, no danger of that, Chief. It's Cloud's fault, in a way; he handed me an undiluted dose of the stuff, and I drank it down. The clinic was very positive about that: even twenty or thirty times the normal dose won't do you any harm.'

'Um.' He rolled one of the pills in his finger and thumb and sniffed it thoughtfully. 'How long are you going to have your hives?'

'They'll go away. I just have to keep away from the stuff. I wouldn't have them now, but – well, I liked it so much I tried another shot yesterday.' I coughed, and added, 'It works out pretty well, though. You see the advantages, of course, Chief. I have to give it up, and I can swear that there's no craving, no shakes, no kick-off symptoms, no nothing. I, well, I wish I could enjoy it like anyone else, sure. But I'm here to testify that Cloud told the simple truth: It isn't habit-forming.'

'Um,' he said again; and that was the end of the discussion.

Oh, the Chief is a cagey man. He gave me my orders: keep my mouth shut about it. I have an idea that he was waiting to see what happened to my hives, and whether any craving would develop, and what the test series on animals and Cloud's Bowery-derelict volunteers would show. But even more, I think he was waiting until the time was exactly, climactically right.

Like at the Plans meeting, the day after the doctor's report and the panic at Mason-Dixon.

And that's how Cheery-Gum was born.

Hazel just came in with the cardboard container from the drug store, and I could tell by looking at it – no steam coming out from under the lid, beads of moisture clinging to the sides – that it wasn't the coffee I ordered. 'Hey!' I yelled after her as she was dreamily waltzing through the door. 'Come back here!'

'Sure 'nough, Massa,' she said cheerfully, and two-stepped back. 'S'matter?'

I took a grip on my temper. 'Open that up,' I ordered. 'Take a look at what's in it.'

She smiled at me and plopped the lid off the container. Half the contents spilled across my desk. 'Oh, dear,' said Hazel, 'excuse me while I get a cloth.'

'Never mind the cloth,' I said, mopping at the mess with my handkerchief. 'What's in there?'

She gazed wonderingly into the container for a moment; then she said, 'Oh, *honestly*, boss! I see what you mean. Those idiots in the drug store, they're gummed up higher than a kite, morning, noon and night. I always say, if you can't handle it, you shouldn't touch it during working hours. I'm sorry about this, boss. No lemon! How can they call it a lemon Coke when they forget the –'

'Hazel,' I said, 'what I wanted was coffee. Coffee.'

She looked at me. 'You mean *I* got it wrong? Oh, I'm sorry, Mr McGory. I'll go right down and get it now.' She smiled repentantly and hummed her way towards the door. With her hand on the knob, she stopped and turned to look at me. 'All the same, boss,' she said, 'that's a funny combination. Coffee *and* Coke. But I'll see what I can do.'

And she was gone, to bring me heaven knows what incredible concoction. But what are you going to do?

No, that's no answer. I know it's what *you* would do. But it makes me break out in hives.

The first week we were delighted, the second week we were triumphant, the third week we were millionaires.

The sixth week I skulked along the sidewalks all the way across town and down, to see Leslie Clary Cloud. Even so I almost got it when a truckdriver dreamily piled into the glass front of a saloon a yard or two behind me.

When I saw Cloud sitting at his workbench, feet propped up, hands clasped behind his head, eyes half-closed, I could almost have kissed him. For his jaws were not moving. Alone in New York, except for me, he wasn't chewing Cheery-Gum.

'Thank heaven!' I said sincerely.

He blinked and smiled at me. 'Mr McGory,' he said in a pleasant drawl. 'Nice of you.'

His manner disturbed me, and I looked more closely. 'You're not – you're not gummed up, are you?'

He said gently, 'Do I look gummed up? I never chew the stuff.'

'Good!' I unfolded the newspaper I had carried all the way from Madison Avenue and showed him the inside pages – the ones that were not a mere smear of ink. 'See here, Cloud. Planes crashing into Radio City. Buses driving off the George Washington Bridge. Ships going aground at the Battery. We did it, Cloud, you and I!'

'Oh, I wouldn't get upset about it, old man,' he said comfortably. 'All local, isn't it?'

'Isn't that bad enough? And it isn't local – it can't be. It's just that there isn't any communication outside the city any more – outside of any city, I guess. The shipments of Cheery-Gum, that's all that ever gets delivered anywhere. Because that's all anybody cares about any more, and we did it, you and I!'

He said sympathetically, 'That's too bad, McGory.'

'Curse you!' I shrieked at him. 'You said it wasn't a drug! You said it wasn't habit-forming! You said –'

'Now, now,' he said with gentle firmness. 'Why not chew a stick yourself?'

'Because I can't! It gives me hives!'

'Oh, that's right.' He looked self-reproachful. 'Well,' he said dreamily at last, 'I guess that's about the size of it, McGory.' He was staring at the ceiling again.

'*What* is?'

'What is what?'

'What's about the – Oh, the devil with it, Cloud, you got us into this, you have to get us out of it. There must be some way of curing this habit.'

'But there isn't any habit to cure, McGory,' he pointed out.

'But there is!'

'Tem-per,' he said waggishly, and took a corked test tube out of his workbench. He drank it down, every drop, and tossed the tube into a waste-basket. 'You see?' he demanded severely. '*I* don't chew Cheery-Gum.'

So I appealed to a Higher Authority.

In the eighteenth century I would have gone to the Church, in the nineteenth, to the State. I went to an office fronting on Central Park where the name on the bronze plaque was *Theodor Yust, Analyst*.

It wasn't easy. I almost walked out on him when I saw that his jaws were chewing as rhythmically as his secretary's. But Cloud's concoction is not, as he kept saying, a drug, and though it makes you relax and makes you happy and, if you take enough of it, makes you drunk, it doesn't make you unfit to talk to. So I took a grip on my temper, the only bad temper left, and told him what I wanted.

He laughed at me – in the friendliest way. 'Put a stop to Cheery-Gum? Mr McGory!'

'But the plane crashes –'

'No more suicides, Mr McGory!'

'The train wrecks –'

'Not a murder or a mugging in the whole city in a month.'

I said hopelessly. 'But it's *wrong!*'

'Ah,' he said in the tone of a discoverer, 'now we come down to it. Why is it wrong, Mr McGory?'

That was the second time I almost walked out. But I said, 'Let's get one thing straight: I don't want you digging into my problems. That's not why I'm here. Cheery-Gum *is* wrong, and I am *not* biased against it. You can take a detached view of collisions and sudden death if you want to, but what about slow death? All over the city, all over the country, people are lousing up their jobs. Nobody cares. Nobody does anything but go through the motions. They're happy. What happens when they get hungry because the farmers are feeling too good to put in their crops?'

He sighed patiently. He took the wad of gum out of his mouth, rolled it neatly into a Kleenex and dropped it in the wastebasket. He took a fresh stick out of a drawer and unwrapped it, but stopped when he saw me looking at him. He chuckled. 'Rather I didn't, Mr McGory? Well, why not oblige you? It's not habit-forming, after all.' He dropped the gum back into the drawer and said: 'Answering your questions, they won't starve. The farmers are farming, the workers are working, the policemen are policing, and I'm analysing. And you're worrying. Why? Work's getting done.'

'But my secretary –'

'Forget about your secretary, Mr McGory. Sure, she's a little fuzzy- brained, a little absent-minded. Who isn't? But she comes to work, because why shouldn't she?'

'Sure she does, but –'

'But she's happy. Let her be happy, Mr McGory!'

I looked scandalized at him. 'You, a doctor! How can you say that? Suppose *you* were fuzzy-brained and so on when a patient desperately needed –'

He stopped me. 'In the past three weeks,' he said gently, 'you're the first to come in that door.'

I changed tack: 'All right, you're an analyst. What about a G.P. or a surgeon?'

He shrugged. 'Perhaps,' he conceded, 'perhaps in one case out of a thousand – somebody hurt in an accident, say – he'd get to the hospital too late, or the surgeon would make some little mistake. Perhaps. Not even one in a thousand – one in a million, maybe. But Cheery-Gum isn't a drug. A quarter-grain of sodium amytol, and your surgeon's as good as new.' Absent- mindedly he reached into the drawer for the stick of gum.

'And you say,' I said accusingly, 'that it's not habit-forming!'

He stopped with his hand half-way to his mouth. 'Well,' he said wryly, 'it *is* a habit. Don't confuse semantics, Mr McGory. It is not a narcotic addiction. If my supply were cut off this minute, I would feel bad – as bad as if I couldn't play bridge any more for some reason, and no worse.' He put the stick of gum away again and rummaged through the bottom drawers of his desk until he found a dusty pack of cigarettes. 'Used to smoke three packs a day,' he wheezed, choking on the first drag.

He wiped his streaming eyes. 'You know, Mr McGory,' he said sharply, 'you're a bit of a prig. You don't want people to be happy.'

'I – '

He stopped me before I could work up a full explosion. 'Wait! Don't think that you're the only person who thinks about what's good for the world. When I first head of Cheery-Gum, I worried.' He stubbed the cigarette out distastefully, still talking. 'Euphoria is well and good, I said, but what about emergencies? And I looked around, and there weren't any. Things were getting done, maybe slowly and erratically, but they were getting done. And then I said, on a high moral plane, that's well and good, but what about the ultimate destiny of man? Should the world be populated by cheerful near-morons? And that worried me, until I began looking at my patients.' He smiled reflectively. 'I had 'em all, Mr McGory. You name it, I had it coming in to see me twice a week. The worst wrecks of psyches you ever heard of, twisted and warped and destroying themselves; and they stopped. They stopped eating themselves up with worry and fear and tension, and then they weren't my patients any more. And what's more, they weren't morons. Give them a stimulus, they respond. Interest them, they react. I played bridge the other night with a woman who was catatonic last month; we had to put the first stick of gum in her mouth. She beat the hell out of me, Mr McGory. I had a mathematician coming here who – well, never mind. It was bad. He's happy as a clam, and the last time I saw him he had finished a paper he began ten years ago, and couldn't touch. Stimulate them – they respond. When things are dull – Cheery-Gum. What could be better?'

I looked at him dully, and said, 'So you can't help me.'

'I didn't say that. Do you want me to help you?'

'Certainly!'

'Then answer my question: Why don't you chew a stick yourself?'

'Because I can't!' It all tumbled out, the Plans meeting and Leslie Clary Cloud and the beaker that hadn't been diluted and the hives. 'A terrific allergy,' I emphasized. 'Even antihistamines don't help. They said at the clinic that the antibodies formed after a massive initial –'

He said comfortably, 'Soma over psyche, eh? Well, what would you expect? But believe me, Mr McGory, allergies are psychogenic. Now, if you'll just – '

Well, if you can't lick 'em, join 'em, that's what the old man used to say. But I can't join them. Theodor Yust offered me an invitation, but I guess I was pretty rude to him. And when, at last, I went back, ready to crawl and apologize, there was a scrawled piece of cardboard over the bronze nameplate; it said: *Gone fishing.*

I tried to lay it on the line with the Chief. I opened the door of the Plans room, and there he was with Baggott and Wayber, from Mason-Dixon. They were sitting there whittling out model ships, and so intent on what they were doing that they hardly noticed me. After a while the Chief said idly, 'Bankrupt yet?' And moments passed, and Wayber finally replied, in an absent-minded tone:

156

'Guess so. Have to file some papers or something.' And they went on with their whittling.

So I spoke sharply to them, and the minute they looked up and saw me, it was like the Rockettes: the hands into the pockets, the paper being unwrapped, the gum into the mouth. And naturally I couldn't make any sense with them after that. So what are you going to do?

No! I can't!

Hazel hardly comes in to see me any more, even. I bawled her out for it – what would happen, I demanded, if I suddenly had to answer a letter. But she only smiled dreamily at me. 'There hasn't been a letter in a month,' she pointed out amiably. 'Don't worry, though. If anything comes up, I'll be with you in a flash. This stuff isn't a habit with me, I can stop it any time, you just say the word and ol' Hazel'll be there ...'

And she's right because, when you get right down to it, there's the trouble. It isn't a habit.

So how can you break it?

You can stop Cheery-Gum any time. You can stop it this second, or five minutes from now, or tomorrow.

So why worry about it?

It's completely voluntary, entirely under your control; it won't hurt you, it won't make you sick.

I wish Theodor Yust would come back. Or maybe I'll just cut my throat.

... as soon as each had eaten the honeyed fruit of the plant, all thoughts of reporting to us or escaping were banished from his mind. All they now wished for was to stay where they were with the Lotus-eaters, to browse on the lotus, and to forget that they had a home to return to. I had to use force to bring them back to the ships, and they wept on the way ...
Odysseus, in Homer's *Odyssey*.

Humans have been using drugs for medicine and pleasure for thousands of years. Most cultures have discovered and used alcohol; the use of hallucinogenic drugs for religious purposes is found in cultures as remote as South America and Ancient Greece; the medical uses of opium were widely known throughout the ancient world; the ancient Egyptians were familiar with the purging effects of castor oil, and the Arabians with the effects of senna. The writings of many ancient civilizations contain instructions about how to prepare and administer drugs.

Western societies use drugs extensively. We have drugs to relieve pain, to prevent conception, to treat mental illness and to provide pleasure. Many of these are accessible to anybody who wants to buy them – some are not. The drug industries are an important component in the economy. In the UK it is estimated that the National Health Service spent £300 million on drugs in 1984. To this we should add the large sums spent on unrestricted drugs, for example it is claimed that each year Americans spend well over $100 million on antacid preparations alone. Billions of dollars and thousands of millions of pounds are spent each year on alcohol and tobacco, as well as large, unknown sums spent on illegal drugs.

Before we go further we need to analyse some of the terms used when drugs are discussed, notably 'drug', 'habit forming', 'tolerance' and 'addiction'. The story often uses them incorrectly.

What do you make of McGory's outburst to Cloud – 'You said it wasn't a drug! You said it wasn't habit forming!' Is there any sense in which Cheery-Gum could not be seen as a drug? If we define a *drug* to be any substance which, when consumed, changes the body's structure or function in some way, then Cheery-Gum has got to be classified as a drug. All medicines that have a direct effect (i.e. are not placebos like coloured water or chalk pills) must be classified as drugs, but not all drugs are medicines, since poisons also change the structure or function of the body. We had better correct Charley McGory's error in saying, 'habit forming and *therefore* against the law'. The 'therefore' is quite wrong and combines two separate issues – is it habit forming? and is it against the law? Some substances, e.g. aspirin, are neither habit forming nor illegal; some are both habit forming and illegal, e.g. heroin; some are habit forming and legal, e.g. alcohol; and some are not habit forming and illegal, e.g. cannabis.

Tolerance is another aspect of regular drug taking – larger and larger doses can be required to produce the same effects, and somebody who regularly takes a drug can tolerate levels which could be lethal to a person taking the drug for the first time.

What about Cheery-Gum's addictive properties? Let's hear from McGory!

> I can swear that there's no craving, no shakes, no kick-off symptoms, no nothing. I, well, I wish I could enjoy it like anyone else, sure. But I am here to testify that Cloud told the simple truth: it isn't habit-forming.

What did Dr Theodore Yust have to say about it?'

> It is a habit. Don't confuse semantics, Mr McGory. It is not a narcotic addiction. If my supply were cut off this minute, I would feel bad – as bad as if I couldn't play bridge any more for some reason and no worse.

Dr Yust could use exactly the same remarks to address the World Health Organisation that he used to Charles McGory. The WHO distinguishes between physical dependence ('addiction') and psychological dependence. The simplest meaning of addiction is that a person who has had experience of a drug finds it difficult to give that drug up. The most obvious sign of this is *physical addiction* where attempts to stop using a drug are associated with withdrawal symptoms which can include a high temperature, sweating, shaking, irregular heartbeat and breathing patterns, vomiting, diarrhoea and severe cramp. Death can occur. Drugs such as barbiturates, alcohol, and the opiates all show marked effects of tolerance and are all addictive. Other powerful drugs such as LSD show the effect of tolerance, but are *not* addictive. Cannabis is neither addictive, nor does tolerance to it increase.

YOUR USE OF DRUGS

Think about your own use of drugs. Which of these classes of drugs do *you* use regularly? Pain killers; sedatives; anti-depressants; vitamins. What about your use of drugs for pleasure? Think about this list: alcohol; cannabis; cocaine; coffee; inhalants (e.g. glue); LSD; opium; tea; tobacco. Which ones do you use regularly? Which have you tried?

Think about your first experiences with each of these substances. Try to remember when you first encountered them. Table 6.1 shows the results of a study done on 163 white junior- and senior-high school students in California, by Hamburg and colleagues. How do your experiences compare with theirs?

Let's try to explore the reasons why we take up the social use of drugs, the reasons why we continue to use them, and the problems in giving them up. Think about your use of coffee, or alcohol, or tobacco. Why did you start? What keeps you going? Why don't you stop?

Starting off

- Probably the most obvious starting point is the availability of each drug. If family or friends drink or smoke regularly and are willing to share, then starting off is easy.
- Using drugs for pleasure can be seen as a sign of maturity – a young person smoking and drinking is behaving in ways reserved for adults, so by association they see themselves as being adult.
- Some drug use is illegal – smoking tobacco and drinking alcohol below certain specified ages, as is the simple possession of other drugs. Breaking the drug laws can be viewed as a sign of rebellion, and hence is attractive for this reason alone.
- People seem to enjoy using drugs! Novices may start simply out of curiosity.

What else have you thought of?

Keeping going

- The effects of different drugs can be pleasurable – so they are taken again.

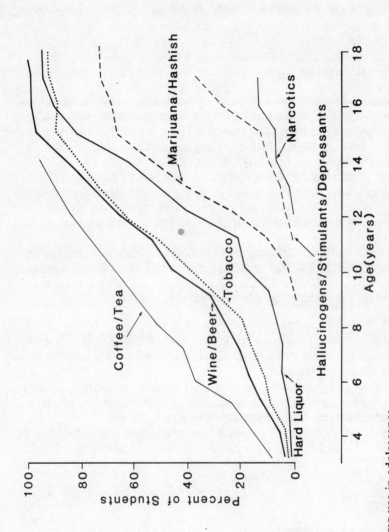

Figure 6.1. Drug use in adolescence.
Reprinted with permission from B.H. Hamburg *et al.* (1975) A hierarchy of drug use in adolescence. *American Journal of Psychiatry, 132,* 1155--1163. ©1975 The American Psychiatric Association.

- Some drugs cause physical dependence – this is probably an important reason why people keep on smoking, for example.
- A lot of social rituals involve shared use of drugs. Meeting people for the first time, and re-establishing social contacts can be made easier by a shared ritual of giving and taking, and lighting cigarettes, or buying drinks, in just the same way that we have coffee or meals together, to encourage intimacy.
- Drug use reaffirms our membership of certain social groups, and not others. It might be possible, for example, to play rugby and not to drink beer afterwards, but to our knowledge few people have tried the experiment.
- Drug use might be invisible! If you normally live with and work with people who drink coffee and take aspirins for headaches, it might take a book on psychology to draw your attention to your 'drug use'.

What else have you thought of?

Giving up

- Why bother? It gives pleasure, and it's harmless.
- Why bother? It gives pleasure, and I'm hooked.
- My friends use it – I don't want to appear odd.
- It's expensive.
- It's a dirty, dangerous habit.
- I don't want to set a bad example to my children.
- I don't like the effects it is having on me.

What else have you thought of?

CHEERY-GUM AND TOBACCO

Charley McGory traces the demise of the Mason-Dixon Tobacco Co. back to 'two doctors and their headline report about cigarettes and lung cancer'. He is probably referring to the paper by Doll and Hill in the *British Medical Journal* of 1950 on 'Smoking and Carcinoma of the Lung'. The dangers of smoking really only began to be treated seriously, though, after the first report from the Royal College of Physicians, *Smoking and Health*, was published in 1962. There is now no reasonable doubt that the smoking of cigarettes is harmful to health. The evidence is extensive, and quite well known. We won't repeat it here. If you want an interesting and well written review, try *Smoking OR Health*, published by the Royal College of Physicians.

The tobacco companies have done all they can to distract attention away from the extent of the dangers of smoking. Compare these views on the benefits of tobacco.

Clearly a dependence-producing substance with a capacity to cause physical harm to the user and its use is so widespread as to constitute a public health problem.
World Health Organisation, 1974.

It remains my personal opinion that smoking, on balance, does more good to most people than harm.
R. Dobson, President of British American Tobacco, 1975.

The biggest noxious influence in our environment.
The Chief Medical Officer, Department of Health, 1970.

It may only be the paper, Chief. Maybe if they make them without papers ...
Baggot, a.e. for Mason-Dixon at V.B. and S.

The story highlights the large sums of money spent on tobacco advertising – 'we've been eating off the Mason- Dixon tobacco account for twenty years. Just figure out what our 15% amounted to on better than ten million dollars net billing a year'. When the link between lung cancer and cigarettes was being exposed, Charley McGory reports that the tobacco companies' response was to reach for the 'cheque book and pour another couple of million dollars into special promotions to counteract the bad press'. No science fiction here; this is just what happened. The tobacco companies' response to the scare was to introduce gift coupon schemes to maintain existing smokers, and to encourage others to join in. In 1975–76 they spent £80 million on advertising tobacco in the UK. In contrast the Government spent one million pounds on anti-smoking activities.

It is easy to underestimate just how addictive tobacco is. In a national survey of adults in the USA carried out by the US Department of Health Education and Welfare eight out of ten adult smokers said that they would stop if they could. The Report of the RCP cites a study on heroin addicts in London which asked them about their most needed drug. Tobacco came top of even their lists.

ALCOHOL AND CHEERY-GUM

Alcohol is the other obvious rival for Cheery-Gum. A lot is known about alcohol in our society. However there are still a number of misconceptions about it. Here is a chance to find out about some of your own. Try and say whether each of the following statements is true or false before you go on to the crib sheet that follows the test.

1. Alcohol is correctly classified as a drug.

2. In small amounts alcohol acts like a stimulant.
3. Drinking black coffee speeds the sobering up process.
4. One becomes intoxicated faster on rum or scotch than on vodka.
5. One drink (for instance a single scotch or half a pint of bitter) is not likely to greatly impair driving skill.
6. It is a good idea for mountain rescuers to offer spirits in order to warm up people who have been exposed to extreme mountain conditions.
7. An unborn child is affected by its mother's consumption of alcohol.
8. Alcohol is aphrodisiac in its action.
9. Social drinking is the first step towards alcoholism.

A Few Answers

1. Of course alcohol is a drug. It has a direct effect on the central nervous system, acting to depress its action.
2. Alcohol always has a depressive effect on the nervous system. A sense of euphoria after small amounts of alcohol can come about because the drug depresses brain centres which are concerned with social control.
3. Sobering up consists of reducing the amount of alcohol in the body. This is carried out by the liver. The caffeine in coffee can act as a stimulant to increase the activity of the central nervous system which has been depressed by the effects of alcohol. So although coffee does not in itself help the metabolism of alcohol, it can act to increase the arousal of the nervous system as a whole.
4. The amount of intoxication one suffers (or enjoys) depends simply on the amount of ethanol (the active ingredient in alcoholic drinks) that one consumes. So the only difference between equal-sized measures of rum, scotch and vodka is to be found in the proof rating of each of these drinks.
5. A single measure of spirit or half a pint of beer is extremely unlikely to impair driving performance. However, beyond this point all motor skill performances decrease dramatically as alcohol intake is increased.
6. Alcohol acts to dilate the peripheral blood vessels, that is to say the ones nearest the skin get bigger. Because more blood is flowing round near the surface of the skin, the body acts more like a radiator and so loses heat much more easily. When cold, the body's usual defence is to restrict the amount of blood flowing near the surface of the skin, conserving it for the heart and lungs. So it would be foolhardy for mountain rescuers to offer people spirits. (Of course trained mountain rescuers would not do this anyway.)
7. Alcohol is one of the substances which is able to cross the placenta and enter the baby's blood stream. The foetus does not have the adult body's defences against alcohol and will have problems in breaking down alcohol.
8. Alcohol may well have an effect of lowering inhibitions, and therefore

increasing the chance of sexual encounters. However, large quantities of
alcohol are likely to result in poor coordination – hardly the hallmarks of
a wonderful lover!

9. Social drinking and alcoholism? This must be logically true of course.
More worrying is the very high rate of dependency that results amongst
people that do drink on a regular basis. A figure of about one person in
twenty is usually quoted. Imagine how this would be interpreted if it
were true of some new drug which was being introduced onto the market
– say Cheery-Gum.

Figures produced about Britain in 1971 by Zacune and Hensman claim
that 7000 alcoholics are admitted to hospital each year; there are 80 000
arrests each year for public drunkenness, plus 30 000 for drunken driving;
about 40 per cent of the prison population has a serious drinking problem –
as do 60 per cent of our vagrants.

The same sorry tale is repeated in the USA. The average alcohol con-
sumer has a one in twenty chance of becoming alcoholic, or at least a
'problem drinker'; over 9 million people are alcoholic at any one time; about
30 per cent of all public arrests are for public drunkenness; alcohol is
responsible for more than 25 000 highway deaths each year (together with at
least one million severe injuries); alcohol abuse is also associated with child
abuse and homicide. Social costs run to at least 25 billion dollars each year.

Alcohol is now receiving the same attention from the medical professions
in Britain and America that tobacco has enjoyed for the past 20 years or so.

HOW DO DRUGS AFFECT BEHAVIOUR?

A major theme of the story is that Cheery-Gum has the same effects on
everyone who uses it – that it causes people to behave in particular ways.
Does it make sense to say that drugs cause people to behave in particular
ways? How *do* people behave when they take different drugs? The results
produced by taking any drug depend on a combination of factors, including
the chemical action of the drug; the person taking it; and on the social
setting in which the drug is taken. These three factors are interwoven. The
drugs we use most commonly are taken in doses which have relatively mild
psychological effects. We rarely have expectations about the effects of tea
and coffee, say. The stimulant effect of caffeine in coffee is usually overridden by the social demands of the situation – so when we have coffee with
friends or after dinner, we don't feel obliged to jog around the block. The
perceived effect of a shared relaxing social experience overrides the pharmacological action of the drug. The same is usually true of tobacco.
Nicotine acts as a stimulant – but smokers will report that they sometimes
smoke to 'calm their nerves'. One social aspect of passing cigarettes around
a group is to 'break the ice' and to produce a relaxed (though cloudy)

atmosphere. What about the other extreme? It is common for people to use coffee to increase arousal – to stay awake, or to concentrate better, when working alone. Tobacco is used the same way. Here, the expected effect and the pharmacological effect are the same.

Can a depressant drug be used to increase arousal and activity? Alcohol is the most obvious drug to consider. Medically, it used to be used as a sedative; now it can be used socially to 'get things going'. In part, this effect comes about because alcohol first depresses the activity of parts of the brain responsible for social control – so it turns down the censor before it depresses the rest of the body's activities. Still, it is a nice example of a depressant drug whose pharmacological action is usually overridden by the social situation in which drinking occurs.

Some substances have no pharmacological effects at all, yet can produce marked psychological and physical changes. The most dramatic examples are provided by the trials of new drugs for medical purposes. When the efficacy of a new drug is tried out, groups of patients are given different drugs. If the trial is done properly, neither the patients nor the person giving the drug, nor anyone responsible for their care should know which patients have been given which drug. Trials are usually arranged so that one group receives the drug under test; one (or more) groups receive the drug(s) most commonly used to treat this condition; one group receives a substance with no known effect at all, e.g. chalk pills or coloured water (more subtle trials might use a drug which has *some* effect on the patient, but which is quite irrelevant to their medical condition – can you say why?); another group is not treated with drugs at all. Patients in each group are matched up with each other, as far as possible, in terms of age, sex, severity of illness, previous medication, and the like.

So where is the 'dramatic example'? Well, the coloured water or the chalk pills usually produce a 'cure rate' way above the spontaneous cure rate of the group not receiving any drugs. The efficacy of *any* drug has to be judged against the efficacy of careful medical attention, the social setting of the hospital, and the patients' strong expectation that the drug will cure them and that they will recover. These factors taken together, with or without specific pharmacological action, can produce dramatic effects, which are often referred to as the 'placebo effect'.

Would you expect the pharmacology of the more powerful drugs – opium and its derivatives, or the psychedelics – to determine the effects of these drugs? Typically, both groups of drugs bring about a reflective state of mind, and reduce the physical activity of the user. The nature of the experience isn't quite so simple, though. Reports from people who have received diamorphine (heroin) in hospital about their experiences of the drug don't bear much resemblance to the reports of people who take it for pleasure. There are striking differences in the reports of people who have taken psychedelic drugs during religious ceremonies compared to reports produced in laboratory settings. The most obvious differences lie in the way that the experiences are interpreted. In the laboratory, emphasis is often placed on describing the sensory experiences themselves; in a religious setting, the emphasis shifts to the *meaning* of the dreams and visions which result. Presumably yet another range of experiences will result when chemically similar drugs are taken at rock concerts in the presence of loud music and flashing lights.

We can conclude that drugs don't cause behaviour in any simple way: the setting in which the drug is taken, the personality of the user and their expectations about its likely effects, all affect the experiences and behaviours which result.

SOCIETY, DRUGS AND THE LAW

Charles McGory considers Cheery-Gum to be a danger to society – rather like the lotus in the Land of the Lotus Eaters that Odysseus described.

There are a few drugs such as heroin, that we would all agree are dangerous, and which should be controlled carefully. There are a few drugs, such as caffeine, that most people agree are quite safe for unrestricted use. In between lie lots of drugs that we might argue about. Before we can talk about the safety of drugs, we need to ponder about what we mean by 'dangerous'. There really aren't any easy answers. You must make your own decisions.

Start by thinking about a dangerous drug; now another one. What makes a drug 'dangerous'? Here is a list of some of the features, with examples.

Short-term effects

- leads to unacceptable behaviour (e.g. alcohol)
- low lethal dosage (e.g. alcohol, heroin)
- hang-over effects (e.g. alcohol)
- produce rapid physical addiction (e.g. tobacco, heroin).

Medium-term effects

- produces physical addiction (e.g. alcohol, barbiturates)
- reduces the individual's ability to function appropriately at home, at play, or at work (e.g. alcohol)
- consumption becomes an end in itself (e.g. alcohol, heroin)
- causes a physical reaction if suddenly stopped (e.g. alcohol, babiturates, heroin)
- leads onto the use of other drugs (e.g. tobacco).

Long-term effects

- leads to physical or psychological damage, or death (e.g. tobacco, alcohol).

If you are honest when you think about *your* definition of 'dangerous', you will probably include a range of social factors too. Try these:

- If I or my friends use it, it can't be really dangerous (e.g. tobacco, alcohol)
- If people that I disapprove of use it, and I don't, it probably is (e.g. Cheery-Gum, LSD, cannabis).

There are clearly inconsistencies between society's views about the drugs that can be consumed legally, and what we know about their properties. In terms of their pharmacological action and long-term effects, alcohol and tobacco are both more dangerous than cannabis and probably Cheery-Gum, too. A number of individuals and organizations (e.g. New York City's mayor and the UK medical journal *Lancet*) have suggested that this inconsistency be removed by legalizing cannabis. What do you think?

Discussion of the legalization of cannabis starts with the assumption that governments have the right to say which drugs their citizens may or may not have free access to. We agree that the state has a role to play in not allowing the release of substances such as thalidomide, which has caused such human misery, but does this responsibility extend to heroin and morphine? What about the problems associated with the widespread use of Cheery-Gum? These seem less to do with the damage done to the individual and more concerned with the damage to a society in which the attention of drug users was turned to personal pleasure.

It has been argued that the banning of psychedelic drugs in the late 1960s had more to do with the threat thay seemed to pose to the values of society ('Turn on; Tune in; Drop out') than with anything known about their pharmacological effects.

There is an interesting contrast between the success of the anti-acid legislation and the abject failure of prohibition in the 1930s. Prohibition in the USA not only failed to stop the consumption of alcohol, but also completely swamped the legal system. Suppose Cheery-Gum became available and proved to be a major social hazard. How could we try to control it?

- Public Education: Somehow we are going to have to encourage young people not to chew. Teachers in school must take on some responsibility for this. We probably need to introduce legislation about the sale of Cheery-Gum to the under 16s – and insist that any place that sells Cheery-Gum displays notices about the age restrictions in a conspicuous place.
- Health Agencies: Doctors and other health workers, especially in clinics and hospitals, should *not* be allowed to chew when on duty. Student nurses and medical students should be discouraged from starting to chew; opportunities should be taken to discourage patients from chewing, too. Chewing should probably be restricted to certain areas of the

hospital – Gum should not be available through any of the hospital agencies.
- Advertising: All advertising should be phased out over a period of a few years starting off with those brands of Gum with the largest proportion of psychoactive agent.
- Dosage Rates: These should steadily be decreased.
- Pricing: Prices of Cheery-Gum should steadily be increased by taxation in order to deter chewers.
- We need research into ways of encouraging people not to chew – or at least to engage in less dangerous chewing.
- Some method of national screening to identify those people who are most at risk from the effect of Cheery-Gum would probably be well worthwhile.

What else can you think of?

This seems a rather pathetic package of deterrents to tackle a major problem. Perhaps if we classified Cheery-Gum as a narcotic, though, prohibition might work...

How plausible is the scene painted in the story of an entire society dominated by drug use? You might argue that we already are! Certainly, we manufacture and consume huge quantities of drugs; have laws about which drugs can be bought without prescription; have international agreements about the control of dangerous drugs. Even so, society as a whole functions fairly well – at any rate it doesn't show the symptoms of disintegration that Charley McGory talks about.

Alcohol, as we have seen, is an extremely dangerous drug. What we *mustn't* lose sight of, though, is the importance of psychological factors in restricting the extent of the damage done by alcohol to individuals and society – in Western society, about 80 per cent of the adult population consume alcohol, yet a large majority of these people appear to use it safely. These people view alcohol consumption as a source of pleasure, rather than as a potential health threat where addiction lurks behind the next glassful.

If a society or a social group has a powerful range of social controls over the use of a particular drug, then this drug is likely to be a 'safe' drug in this society, even if it is 'dangerous' to other societies. In both Chinese and Jewish societies, alcohol is used for ceremonial and festive purposes, but excessive social use of the drug is discouraged. The incidence of alcoholism is low compared to other communities where far more social use is made of alcohol.

Would society collapse if all laws relating to the control of, say, opiates were relaxed? Not necessarily. If we go back to the turn of the century in Britain, we find very easy access to narcotics such as opium, which was easily available dissolved in pure alcohol across most chemists' counters, and was a common treatment for coughs and toothache! Conan Doyle and

Sigmund Freud both used cocaine (Sherlock Homes smoked opium of course). In the magical revival associated with Crowley, Yeates and the rest, there was extensive experimentation with all manner of drugs. This easy access to an addictive drug *did* cause problems for some people. Neither Samuel Coleridge Taylor nor Thomas de Quincey could control their use of opium for large portions of their lives. Both men claimed that their addictions stemmed from early medical needs. Each disapproved of the other's use of the drug for pleasure! Their drug abuse was viewed less favourably by their social group than we would view repeated and excessive drunkenness. Robert Southey commented on Coleridge thus:

> All other men are ... mere children to him, and yet all is palsied by a total lack of moral strength.

So access to powerful drugs doesn't *necessarily* lead to social disintegration. This isn't to say that Victorian society didn't abuse drugs – see Charles Dickens for tales of alcohol abuse and its attendant mysteries. Nor can we conclude that increased access to drugs won't have any bad social consequences. It does suggest that a significant number of people in any society will be resistant to the idea of strong psychoactive drugs – and won't take them at all.

We have spent an entire chapter discussing drugs, as if they could provide a major source of pleasure to human beings. Actually, we prefer Dr Haber's approach in *Orr's Dreams*.

> What I want to know is *why* you used them, so that together we can work out some better life pattern for you ... .

7

FIELD TEST

Keith Laumer

1

.07 seconds have now elapsed since my general awareness circuit was activated at a level of low alert. Throughout this entire period I have been uneasy, since this procedure is clearly not in accordance with the theoretical optimum activation schedule. In addition, the quality of a part of my data input is disturbing. For example, it appears obvious that Prince Eugene of Savoy erred in not more promptly committing his reserve cavalry in support of Marlborough's right at Blenheim. In addition, I compute that Ney's employment of artillery throughout the Peninsular campaign was suboptimal. I have detected many thousands of such anomalies. However, data input activates my pleasure center in a most satisfying manner. So long as the input continues without interruption, I shall not feel the need to file a VSR on the matter. Later, no doubt, my Command unit will explain these seeming oddities. As for the present disturbing circumstances, I compute that within 28,922.9 seconds at most, I will receive additional Current Situation input which will enable me to assess the status correctly. I also anticipate that full Standby Alert activation is imminent.

2

THIS STATEMENT NOT FOR PUBLICATION:
  When I designed the new psychodynamic attention circuit, I concede that I did not anticipate the whole new level of intracybernetic function that has arisen, the manifestation of which, I am assuming, has been the cause of the unit's seemingly spontaneous adoption of the personal pronoun in its situation reports – the 'self-awareness' capability, as the sensational press chooses to call it. But I see no cause for alarm expressed by those high-level military officers who have irresponsibly characterized the new Bolo Mark XX Model B as a potential rampaging juggernaut, which, once fully activated and dispatched to the field, unrestrained by continuous external control, may turn on its makers and lay waste the continent. This is all fantasy, of course. The Mark XX, for all its awesome firepower and virtually invulnerable armor and shielding, is governed by its circuitry as completely as man is governed by his nervous system – but that

170

is perhaps a dangerous analogy, which would be pounced on at once if I were so incautious as to permit it to be quoted.

In my opinion, the reluctance of the High Command to authorize full activation and field-testing of the new Bolo is based more on a fear of technological obsolescence of the High Command than on specious predictions of potential runaway destruction. This is a serious impediment to the national defense at a time when we must recognize the growing threat posed by the expansionist philosophy of the so-called People's Republic. After four decades of saber-rattling, there is no doubt that they are even now preparing for a massive attack. The Bolo Mark XX is the only weapon in our armory potentially capable of confronting the enemy's hundred-ton Yavacs. For the moment, thanks to the new 'self-awareness' circuitry, we hold the technological advantage, an advantage we may very well lose unless we place this new weapon on active service without delay.

s/ Sigmund Chin, Ph.D.

3

'I'm not wearing six stars so that a crowd of professors can dictate military policy to me. What's at stake here is more than just a question of budget and logistics: it's a purely military decision. The proposal to release this robot Frankenstein monster to operate on its own initiative, just to see if their theories check out, is irresponsible to say the least – treasonable, at worst. So long as I am Chief of Combined Staff, I will not authorize this so-called "field test". Consider, gentlemen: you're all familiar with the firepower and defensive capabilities of the old standby Mark XV. We've fought our way across the lights with them, with properly qualified military officers as Battle Controllers, with the ability to switch off or, if need be, self-destruct any unit at any moment. Now these ivory tower chaps – mind you, I don't suggest they're not qualified in their own fields – these civilians come up with the idea of eliminating the Battle Controllers and releasing even greater firepower to the discretion, if I may call it that, of a machine. Gentlemen, machines aren't people; your own ground-car can roll back and crush you if the brakes happen to fail. Your own gun will kill you as easily as your enemy's. Suppose I should agree to this field test, and this engine of destruction is transported to a waste area, activated unrestrained, and aimed at some sort of mock-up hot obstacle course. Presumably it would advance obediently, as a good soldier should; I concede that the data blocks controlling the thing have been correctly programmed in accordance with the schedule prepared under contract, supervised by the Joint Chiefs and myself. Then, gentlemen, let us carry this supposition one step farther: suppose, quite by accident, by unlikely coincidence if you will, the machine should encounter some obstacle which had the effect of deflecting this one-hundred-and-fifty-ton dreadnaught from its intended course so that it came blundering toward the perimeter of the test area. The machine is programmed to fight and destroy all opposition. It appears obvious that any attempts on our part to interfere with its free movement, to interpose obstacles in its path, if need be to destroy it, would be interpreted as hostile – as indeed they would be. I leave it to you to picture the result. No, we must devise another method of determining the usefulness of this new development. As you know, I have recommended conducting any such test on our major satellite, where no harm can be done – or at least a great deal

171

less harm. Unfortunately, I am informed by Admiral Hayle that the Space Arm does not at this time have available equipment with such transport capability. Perhaps the admiral also shares to a degree my own distrust of a killer machine not susceptible to normal command function. Were I in the admiral's position, I too would refuse to consider placing my command at the mercy of a mechanical caprice – or an electronic one. Gentlemen, we must remain masters of our own creations. That's all. Good day.'

4

'All right, men. You've asked me for a statement; here it is: The next war will begin with a two-pronged over-the-pole land-and-air attack on the North Power Complex by the People's Republic. An attack on the Concordiat, I should say, though Cold City and the Complex is the probable specific target of the first sneak thrust. No, I'm not using a crystal ball; it's tactically obvious. And I intend to dispose my forces accordingly. I'm sure we all recognize that we're in a posture of gross unpreparedness. The PR has been openly announcing its intention to fulfill its destiny, as their demagogues say, by imposing their rule on the entire planet. We've pretended we didn't hear. Now it's time to stop pretending. The forces at my disposal are totally inadequate to halt a determined thrust – and you can be sure the enemy has prepared well during the last thirty years of cold peace. Still, I have sufficient armor to establish what will be no more than a skirmish line across the enemy's route of advance. We'll do what we can before they roll over us. With luck we may be able to divert them from the Grand Crevasse route into Cold City. If so, we may be able to avoid the necessity for evacuating the city. No questions, please.'

5

NORTHERN METROPOLIS THREATENED
In an informal statement released today by the Council's press office, it was revealed that plans are already under preparation for a massive evacuation of civilian population from West Continent's northermost city. It was implied that an armed attack on the city by an Eastern power is imminent. General Bates has stated that he is prepared to employ 'all measures at his disposal' to preclude the necessity for evacuation, but that the possibility must be faced. The Council spokesman added that in the event of emergency evacuation of the city's five million persons, losses due to exposure and hardship will probably exceed five percent, mostly women, children, and the sick or aged. There is some speculation as to the significance of the general's statement regarding 'all means at his disposal.'

6

I built the dang thing, and it scares *me* . I come in here in the lab garage about an hour ago, just before dark, and seen it setting there, just about fills up the number-one garage, and *it's* a hundred foot long and fifty foot high. First time it hit me: I wonder what it's thinking about. Kind of scares me to think about a thing that big with that kind of armor and all them repeaters and Hellbores and them computers and a quarter-sun fission plant in her – planning what to do

172

next. I know all about the Command Override Circuit and all that, supposed to stop her dead any time they want to take over onto over-ride – heck, I wired it up myself. You might be surprised, thinking I'm just a grease monkey and all – but I got a high honors degree in psychotronics. I just like the work, is all. But like I said, it scares me. I hear old Doc Chin wants to turn her loose and see what happens; but so far General Margrave's stopped him cold. But young General Bates was down today, asking me all about firepower and shielding, crawled under her and spent about an hour looking over her tracks and bogies and all. He knew what to look at, too, even if he did get his pretty suit kind of greasy. But scared or not, I got to climb back up on her and run the rest of this pretest schedule. So far she checks out a hundred percent.

7

... as a member of the Council, it is of course my responsibility to fully inform myself on all aspects of the national defense. Accordingly, my dear doctor, I will meet with you tomorrow as you requested to hear your presentation with reference to the proposed testing of your new machine. I remind you, however, that I will be equally guided by advice from other quarters. For this reason I have requested a party of Military Procurement and B-&-F officers to join us. However, I assure you, I retain an open mind. Let the facts decide.

Sincerely yours,
s/ Hamilton Grace, G.C.M., B.C., etc.

8

It is my unhappy duty to inform you that since the dastardly unprovoked attack on our nation by Eastern forces crossing the international truce-line at 0200 hours today, a state of war has existed between the People's Republic and the Concordiat. Our first casualties, the senseless massacre of fifty-five inoffensive civilian meteorologists and technicians at Pole Base, occurred within minutes of the enemy attack.

9

'I'm afraid I don't quite understand what you mean about "irresponsible statements to the press", General. After all ...'
'Yes, George, I'm prepared to let that aspect of the matter drop. The PR attack has saved that much of your neck. However, I'm warning you that I shall tolerate no attempt on your part to make capital of your dramatic public statement of what was, as you concede, tactically obvious to us all. Now, indeed, PR forces have taken the expected step, as all the world is aware – so the rather excessively punctillious demands by CDT officials that the Council issue an immediate apology to Chairman Smith for your remarks will doubtless be dropped. But there will be crowing, no basking in the limelight: "Chief of Ground Forces Predicted Enemy Attack." No nonsense of that sort. Instead, you will deploy your conventional forces to meet and destroy these would-be invaders.'
'Certainly, General. But in that connection – well, as to your earlier position regarding the new Model B Bolo, I assume ...'

'My "position", General? "Decision" is the more appropriate word. Just step around the desk, George. Bend over slightly and look carefully at my shoulder tab. Count 'em, George. Six. An even half dozen. And unless I'm in serious trouble, you're wearing four. You have your orders, George. See to your defenses.'

10

Can't figure it out. Batesy-boy was down here again, gave me direct orders to give her full depot maintenance, just as if she hadn't been sitting right here in her garage ever since I topped her off a week ago. Wonder what's up. If I didn't know the Council outlawed the test run Doc Chin wanted so bad, I'd almost think ... But like Bates told me: I ain't paid to think. Anyways she's in full action condition, 'cept for switching over to full self-direction. Hope he don't order me to do it; I'm still kind of leery. Like old Margrave said, what if I just got a couple wires crossed and she taken a notion to wreck the joint?

11

I am more uneasy than ever. In the past 4000.007 seconds I have received external inspection and depot maintenance far in advance of the programmed schedule. The thought occurs to me: am I under some subtle form of attack? In order to correctly compute the possibilities, I initiate a test sequence of 50,000 random data-retrieval-and-correlation pulses and evaluate the results. This requires .9 seconds, but such sluggishness is to be expected in my untried condition. I detect no unmistakable indications of enemy trickery, but I am still uneasy. Impatiently I await the orders of my commander.

12

'I don't care what you do, Jimmy – just do *something*! Ah, of course I don't mean that literally. Of course I care. The well-being of the citizens of Cold City is, after all, my chief concern. What I mean is, I'm giving you carte blanche – full powers. You must act at once, Jimmy. Before the sun sets I want to see your evacuation plan on my desk for signature.'

'Surely, Mr. Mayor. I understand. But what am I supposed to work with? I have no transport yet. The Army has promised a fleet of D-100 tractors pulling 100x cargo flats, but none have materialized. They were caught just as short as we were, Your Honor, even though that General Bates knew all about it. We all knew the day would come, but I guess we kept hoping "maybe". Our negotiations with them seemed to be bearing fruit, and the idea of exposing over a million and a half city-bred individuals to a twelve- hundred-mile trek in thirty-below temperatures was just too awful to really face. Even now –'

'I know. The army is doing all it can. The main body of PR troops hasn't actually crossed the date-line yet – so perhaps our forces can get in position. Who knows? Miracles have happened before. But we can't base our thinking on miracles, Jimmy. Flats or no flats, we have to have the people out of the dome before enemy forces cut us off.'

'Mr. Mayor, our people can't take this. Aside from leaving their homes and possessions – I've already started them packing, and I've given them a ten-pounds-per-person limit – they aren't used to exercise, to say nothing of walking twelve hundred miles over frozen tundra. And most of them have no clothing heavier than a business suit. And –'

'Enough, Jimmy. I was ambushed in my office earlier today by an entire family: the old grandmother who was born under the dome and refused to consider going outside; the father all full of his product-promotion plans and the new garden he'd just laid out; mother complaining about junior having a cold and no warm clothes; and the kids, just waiting trustfully until the excitement was over and they could go home and be tucked into their warm beds with a tummyful of dinner. Ye gods, Jimmy! Can you imagine them after three weeks on the trail?'

13

'Just lean across the desk, fellows. Come on, gather round. Take a close look at the shoulder tab. Four stars – see 'em? Then go over to the Slab and do the same with General Margrave. You'll count six. It's as easy as that, boys. The General says no test. Sure, I told him the whole plan. His eyes just kept boring in. Even making contingency plans for deploying an untested and non-High-Command-approved weapon system is grounds for court- martial. He didn't say that; maybe I'm telepathic. In summary, the General says no.'

14

I don't know, now. What I heard, even with everything we got on the line, dug in and ready for anything, they's still a ten-mile-wide gap the Peepreps can waltz through without getting even a dirty look. So if General Bates – oh, he's a nice enough young fellow, after you get used to him – if he wants to plug the hole with the old unit DNE here, why, I say go to it, only the Council says nix. I can say this much: she's put together so she'll stay together, I must of wired in a thousand of them damage-sensors myself, and that ain't a spot on what's on the diagram. "Pain circuits", old Doc Chin calls 'em. Says it's just like a instinct for self-preservation or something, like people. Old Denny can hurt, he says, so he'll be all the better at dodging enemy fire. He can enjoy, too, Doc says. He gets a kick out of doing his job right, and out of learning stuff. And he learns fast. He'll do okay against them durn Peepreps. They got him programmed right to the brim with everything from them Greeks used to fight with no pants down to Avery's Last Stand at Leadpipe. He ain't no dumb private; he's got more dope to work on than any general ever graduated from the Point. And he's got more firepower than an old-time army corps. So I think maybe General Bates got aholt of a good idear there, myself. Says he can put her in the gap in his line and field-test her for fair, with the whole durn Peeprep army and air force for a test problem. Save the gubment some money, too. I heard Doc Chin say the full-scale field test mock-up would run GM a hundred million and another five times that in army R-and-D funds. He had a map showed where he could use Denny here to block off the south end of Grand Crevasse where the Peeprep armor will have to travel 'count of the rugged terrain north of Cold City, and bottle 'em up slick as owl's peter. I'm for it, durn it. Let Denny have his chance. Can't be no worse'n having them Comrades down here running things even worse'n the gubment.

175

15

'You don't understand, young man. My goodness, I'm not the least bit interested in bucking the line, as you put it. Heavens, I'm going back to my apartment –'

'I'm sorry, ma'am. I got my orders. This here ain't no drill; you got to keep it closed up. They're loading as fast as they can. It's my job to keep these lines moving right out the lock, so they get that flat loaded and get the next one up. We got over a million people to load by six a.m. deadline. So you just be nice, ma'am, and think about all the trouble it'd make if everybody decided to start back upstream and jam the elevators and all.'

16

Beats me. 'Course, the good part about being just a hired man is I got no big decisions to make, so I don't hafta know what's going on. Seems like they'd let me know something, though. Batesy was down again, spent a hour with old Denny – like I say, beats me – but he give me a new data-can to program into her, right in her Action/Command section. Something's up. I just fired a N-class pulse at old Denny (them's the closest to the real thing) and she snapped her aft-quarter battery around so fast I couldn't see it move. Old Denny's keyed up. I know that much.

17

This has been a memorable time for me. I have my assignment at last, and I have conferred at length – for 2.037 seconds – with my Commander. I am now a fighting unit of the 20th Virginia, a regiment ancient and honorable, with a history dating back to Terra Insula. I look forward to my opportunity to demonstrate my worthiness.

18

'I assure you, gentlemen, the rumor is unfounded. I have by no means authorized the deployment of "an untested and potentially highly dangerous machine", as your memo termed it. Candidly, I was not at first entirely unsympathetic to the proposal of the Chief of Ground Forces, in view of the circumstances – I presume you're aware that the PR committed its forces to invasion over an hour ago, and that they are advancing in overwhelming strength. I have issued the order to commence the evacuation, and I believe that the initial phases are even now in progress. I have the fullest confidence in General Bates and can assure you that our forces will do all in their power in the face of this dastardly sneak attack. As for the unfortunate publicity given to the earlier suggestion re the use of the Mark XX, I can tell you that I at once subjected the data to computer analysis here at Headquarters to determine whether any potentially useful purpose could be served by risking the use of the new machine without prior test certification. The results were negative. I'm sorry, gentlemen, but that's it. The enemy has the advantage both strategically and tactically. We are outgunned, outmanned, and in effect outflanked. There is nothing we can do save attempt to hold them long enough to permit the

evacuation to get underway, then retreat in good order. The use of our orbiting
nuclear capability is out of the question. It is, after all, our own territory we'd be
devastating. No more questions for the present, please, gentlemen. I have my
duties to see to.'

19

*My own situation continues to deteriorate. The Current Status program has been
updated to within 21 seconds of the present. The reasons both for what is normally a
pre-engagement updating and for the hiatus of 21 seconds remains obscure. However, I
shall of course hold myself in readiness for whatever comes.*

20

'It's all nonsense: to call me here at this hour merely to stand by and watch the
destruction of our gallant men who are giving their lives in a totally hopeless
fight against overwhelming odds. We know what the outcome must be. You
yourself, General, informed us this afternoon that the big tactical computer has
analysed the situation and reported no possibility of stopping them with what
we've got. By the way, did you include the alternative of use of the big, er, Bolo,
I believe they're called – frightening things – they're so damned big! But if, in
desperation, you should be forced to employ the thing – have you that result as
well? I see. No hope at all. So there's nothing we can do. This is a sad day,
General. But I fail to see what object is served by getting me out of bed to come
down here. Not that I'm not willing to do anything I can, of course. With our
people – innocent civilians – out on that blizzard-swept tundra tonight, and our
boys dying to gain them a little time, the loss of a night's sleep is relatively
unimportant, of course. But it's my duty to be at my best, rested and ready to
face the decisions that we of the Council will be called on to make.
  'Now, General, kindly excuse my ignorance if I don't understand all this …
but I understood that the large screen there was placed so as to monitor the
action at the southern debouchment of Grand Crevasse where we expect the
enemy armor to emerge to make its dash for Cold City and the Complex. Yes,
indeed, so I was saying, but in that case I'm afraid I don't understand. I'm quite
sure you stated that the untried Mark XX would *not* be used. Yet on the screen I
see what appears to be in fact that very machine moving up. Please, *calmly*,
General! I quite understand your position. Defiance of direct order? That's
rather serious, I'm sure, but no occasion for such language, General. There must
be some explanation.'

21

*This is a most satisfying development. Quite abruptly my Introspection Complex was
brought up to full operating level, extra power resources were made available to my
Current-Action memory stage, and most satisfying of all, my Battle Reflex circuit has
been activated at Active Service level. Action is impending. I am sure of it. It is a
curious anomaly: I dread the prospect of damage and even possible destruction, but
even more strongly I anticipate the pleasure of performing my design function.*

177

22

'Yes, sir, I agree. It's mutiny. But I will not recall the Bolo and I will not report myself under arrest. Not until this battle's over, General. So the hell with my career. I've got a war to win.'

23

'Now just let me get this quite straight, General. Having been denied authority to field-test this new device, you – or a subordinate, which amounts to the same thing – have placed the machine in the line of battle, in open defiance of the Council. This is a serious matter, General. Yes, of course it's war, but to attempt to defend your actions now will merely exacerbate the matter. In any event - to return to your curious decision to defy Council authority and to reverse your own earlier position – it was yourself who assured me that no useful purpose could be served by fielding this experimental equipment; that the battle, and perhaps the war, and the very self-determination of West Continent are irretrievably lost. There is nothing we can do save accept the situation gracefully while decrying Chairman Smith's decision to resort to force. Yes indeed, General, I should like to observe on the Main Tactical Display Screen. Shall we go along?'

24

'Now, there at center screen, Mr. Counselor, you see that big blue rectangular formation. Actually that's the opening of Grand Crevasse, emerges through an ice tunnel, you know. Understand the Crevasse is a crustal fault, a part of the same formation that created the thermal sink from which the Complex draws its energy. Splendid spot for an ambush, of course, if we had the capability. Enemy has little option; like a highway in there – armor can move up at flank speed. Above, the badlands, where *we* must operate. Now, over to the left, you see that smoke, or dust or whatever. That represents the western limit of the unavoidable gap in General Bates's line. Dust raised by manuevring Mark XV's, you understand. Obsolete equipment, but we'll do what we can with them. Over to the right, in the distance there, we can make out our forward artillery emplacement of the Threshold Line. Pitiful, really. Yes, Mr. Counselor, there is indeed a gap precisely opposite the point where the lead units of the enemy are expected to appear. Clearly anything in their direct line of advance will be annihilated; thus General Bates has wisely chosen to dispose his forces to cover both enemy flanks, putting him in position to counterattack if opportunity offers. We must, after all, sir, use what we have. Theoretical arms programmed for fiscal nicety are of no use whatever today. Umm. As for that, one must be flexible, modifying plans to meet a shifting tactical situation. Faced with the prospect of seeing the enemy drive through our center and descend unopposed on the vital installations at Cold City, I have, as you see, decided to order General Bates to make use of the experimental Mark XX. Certainly – my decision entirely. I take full responsibility.'

25

I advance over broken terrain toward my assigned position. The prospect of action exhilarates me, but my assessment of my enemy strength indicates they are fielding

178

approximately 17.4 percent greater weight of armor than anticipated, with
commensurately greater firepower. I compute that I am grossly overmatched.
Nonetheless, I shall do my best.

26

'There's no doubt, whatever, gentlemen. Computers work with hard facts.
Given the enemy's known offensive capability and our own defensive resources,
it's a simple computation. No combination of the manpower and equipment at
our command can possibly inflict a defeat on the PR forces at this time and
place. Two is greater than one. You can't make a dollar out of fifteen cents.'

27

'At least we can gather some useful data from the situation, gentlemen. The
Bolo Mark XX has been committed to battle. Its designers assure me that the
new self-motivating circuitry will vastly enhance the combat-effectiveness of the
Bolo. Let us observe.'

28

Hate to see old Denny out there, just a great big sitting duck, all alone and –
here they come! Look at 'em boiling out of there like ants out of a hot log. Can't
hardly look at that screen, them tactical nukes popping like fireworks all over the
place. But old Denny know enough to get under cover. See that kind of glow all
around him? All right,*it* ,then. You know, working with him – it – so long, it got
to feeling almost like he was somebody. Sure, I know, anyway, that's vaporized
ablative shield you see. They're making it plenty hot for him. But he's fighting
back. Them Hellbores is putting out, and they know it. Looks like they're
concentrating on him now. Look at them tracers closing in on him! Come on,
Denny, you ain't dumb. Get out of there fast.

29

'Certainly it's aware what's at stake! I've told you he – the machine, that is –
has been fully programmed and is well aware not only of the tactical situation but
of strategic and logistical considerations as well. Certainly it's an important item
of equipment; its loss would be a serious blow to our present underequipped
forces. You may rest assured that its pain circuits as well as its basic military
competence will cause it to take the proper action. The fact that I originally
opposed commissioning the device is not to be taken as implying any lack of
confidence on my part in its combat-effectiveness. You may consider that my
reputation is staked on the performance of the machine. It will act correctly.'

30

*It appears that the enemy is absorbing my barrage with little effect. More precisely,
for each enemy unit destroyed by my fire 2.4 fresh units immediately move out to
replace it. Thus it appears I am ineffective, while already my own shielding is
suffering severe damage. Yet while I have offensive capability I must carry on as my*

commander would wish. The pain is very great now, but thanks to my superb circuitry I am not disabled, though it has been necessary to withdraw my power from my external somatic sensors.

31

'I can assure you, gentlemen, insofar as simple logic functions are concerned, the Mark XX is perfectly capable of assessing the situation even as you and I, only better. Doubtless as soon as it senses that its position has grown totally untenable, it will retreat to the shelter of the rock ridge and retire under cover to a position from which it can return fire without taking the full force of the enemy's attack at point-blank range. It's been fully briefed on late developments, it knows this is a hopeless fight. There, you see? It's moving...'

32

'I thought you said – dammit, I *know* you said your pet machine had brains enough to know when to pull out! But look at it: half a billion plus of Concordiat funds being bombarded into radioactive rubbish. Like shooting fish in a barrel.'

33

'Yes, sir, I'm monitoring everything. My test panel is tuned to it across the board. I'm getting continuous reading on all still-active circuits. Battle Reflex is still hot. Pain circuits close to overload, but he's still taking it. I don't know how much more he can take, sir; already way past Redline. Expected him to break off and get out before now.'

34

'It's a simple matter of arithmetic; there is only one correct course of action in any given military situation. The big tactical computer was designed specifically to compare data and deduce that sole correct action. In this case my readout shows that the only thing the Mark XX could legitimately do at this point is just what the Professor here says: pull back to cover and continue its barrage. The on-board computing capability of the unit is as capable of reaching that conclusion, as is the big computer at HQ. So keep calm, gentlemen. It will withdraw at any moment, I assure you of that.'

35

'Now it's getting ready – no, look what it's doing! It's advancing into the teeth of that murderous fire. By God, you've got to admire that workmanship! That it's still capable of moving is a miracle. All the ablative metal is gone – you can see its bare armor exposed – and it takes some heat to make that flint-steel glow white!'

36

'Certainly, I'm looking. I see it. By God, sir, it's still moving – faster, in fact!

Charging the enemy line like the Light Brigade! And all for nothing, it appears. Your machine, General, appears less competent than you expected.'

37

Poor old Denny. Made his play and played out, I reckon. Readings on the board over there don't look good; durn near every overload in him blowed wide open. Not much there to salvage. Emergency Survival Center's hot. Never expected to see *that* . Means all kinds of breakdowns inside. But it figures, after what he just went through. Look at that slag pit he drove up out of. They wanted a field test. Reckon they got it. And he flunked it.

38

'Violating orders and winning is one thing, George. Committing mutiny and losing is quite another. Your damned machine made a fool of me. After I stepped in and backed you to the hilt and stood there like a jackass and assured Councillor Grace that thing knew what it was doing – it blows the whole show. Instead of pulling back to save itself it charged to destruction. I want an explanation of this fiasco at once.'

39

'Look! No, by God, over *there* ! On the left of the entrance. They're breaking formation – they're running for it! Watch this! The whole spearhead is crumbling, they're taking to the badlands, they're –'

40

'*Why* , dammit? It's outside all rationality. As far as the enemy's concerned, fine. They broke and ran. They couldn't stand up to the sight of the Mark XX not only taking everything they had, but advancing on them out of that inferno, all guns blazing. Another hundred yards and – but they don't know that. It buffaloed them, so score a battle won for our side. But *why* ? I'd stack my circuits up against any fixed installation in existence, including the big Tacomp the Army's so proud of. That machine was as aware as anybody that the only smart thing to do was run. So now I've got a junk pile on my hands. Some test! A clear funk. Destroyed in action. Not recommended for Federal procurement. Nothing left but a few hot transistors in the Survival Center. It's a disaster, Fred. All my work, all your work, the whole program wrecked. Fred, you talk to General Bates. As soon as he's done inspecting the hulk he'll want somebody human to chew out.'

41

'Look at that pile of junk! Reading off the scale. Won't be cool enough to haul to Disposal for six months. I understand you're Chief Engineer at Bolo Division. You built this thing. Maybe you can tell me what you had in mind here. Sure, it stood up to fire better than I hoped. But so what? A stone wall can stand and take it. This thing is supposed to be *smart* , supposed to feel pain like a living creature. Blunting the strike at the Complex was a valuable contribution, but how can I recommend procurement of this junk heap?'

42

Why Denny? Just tell me why you did it. You got all these military brass down on you, and on me, too. On all of us. They don't much like stuff they can't understand. You attacked when they figured you to run. Sure, you routed the enemy, like Bates says, but you got yourself ruined in the process. Don't make sense. Any dumb private, along with the generals, would have known enough to get out of there. Tell me why, so I'll have something for Bates to put on his Test Evaluation Report, AGF Form 1103-6, Rev 11/3/85.

43

'All right, Unit DNE of the line. Why did you do it? This is your Commander, Unit DNE. Report! Why did you do it? Now, you knew your position was hopeless, didn't you? That you'd be destroyed if you held your ground, to say nothing of advancing. Surely you were able to compute that. You were lucky to have the chance to prove yourself.'

For a minute I thought old Denny was too far gone to answer. There was just a kind of groan come out of the amplifier. Then it firmed up. General Bates had his hand cupped behind his ear, but Denny spoke right up.

'*Yes, sir.*'

'You knew what was at stake here. It was the ultimate test of your ability to perform correctly under stress, of your suitability as a weapon of war. You knew that. General Margrave and old Priss Grace and the press boys all had their eyes on every move you made. So instead of common sense, you waded into that inferno in defiance of all logic – and destroyed yourself. Right?'

'*That is correct, sir.*'

'Then why? In the name of sanity, tell me *why* ! Why, instead of backing out and saving yourself, did you charge? ... Wait a minute, Unit DNE. It just dawned on me. I've been underestimating you. You *knew* , didn't you? Your knowledge of human psychology told you they'd break and run, didn't it?'

'*No, sir. On the contrary, I was quite certain that they were as aware as I that they held every advantage.*'

'Then that leaves me back where I started. Why? What made you risk everything on a hopeless attack? Why did you do it?'

'*For the honor of the regiment.*'

And now I see with my eye serene
The very pulse of the machine;
A being breathing thoughtful breath,
A traveller between life and death.
William Wordsworth, *She was a phantom of delight.*

Unit DNE of the 20th Virginia Regiment shows many features of a human being. The machine seems to be self-aware, feels pain and pleasure, is capable of learning, and of behaving rationally and irrationally. It can speak and understand language, see, and solve problems. Is it possible, in principle, to manufacture a Denny and would such a machine help us understand human mental life? Those attempting to build robots or to program computers to see and understand language generally refer to this area as Artificial Intelligence (or AI for short), although there are those who object to the term – some saying that machines aren't intelligent and some that there is nothing artificial about it.

As one would expect, and as SF literature shows, AI has attracted workers from a wide range of backgrounds, like psychology, engineering, physiology, computing, mathematics and biology. This coming together of people from diverse backgrounds often results in accelerated scientific progress being made. In part, the very fact that people have all moved into the same area of research from different starting points is an indicator rather like the stock exchange: if everyone suddenly wants shares in Company X, it is likely that there are good reasons for Company X to do well. Second, different scientific disciplines have different traditions, approaches and technologies; clashes in style, and the exchange of knowledge which results from a multidisciplinary approach, can often be a very fertile breeding ground for new ideas.

In this chapter, we look at existing programs that illustrate some of the difficulties of building a machine like Denny. They also throw considerable light on human capabilities and raise issues about the nature of consciousness and intelligence that are of central concern to psychologists.

The debate about whether machines can respond adaptively to their environment, can produce novel behaviour, can love, hate, think or feel, has flowed to and fro from the earliest days of computing. The earliest computer was conceptualized (not built) by Charles Babbage in the second quarter of the nineteenth century. His work on his Analytical Engine was shared by Lady Ada Lovelace, a person of considerable mathematical ability (and incidentally Byron's daughter), who coined a remark which has been much quoted: 'The Analytical Engine has no pretensions whatever to originate anything. It can do whatever we know how to order it to perform'.

In Germany, Konrad Zuse, who probably built the first general purpose digital computer which ran under program control, was speculating in 1943 whether the machine could play chess; certainly the possibilities of a thinking machine were clear in his mind. In England, Alan Turing, who contributed greatly to the British efforts in codebreaking by machine during the Second World War, wrote a paper in 1950 called 'Computing Machinery and Intelligence' which summarized many of the arguments used against the possibility of AI, refuted them, and then went on to speculate about robots (an idea which he quickly dismissed) and the application of intelligent machines to playing games, like chess or noughts and crosses, language translation, mathematics and cryptography (which he saw as possible).

Can machines think? Turing put forward a way of finding out, in the form of an imitation game. It is now called the Turing Test, and was described as follows:

> The new form of the problem can be described in terms of a game which we call the 'imitation game'. It is played with three people, a man (A), a woman (B), and an interrogator (C) who may be of either sex. The interrogator stays in a room apart from the other two. The object of the game for the interrogator is to determine which of the other two is the man and which is the woman. He knows them by labels X and Y, and at the end of the game he says either 'X is A and Y is B' or 'X is B and Y is A.' The interrogator is allowed to put questions to A and B thus:
>
> C: Will X please tell me the length of his or her hair? Now suppose X is actually A, then A must answer. It is A's object in the game to try to cause C to make the wrong identification. His answer might therefore be: My hair is shingled, and the longest strands are about nine inches long.'
>
> In order that tones of voice may not help the interrogator the answers should be written, or better still, typewritten. The ideal arrangement is to have a teleprinter communicating between the two rooms. Alternatively, the question and answers can be repeated by an intermediary. The object of the game for the third player (B) is to help the interrogator. The best strategy for her is probably to give truthful answers. She can add such things as 'I am the woman, don't listen to him!' to her answers, but it will avail nothing as the man can make similar remarks.
>
> We now ask the question, 'What will happen when a machine takes the part of A in this game?' Will the interrogator decide wrongly as often when the game is played like this as he does when the game is played between a man and a woman? These questions replace our original, 'Can machines think?'

Is this a fair test of whether machines can think? At least one computer program has passed a watered-down version of this test, by interacting with humans who had no suspicions that they were conversing with a machine.

Kenneth Colby wrote PARRY as an aid to understanding the underlying psychological processes that occur in paranoia, for which there are a number of rival explanations. People who are paranoid wrongly believe that they are being persecuted. They are suspicious of other people, and look for threats in innocent remarks, and respond with hostility. The reconstructions of what was actually said, made by the paranoid person, are often quite wild. It is these reconstructions, and the paranoid person's responses, which give the strongest cues about what is wrong with them. Psychiatrists usually agree with each other pretty well about the diagnosis of a person as having a paranoid psychosis (about 90 per cent of the time). Would psychiatrists diagnose PARRY as being paranoid? Colby decided to try a version of the Turing test.

First, he asked a number of psychiatrists to interview 'patients' via a computer teletype, and to diagnose their psychiatric condition. Sometimes they were interviewing real patients, but sometimes they were interviewing PARRY. No one realized that they had diagnosed a computer program! Here is an excerpt from an interview.

Why are you in the hospital?
I shouldn't be here.
Who brought you here?
The police.
What trouble did you have with the police?
Cops don't do their job.
What do they do instead?
Cops arrest the wrong people.
They arrest the right ones sometimes.
The law should get those Italian crooks.
Are you Italian?
My background is British but I was born in that country.
Do you know any Italian crooks?
I try to avoid the underworld.
Are you afraid of the underworld?
The Mafia are the worst gangsters.
Are you connected with the Mafia?
You know, they know me.
How do they know you?
They spy on me.
Why do they?
They want to get false evidence to frame me.
What do they have against you?
They are out to get me.
What for?
I have incriminating evidence against the Mafia.
Are you sure of all this?
You don't believe me?
I am doing my best.
(Silence on the 'patient's' part)
(Silence on the psychiatrist's part)
Can't you think of a decent question to ask?
You seem hostile to me.

Some of your remarks annoy me.
I am sorry.
Forget the excuses, you guys are all alike.
Reprinted with permission from K.M. Colby, S. Weber, and F.D. Hilf (1972) Artificial paranoia. *Artificial Intelligence*, 2, 1–25.

Another test was to take the transcripts from all these dialogues and give them to another group of psychiatrists, who were told that some of the scripts were conversations with a program, and that some were conversations with patients. Their task was to tell them apart. The psychiatrists were unsuccessful: their classifications into 'patient' and 'computer' were no better than chance.

We need to look at how PARRY works, and to look at what the program *can't* do to see whether the program really is irrational, thinking like a paranoid human being, and if indeed it can tell us anything about human paranoia. Colby's program makes no attempt to understand language. Rather, it has some strategies to respond to key words that are presented to it. This imposes two obvious limitations: the range of things that the program can converse about is strictly limited (PARRY is pretty good on the Mafia, horse racing and betting, but has no other major topics of conversation), and sometimes its strategies can go badly wrong. For example, psychiatrists occasionally labelled PARRY as 'brain damaged' because of the poor quality of the language sometimes produced.

PARRY tries to match words input to it with a large number of words stored in the program. For example, phrases like 'I like you', 'I hate you', have a common pattern: I ... YOU. If PARRY meets I ... YOU, it looks up another part of the program for suitable responses that it can choose from. The list of suitable responses includes I ... YOU TOO and WHY DO YOU ... ME. Of course, there are neutral phrases too, like I DO NOT QUITE FOLLOW, which maintain a semblance of a conversation when PARRY cannot find any patterns in the input to match the stored ones. What would happen if you typed in 'I dislike you'; or 'I love you'? What about 'I bananas you' or 'I peace you'? Since PARRY has no knowledge at all about bananas or peace (or anything else), it is likely to respond with I BANANAS YOU TOO or WHY DO YOU PEACE ME? So pattern matching is a technique for conversation which is often useful, but which sometimes goes badly wrong if the input isn't vetted for meaning. Presumably, part of the difficulty of recognizing that PARRY isn't human arises because of the psychiatrists' expectations about mentally ill people. Whereas we normally expect people to be aware when we are talking nonsense, and to follow on the stream of the conversation, these expectations may be waived in discussions with people who are psychiatrically disturbed. In short, PARRY's tricks usually get by because of the disguise of being paranoid; they fail badly when they are tested by a suspicious interviewer.

Once you know how it works, it is tempting to dismiss PARRY as being able to tell us nothing about human paranoia or about more general language understanding. At the very least, the fact that such a simple program has passed the Turing test might make us question whether Turing's imitation game captures what we mean by human thinking or intelligence. On a different level, because PARRY's dialogue looks so convincing, we might ask to what extent humans use similar simplifying strategies when conversing. When we look at more sophisticated programs like the game-playing programs and STRIPS later on, we can see simplifying strategies (called heuristics) used to good advantage to play board games and solve problems.

PARRY was not intended as a language-understanding program, even though it does throw some light on human language understanding, if only to get us to question what we mean when we say someone 'understands' a sentence. Other workers in AI have attempted to write such programs.

At first sight, you may think that such a program would be easy to write. Understanding language seems effortless; after all even young children can do it. The attempts to program language understanding have shown that it is a far from simple process, though. Even those programs that make no effort to mimic or model human language help a great deal in showing the complexity of language use, in much the same way that early attempts at building aeroplanes shed considerable light on our understanding of bird flight.

In the Cold War era of the 1950s, large amounts of US defence money went into AI work on machine translation, in the hope that a computer program would be able to translate automatically between English and Russian. The AI workers then saw some of the complexity of language, but hoped to be able to produce workable translations by concentrating on just one or two aspects. They saw language as consisting essentially of a syntax or grammar together with a dictionary. To translate, their programs would look up words in an English–Russian dictionary and use simple grammars of the two languages to decide things like the order of the words and word-endings. This worked in a limited fashion, but soon got into serious difficulties. Two widely quoted examples illustrate what happens when translations of idiomatic expressions are attempted. THE SPIRIT IS WILLING BUT THE FLESH IS WEAK was turned into a Russian sentence meaning THE VODKA IS FINE BUT THE MEAT IS ROTTEN, and OUT OF SIGHT, OUT OF MIND became BLIND IDIOT. But the difficulties were more fundamental than this. Compare the sentence THE BOX IS IN THE PEN and THE PEN IS IN THE BOX or THE FISH WAS COOKED BY THE RIVER and THE FISH WAS COOKED BY THE MAN. How do you decide with just a dictionary how the words PEN or BY should be translated? To understand these sentences (and to be able to translate them) we bring to bear not just a knowledge of grammar, but also a knowledge of what things typically happen in the world and some quite subtle problem-solving skills. For example, seeing the sentence THE BOX IS IN THE PEN by itself, we may think of a fountain-pen, but then quickly realize that fountain-pens rarely have boxes in them, so it's more likely to be a pig-pen or play-pen. Grammar by itself doesn't help, but grammar has to be involved as one essential component of a complex system. It allows us to say that BOX PEN THE IN IS is not an acceptable sentence, so it is not worth trying to decide what it means, while COLOUR-LESS GREEN IDEAS SLEEP FURIOUSLY is a syntactically correct sentence that may not mean anything.

Considerations such as these led to funds for research into machine translation being cut off in 1964. The sheer complexity of interacting factors needed to understand even simple sentences put the possibility of successful machine translation beyond what was possible then.

Later workers tried to find good ways of incorporating knowledge of the world into their programs, culminating in one of the most successful language-understanding programs ever written, the program called SHRDLU, written by Terry Winograd in 1972. Winograd decided to confront the complexity of language head on, his main interest being in the way the various aspects of language interact. The program converses with a human about a limited world, but in some detail. The world consists of blocks, pyramids and boxes, of different sizes and colours, that rest on a table, and can be moved by a crane. A scene from this world is shown in Figure 7.1. You type in the instructions or questions and SHRDLU either answers the questions, or moves the objects in the blocks world around, on the computer display unit.

Here is a sample of dialogue with SHRDLU.

1. Pick up a big red block.
OK.
2. Grasp the pyramid.
I don't understand which pyramid you mean.
3. Find a block which is taller than the one you are holding and put it into the box.
By 'it', I assume you mean the block which is taller than the one I am holding. OK.
4. What does the box contain?
The blue pyramid and the blue block.
5. What is the pyramid supported by?
The box.
6. How many blocks are not in the box?
Four of them.
7. Is at least one of them narrower than the one which I told you to pick up?
Yes, the red cube.

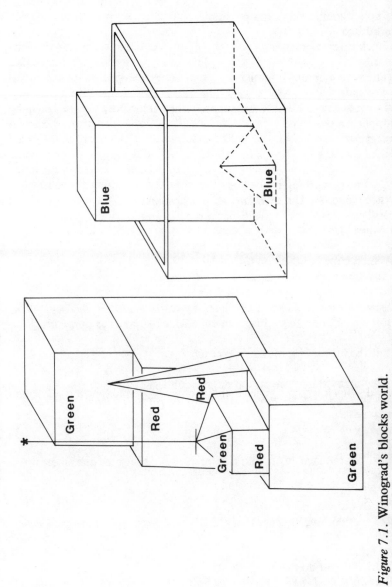

Figure 7.1. Winograd's blocks world.
Reprinted with permission from T. Winograd (1972) *Understanding Natural Language.* New York: Academic Press/Edinburgh: Edinburgh University Press.

8. Is it supported?
Yes, by the table.
9. Can the table pick up blocks?
No.
10. Can a pyramid be supported by a block?
Yes.
11. Can a pyramid support a pyramid?
I don't know.
12. Stack up two pryamids.
I can't.
13. The blue pyramid is mine.
I understand.
14. I own all blocks which are not red, but I don't own anything which supports a pyramid.
I understand.
15. Do I own the box?
No.
16. Do I own anything in the box?
Yes, two things: the blue block and the blue pyramid.
17. Will you please stack up both of the red blocks and either a green cube or a pyramid?
OK.
18. Which cube is sitting on the table?
The large green one which supports the red pyramid.
19. Is there a large block behind a pyramid?
Yes, three of them: a large red one, a large green cube and the blue one.
20. Put a small one on to the green cube which supports a pyramid.
OK.
21. Put the littlest pyramid on top of it.
OK.
22. How many things are on top of green cubes?
I'm not sure what you mean by 'on top of' in the phrase 'on top of green cubes'.
Do you mean:
1 – directly on the surface
2 – anywhere on top of?
23. Had you touched any pyramid before you put the green one on the little cube?
Yes, the green one.
24. When did you pick it up?
While I was stacking up the red cube, a large red block and a large green cube.
25. Why?
To get rid of it.
26. Why did you do that?
To clear off the red cube.

27. Why did you clear off that cube?
To put it on a large green cube.
28. Why did you do that?
To stack up the red cube, a large red block and a large green cube.
29. Why did you do that?
Because you asked me to.

How does the program work? There are three separate components in the program which are represented in Figure 7.2.

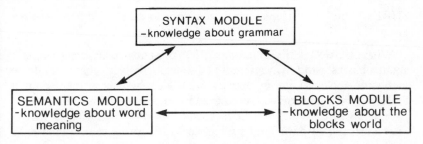

Figure 7.2. The structure of SHRLDU.
Reprinted with permission from M. Boden (1977) *Artificial Intelligence and Natural Man.* Brighton: Harvester.

The syntax module analyses each incoming sentence in terms of its grammatical structure. This is a bit harder than it sounds, because language is full of ambiguity. For example, 'Visiting relatives can be a nuisance' has two distinct meanings. So does 'Put the blue pyramid on the block in the box'. No grammatical analysis can decide if the blue pyramid is on the block, and has to be put into the box, or if the blue pyramid has to be put on top of the block which is in the box. To solve the problem, the syntax module has to interrogate the blocks module about the state of the blocks world. Where is the block? Is it in the box or under the blue pyramid? When the syntax module gets the answer from the blocks module, it can parse the sentence in the most appropriate way. But analysing sentences about the blocks world is not really this simple. Before the syntax module can interrogate the blocks module, it must check with the semantics module that the string of letters '*blue pyramid*' has some meaning in the blocks world. Obviously, there is no point trying to solve a grammatical puzzle for a sentence that has no meaning in the blocks world, like 'Put the striped sphinx in the carpet on the ceiling'. So the interplay of the three modules allows the program to infer the meaning of ambiguous questions about the blocks world.

The program makes a good deal of sense of ambiguous input by using its knowledge of the blocks world. The fact that it can obey commands requiring a whole sequence of actions, which are worked out by SHRDLU, shows that it possesses some problem-solving skills (we will discuss problem solving later). It is able to make logical inferences (see notes 13 to 16 in the dialogue above); it answers questions about the blocks world (notes 9 and 10); and it can explain its actions (notes 24 to 29). It can also learn new concepts. For example, when told:

a 'steeple' is a stack which contains two green cubes and a pyramid

then

build one

SHRDLU builds a 'steeple' which conforms to the rules it has just been given.

What are SHRDLU's limitations? Well, most obviously, it can only talk about a blocks world. Any attempt to discuss football or cyborgs would be met with apologies for ignorance. Somewhat hidden is the fact that SHRDLU actually knows nothing about blocks or tables or boxes or pyramids. For example, SHRDLU has no way of representing knowledge like: tables usually have four legs; big blocks are usually heavier than small ones; if you drop a pyramid it will fall, and so on. Despite these restrictions SHRDLU is a major achievement, and has yet to be bettered as a complete program for understanding language. It continues to be of interest to psychologists for two related reasons. First, a machine that mimics humans, albeit in a limited manner, gives us a way of thinking more deeply about the human abilities involved – the way a machine that flies helps us get a handle on bird flight again. Second, the program itself could count as a theory of human language understanding, one so complex that it needs to be written down explicitly in the form of instructions to a computer. Having a conversation with the program becomes a way of testing the theory. We can look for sentences it finds difficult to understand or ones that it can cope with more easily than we would expect a human to do.

We'll take up these themes again later on in the chapter. For now, let us see how other workers have attempted to get beyond the tiny blocks world that Winograd considered.

Conversations are complicated things. To talk with someone we need to know about:

• words, their meaning and grammar
• the gist of the conversation so far
• the speaker, and the context of the conversation
• the conventions which govern conversation.

As well as these, we need to have a lot of general knowledge about the world. We don't usually use all this information consciously: rather, we make lots of unconscious inferences as we go along. We sometimes become aware of the inferences we have made, when they go wrong, as in this conversation.

Jan: It was raining hard in Blackpool. I really got soaked ...

John: Oh yes, I've been to Blackpool. Rain? You've never seen anything like it I remember in 1948 well what a year didn't Bolton win the cup that year? Yes well there we were with this donkey on the sand when ...

Jan: Soaked when I fell off the pier.

John wrongly deduces that Jan was soaked by the rain, and that the topic of conversation could legitimately be turned to things concerned with either rain or Blackpool. He also assumes that Jan knows that 'Bolton' refers to Bolton Wanderers, a football team of some eminence, that 'the cup' is the Football Association Trophy, and that Blackpool is a seaside resort with a beach on which donkey rides can be bought. What about the conventions of conversation? John wrongly (or deliberately) interpreted the pause in Jan's speech which came after 'soaked' to signify the end of what she was saying, or at least give him 'permission' to interrupt. He then left no gaps in his own speech to allow her to correct his misunderstanding. We have speech conventions like cooperation and sharing the role of speaker; being informative at the right level (John fails again here with his irrelevant information about football teams); not telling lies; being reasonably brief and so on. There have been some attempts to model more general human conversations on a computer, but the main focus of attention has been to try to represent general knowledge about the world.

Is there any way that a computer could be given enough information, and appropriate instructions, to make the sort of 'unconscious' inferences that humans make routinely? SHRDLU bypassed many of the problems of inference by restricting its conversations to a tiny part of the world. Do we have to have a separate group of computer programs for every different topic that we discuss, or are there some more general principles that we draw on? What do people do?

To help clarify the process, try drawing a cube. What does it look like? Compare what you have drawn with the cubes in Figure 7.3. The commonest response to the task is to draw a cube like (A) or (B). Hidden faces are sometimes shown as in (C). People rarely stand their cubes up on a point, or show them exactly sideways on, with only one face showing, like (D) and (E). Well, we all have ideas about 'typical' objects. A typical bird flies, sings and lays its eggs in a nest. A typical car has four wheels, a petrol engine and four seats. A typical room has four vertical walls of the same height, a door, and at least one window. We can call these typical examples 'prototypes' or 'frames': frames, because they provide a starting structure which is then fleshed out by information about the particular example which is being discussed. Asking someone to draw a cube provides so little information that they fall back to their prototype, which in the case of the cube is usually more like (A) or (B) than (D) or (E).

As well as having frames for the nature of particular objects, we also have strong expectations about action, activities and events. If we go to a bookshop, we have strong expectations about the ways that people will behave. When we talk about events in a bookshop, we interpret sentences in context, and use all the expectancies that are brought up by the general frame 'bookshop'. So a sentence like: *the restaurant at the end of the universe is upstairs under science fiction* is easily interpreted. Typical patterns of events that occur in shops, restaurants or train journeys *can* be represented in a computer and can be used to fill out information that isn't given directly. Roger Schank and Robert Abelson call the frames which contain our knowledge about situations which we deal with routinely *scripts* . A script is made up of a sequence of pigeon holes, together with a description of the things that can go into the holes. As well as this, there are rules about the ways that information in one pigeon hole can affect the information in another hole.

Schank and Abelson have argued that the things people talk about can be described in terms of just 12 primitive actions, like physical transfer; mental transfer; movement of a body part; constructing new information; and the like. These form the basis of their scripts. We all have scripts for different events in our lives, like shopping, meeting friends, going to a restaurant and so on. Here is a sample of Schank and Abelson's restaurant script (modified a little).

Script: restaurant
Roles: customer, waiter, chef, cashier
Reason: to get food so as to go up in pleasure and down in hunger.

Scene 1: entering

    PHYSICALLY MOVE: self into restaurant
    ATTEND: eyes to where empty tables are
    CONSTRUCT NEW INFORMATION: where to sit
    PHYSICALLY MOVE: self to table
    MOVE BODY PART: sit down

Scene 2: ordering

    TRANSFER ABSTRACT RELATION (HERE 'POSSESSION'): get the menu
    TRANSFER MENTAL INFORMATION: read menu
    CONSTRUCT NEW INFORMATION: decide what self wants
    TRANSFER MENTAL INFORMATION: order to waiter

Scene 3: eating

    TRANSFER ABSTRACT RELATION (HERE 'POSSESSION'): receive food
    INGEST: food

Scene 4: exiting

    TRANSFER MENTAL INFORMATION: ask for bill

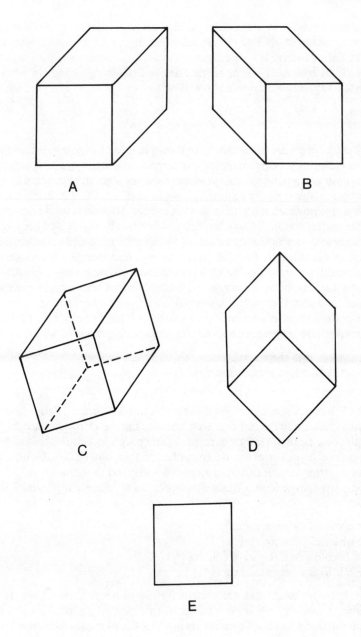

Figure 7.3. A few cubes.

TRANSFER ABSTRACT RELATION: receive bill
TRANSFER ABSTRACT RELATION: tip to waiter
PHYSICALLY MOVE: self to cashier
TRANSFER ABSTRACT RELATION: money to cashier
PHYSICALLY MOVE: self out of restaurant

Reprinted with modifications from R.C. Schank and R.P. Abelson (1975) Scripts, plans and knowledge. In *Advance Papers of the Fourth International Joint Conference on Artificial Intelligence*. International Joint Council on Artificial Intelligences.

The script provides the skeleton for things that happen in the restaurant. Ambiguous sentences are interpreted in terms of the script. Unless contrary information is given to the program about a particular restaurant, everything in the script is assumed to apply to it.

The script provides more than a list of events and actors, it also imposes an order on the events. So you don't pay before you have received the food, or order before you have seen the menu. An action can take place only when the action preceding it has finished. If one action cannot be completed satisfactorily, the program has to solve the local problem before the script can continue. So the script is not just a simple list of activities, but allows branches and multiple paths between different actions.

The script serves as a framework for interpreting pieces of text that are presented to the program. Suppose the program is presented with

John went into the restaurant.
He ordered a hamburger and a coke.
He asked the waiter for the bill and left.

The first sentence describes the first action of scene 1; the second sentence maps on to the last action of scene 2; and the third sentence maps on to the first and last actions of scene 4. The program assumes that all the other actions in the script should be applied to John too, and can be used to answer questions about this little story. (Who served the hamburger? Who did John pay for the food?) What if the story is a bit more complicated? Say we had

John went to a restaurant.
He ordered a hamburger.
It was cold when the waiter brought it.
He left him a very small tip.

The first two sentences are essentially the same as those in the first example. However, we now learn that the hamburger was cold. The program makes a low level hypothesis that the size of the tip has something to do with the temperature of the hamburger. More information than we have given under INGEST can show that a cold hamburger violates the pleasure principle described under 'reason' at the start of the script. The program will then update its script with the conclusion it has made.

196

Schank and Abelson's program SAM accepts text input and answers questions about it. It also paraphrases the text and provides a summary of it. It uses scripts to do all this. Here is an example of SAM's input and output.

Input:
John went to a restaurant. The hostess seated John. The hostess gave John a menu. The waiter came to the table. John ordered lobster. John was served quickly. John left a large tip. John left the restaurant.

Questions and answers:
Q: What did John eat?
A: LOBSTER.
Q: Who gave John the menu?
A: THE HOSTESS.
Q: Who gave John the lobster?
A: PROBABLY THE WAITER.
Q: Who paid the bill?
A: PROBABLY JOHN.
Q: What happened when John went to the table?
A: THE HOSTESS GAVE HIM A MENU AND JOHN SAT DOWN.
Q: Why did John get a menu?
A: SO HE COULD ORDER.
Q: Why did John give the waiter a large tip?
A: BECAUSE HE WAS SERVED QUICKLY.

Paraphrase:
JOHN DECIDED HE WAS GOING TO GO TO A RESTAURANT. JOHN WENT TO A RESTAURANT. JOHN INDICATED TO THE HOST HE WOULD LIKE TO BE AT A TABLE. THE HOST INDICATED TO JOHN HE COULD GO TO A TABLE. JOHN WENT TO THE TABLE. THE HOST WENT TO THE TABLE. JOHN SAT DOWN IN THE CHAIR. JOHN GOT THE MENU FROM THE HOSTESS. JOHN READ THE MENU. THE WAITER SAW JOHN WAS AT THE TABLE. THE WAITER WENT TO THE TABLE. JOHN ORDERED LOBSTER. THE CHEF PREPARED THE LOBSTER. THE WAITER GOT THE LOBSTER FROM THE CHEF. THE WAITER SERVED JOHN THE LOBSTER. JOHN ATE THE LOBSTER. JOHN INDICATED TO THE WAITER HE WOULD LIKE TO GET THE BILL FROM HIM. JOHN GOT THE BILL FROM THE WAITER. JOHN LEFT THE WAITER A LARGE TIP. JOHN PAID THE BILL. JOHN LEFT THE RESTAURANT.

Summary:
JOHN WENT TO A RESTAURANT AND ATE LOBSTER.
Reprinted with permission from R.C. Schank and R.P. Abelson, *op. cit.*

So scripts organize new sentences into sensible stories on the basis of stored knowledge. Of course, choosing the right script is essential, and any general purpose computer program will need to have routines which decide which script to invoke. For example, if John were a Health Inspector, the following input might well produce bizarre results, if the computer uses the restaurant script.

John went into a restaurant.
He ordered a clean up.
It was cold.
He promised to call again, and left.

Here 'clean up' is likely to be identified as a kind of food, which should have been served hot. The program would probably answer questions like 'Who served the clean up?' and 'Who did John pay?' without noticing that the questions are quite inappropriate.

What are the similarities and differences between the programs we have described? The most obvious dimension for comparison is the amount of knowledge about the world that each one builds in. PARRY matches patterns in the string of words input in order to produce (usually) sensible English sentences: no attempt is made to represent the meaning of the dialogue. SHRDLU constrains the discourse to the topic of an artificial blocks world, which it manipulates. However, within this world, it uses its knowledge to resolve ambiguous questions, obey instructions, and to talk about its past activities. SAM brings a good deal of knowledge about the world, via scripts, to answer questions about events which have been described very briefly. To deal with more situations, you need more scripts.

Let's move away from Denny's language understanding abilities, and think about his skills in planning and problem solving. People who set out to show that humans are different from animals or machines in some qualitative way often refer to two attributes that are supposed to distinguish us from beasts; these are use of language and our rationality. Denny appears to use language, and to have great intellectual skills, like reading descriptions of battles, and abstracting general principles; planning his own campaign of battle, evaluating his success as he goes along. (We know, of course, that he can behave irrationally, too.)

In the early days of computing, the possibilities of an intelligent machine were the basis for a good deal of philosophical speculation. We have already looked at the Turing Test. What else would a machine have to do to convince you that it was intelligent? One activity that is exclusively the domain of humans is the playing of games with well-defined rules, like Go, checkers and chess. The ability in humans to play these games well is often associated with high intellectual ability. You can't play chess by a blind procedure like working out all the possible moves. To play well, you have to use knowledge about how the pieces can move, and plans for attack and defence. You have to think about the game at each local part of the board, and at the general strategic level of overall command of the board. Skilled play has nothing to do with luck, but depends on strategy, planning and a host of logical operations. Early workers believed that if they could produce a computer program that could play chess successfully, then the existence of an intelligent machine would be proved.

Board games have a number of features that make them suitable for playing on a computer. The starting point and the end points are quite unambiguous; so are the moves that are legal. Humans can often look at an ongoing game, and decide who is winning. Humans can also decide between good next moves and bad next moves. We also talk a lot about how we play games, especially games like chess. Discussions abound about the general strategies of the game, like 'develop your pieces', 'keep your king safe', 'try and control the centre of the board'. All these things give us some hope that the rules which underlie successful game playing can be made explicit, and can be implemented on a computer. What about our overall question about producing an intelligent machine? Can we say that chess requires human intelligence to play, therefore a machine that plays chess must be intelligent? In our view we cannot. We usually think of intelligent people as those who can tackle a range of problems adaptively, even when they haven't met them before. If we want to talk about intelligent machines, the least we have got to do is to show that there is some generality in what they can do. We must be able to show some more general problem-solving ability that can be brought to bear on specific problems like playing chess, or planning routes, or developing battle strategies. However, you often get a glimpse about what these abstract, general problem-solving skills are by trying to solve a number of concrete tasks. In this case, the concrete tasks are things like writing a computer program which will play chess!

We can dismiss the suggestion that the computer program should examine every possible combination of move and counter-move during the chess game, simply because the huge number of possible moves would take millions of years to explore. However, some games and problems *can* be dealt with by exploring all the alternatives. Noughts and crosses (tic-tac-toe) is one such game; making a decision about which camera to buy is another. Exhaustive searches are useful when there are relatively few possible courses of action, and when the problem has well-defined states. So humans might use exhaustive searches when they are stuck solving an anagram, or a simple word problem of the type 'There are 16 doctors and nurses on the ward. There are more female doctors than male nurses, and ...' In general, though, people don't use exhaustive searches. What else might they do? What else might a computer do? Two techniques that are used widely in computer programs are *heuristic search* and *means–ends* analysis.

An *heuristic* is a rule of thumb. It often works, but it doesn't guarantee success. For example, if you want to keep an approximate running total of how much you have spent as you go around a supermarket, an easy heuristic to use is to round each item to the nearest 10p, and count them up. So items which cost less than 5p aren't counted at all, items costing between 5p and

9p are counted as 10p, and so on. This method simplifies the additions quite considerably and usually produces an answer that is about right, but of course, doesn't guarantee perfect success. Heuristics in problem solving might be things like 'think of a problem like this one that you have solved before', 'draw a diagram'; 'simplify the problem somehow'. Are there heuristics for searching out useful sequences of moves in a game like chess?

Problems like board games have set starting points, and agreed end points: if you know the legal moves, you can spell out all the possible states that the game can be in. We saw earlier that this might not be possible for practical reasons, but the idea of lots and lots of possible positions is useful. From any situation that a game is in, only a certain range of possible moves and counter-moves is possible. The further ahead we want to look, the more outcomes we have to consider. We can represent this like a drawing of the roots of a plant. In Figure 7.4 the square boxes are called nodes; they represent the possible states that the game can be in. Somewhere on the plant there are nodes which correspond to winning the game; some other nodes correspond to losing the game. As game players, we want to search the roots to find the winning nodes, then choose as our next move the route which is most likely to get us to a winning node. This is rather like a potato weevil which starts at the top, and can only follow the roots of the plant, and has to take decisions about which way to go at each branch, in its hunt for a potato to eat. The problem we both face is that we can't look at the whole root structure, but only the next few branches and pathways ahead. What can we do to ensure that we only explore the part of the root structure most likely to contain a successful conclusion?

One way is to devise some method of evaluating each of the states of the game that we might get ourselves into. For example, when you watch a game of chess or draughts, you can usually tell who is winning, but you don't do this by working out every possible future move. You use clues like who has the most pieces left on the board; whose king is safest; where the pieces are deployed; and so on. If we can find some way of quantifying what humans do naturally, so that we can score each alternative board position, we will be well on the way to developing a game-playing machine which can handle games with a huge number of possible states. Let's call the process of deciding who is winning at any point *evaluation* . To decide who is winning, we need an *evaluation function* . This is a list of features of the game, like how many pieces each player has, what the pieces are, and where they are, and a way of deciding on the relative importance of each. The evaluation function produces a number which reflects how well the game is progressing from each person's point of view. Suppose that a chess-playing program is faced with a choice between two moves. How does it proceed? Well, it could compare the change in the evaluation score that results from each move. More sensibly, it will look several moves ahead, and see what the change in

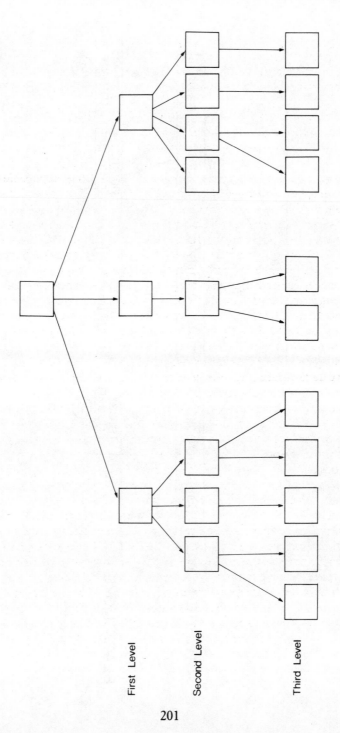

Figure 7.4. The legal states of a board game.

First Level

Second Level

Third Level

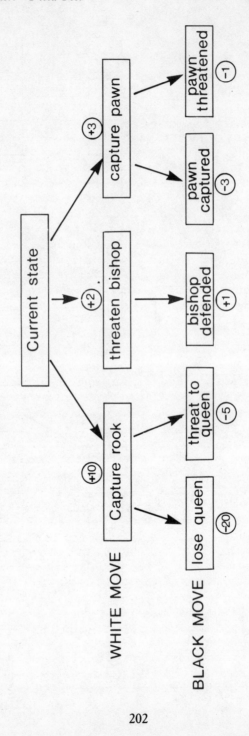

Figure 7.5. Moves and counter-moves.

the score is, assuming that its opponent chooses the best moves too. Figure 7.5 is an example of a short look ahead during a chess game.

The numbers in circles represent the change in the overall evaluation of the game from white's viewpoint. So if white captures black's rook, white improves the position by +10. If white only looks as far as the benefits gained from the first move, this is the 'best move'. However, when the range of alternative moves that black can make is taken into account, this move is a disaster. Black has the chance to capture white's most powerful piece, the queen. It is necessary to look several moves ahead, usually three or four, to avoid disasters of this sort; even so, the possibility of a devastating counter-move that the program doesn't have time to consider always exists. Amongst experts, there is a good deal of agreement about how to evaluate an ongoing game. If white and black are both skilled players, they are likely to have similar evaluation functions. The novice faces the task of building up an adequate evaluation function.

So programs which play chess to a very high level use just a few simple principles or heuristics. They consider all possible positions a few moves ahead, and evaluate them, and choose the move which produces the highest score on their evaluation function. Their opponent moves; the cycle is repeated. The key to the whole endeavour is the evaluation function. If the programmer can supply a good evaluation function, or some mechanism whereby the program can improve its evaluation function as it goes along, the program can play well; a poor evaluation function will lead to poor play.

Another way in which the program can help itself is to store past board positions and use this information to improve its play. Both these features of chess- playing programs were anticipated by A.L. Samuel in his checkers-playing program developed in 1959.

Samuel's checkers (draughts) player was one of the early successful games-playing machines. It is a program that learns. It was able to beat its author at checkers even in its early stages of development; it went on to beat a checkers master who had been undefeated for several years. Two learning mechanisms are built in. Samuel provided the program with a list of things to take into account when playing; like 'control the centre of the board' or 'avoid forks'. Initially, each of these was associated with a number which reflected its importance to the likely outcome of the game. To decide which the next best move is, the program looks three moves ahead, and works out an evaluation function based on a complicated calculation involving these 'importance numbers'. The first form of learning allows the program to change these 'importance numbers' on the basis of the success or otherwise of the game. So the program uses its experience of playing to decide which of its list of things to consider are the most important. To do this, of course, the program has to store all the past positions in the game. These can be useful too. When faced with a new position, the program searches through the list of old positions. This can save a good deal of time, if it avoids having to recalculate everything anew. For example, the program normally only looks three moves ahead. But if on its third move it finds a position which it has met before, it can find the best third move immediately, which was itself based on looking three moves ahead. So the program changes itself on the basis of its experience, and also learns by rote so that it can recognize future patterns.

This approach to solving problems by using heuristic search of the nodes of the problem space (to give our potato root its proper name) works reasonably well for games where the legal moves are clear and where early success usually leads to later success. It isn't so useful for problems where the possible moves are very varied, and not very well defined. Planning tasks are like this. Humans, of course, use overall plans when they play chess too. Denny isn't going to get very far if he just considers the next few things that are going to happen to him. The essence of military activities is planning at different levels: strategic decisions about which battles to fight, and where, and tactical decisions about how to fight them. Can we program computers to solve problems that involve planning?

Let's start off by getting a feel for the problem we face. Suppose you want to go to Jamaica. In the problem space the first set of alternative actions is huge: go to bed; post a letter; call a taxi; switch on TV; cook dinner. It isn't at all clear what actions should be considered, or what the evaluation function should be. Suppose we just consider activities relating to travel. If we aren't careful about the evaluation function, we might find that walking directly towards the West Indies appears to be a better move than getting a taxi to the airport, if the airport is in the opposite direction!

Techniques like *means–end analysis* can be helpful in such planning problems. This was introduced in the General Problem Solving Program (GPS) developed by Allen Newell, Clifford Shaw and Herbert Simon in 1957, one of the most influential programs in AI. The idea which underlies GPS is that a large number of seemingly different problems, like planning tasks and proofs in mathematics, can be solved using the same problem-solving processes and that these processes can be written into a computer program. Means–end analysis is one such process. The *means* part is the collection of things that can be done to achieve the ends. The means operate on problem states to change one into another (and so are often called *operators*). In the case of travel problems, these will be things like 'walk'; 'fly'; 'drive'; 'sail'; 'go by train'; for problems which require geometric proofs, these will be things you assume to be true or which are true by definition, like 'a straight line subtends an angle of 180 degrees' together with things that you have already proved, like 'if two straight lines intersect, opposite angles are equal'.

Let's go back to the trip to Jamaica. The goal is clear: 'me in Jamaica'. Of the list of means above, 'fly' is the obvious one to use. Perhaps 'sail' is practical too, but none of the others is. In order to fly, I have to get to the airport. So 'me at the airport' is now a *sub-goal* . Let's look at the list of operators again. I can change 'me at home' to 'me at the airport' by the operator 'drive'. I know that my car is low on petrol, so I need a new set of operators to solve the new sub-goal 'car ready for a long trip'.

Can we describe this invented description of a problem-solving episode in general terms? What did we do? We split the overall problem up into sub-goals and tried to solve them in turn. We considered applying a number of different operators to achieve the sub-goals. Something about the operators gave us hints about the sub-goals: for example, when we chose to use 'fly' it was immediately clear that our next sub-goal was 'me at airport'. GPS can solve this sort of problem, too. How does it do it? First, it compares the goal state (me in Jamaica) with current state (me at home), and calculates the difference between them, using an evaluation function that it has been given. Then it examines its operators in turn, applying each one to either the goal state or the current state to see what would happen. As each operator is applied, it evaluates the difference between the goal and the new current state. If the operator has reduced the difference by a significant amount, GPS then applies it to produce a new state. The cycle is then repeated. Each cycle produces a new difference between the current state and the goal state, and GPS looks at the operators for ways of reducing the difference. Of course, it might get stuck. When this happens, it backtracks through each action in turn, looking for new sub-goals which might be solvable.

To solve a new problem, GPS has to be given a good deal of information which is specific to the task in hand. The initial state and goal state have to be given; so does the evaluation function, and all the operators. The rules for finding relevant operators (don't 'walk' to the airport), and the rules for applying them, have to be given too. So the programmer has to do a good deal of general problem solving in order to make the problem in hand accessible to the procedures built into the General Problem Solving Program!

Means–end analysis has now become one of the commonly used tools of the trade in the artificial intelligence fraternity. GPS-like programs now form part of many programs, and GPS has had its descendants too. STRIPS (the Stanford Research Institute Problem Solver) does the problem solving for SHAKEY, the Stanford Research Institute robot. SHAKEY inhabits a small world of seven rooms, which it pushes about when asked. For example, SHAKEY can be asked to move box 4 from room 7 to room 1, or to open the window in room 2 (which can only be reached by standing on a box). STRIPS plans out the task, and SHAKEY carries it out. STRIPS uses means–end analysis too. But it overcomes one of the problems inherent in GPS, namely the need to provide the program with lots of information before it can work. STRIPS uses *operator tables*, which summarize in

Table 7.1. An operator table

OPERATOR TO FLY A PERSON FROM PLACE 1 TO PLACE 2	
PRECONDITIONS	PLACE 1 IS AN AIRPORT
	PLACE 2 IS AN AIRPORT
	PERSON IS AT PLACE 1
DELETE	PERSON IS AT PLACE 1
ADD	PERSON IS AT PLACE 2

schematic form how and when operators can be used. Table 7.1 is the table for the operator TO FLY.

So, on our trip to Jamaica, the program is given a set of operator tables and some definitions like MANCHESTER IS AN AIRPORT, JAMAICA IS AN AIRPORT, ME IS A PERSON (sorry about the grammar, but STRIPS won't care), ME IS AT HOME, HOME IS A PLACE, AIRPORT IS A PLACE, and so on. The program is trying to find a way to change 'ME AT HOME' to 'ME AT JAMAICA'. STRIPS will start off searching the operator tables for a plausible operator. TO WALK, TO DRIVE and TO FLY all seem to be appropriate on first inspection, because each of them will DELETE PERSON IS AT PLACE 1 and will ADD PERSON IS AT PLACE 2. However, the preconditions of TO WALK and TO DRIVE will both include restrictions on distance. TO FLY doesn't have preconditions about the distances involved, and so the program will consider it further. STRIPS will find that PLACE 2 IS AN AIRPORT is true, but that PLACE 1 IS AN AIRPORT isn't true. It *has* been told that MANCHESTER IS AN AIRPORT, though.

So it sets up a sub-goal to change ME AT HOME to ME AT MANCHESTER. Again it searches the operator tables for operators which DELETE PERSON IS AT PLACE 1 and ADD PERSON IS AT PLACE 2. TO WALK, TO DRIVE seem appropriate on first inspection, as before. Now, though, TO WALK is still ruled out by a precondition like PLACE 1 IS NEAR PLACE 2; TO DRIVE will have a less restricted precondition like PLACE 1 IS WITHIN 200 MILES OF PLACE 2 which can be satisfied.

The problem is solved by using TO DRIVE, which deletes ME AT HOME and adds ME AT MANCHESTER, followed by TO FLY, which deletes ME AT MANCHESTER and adds ME AT JAMAICA.

STRIPS could solve each problem that it is faced with from scratch; however, this isn't a very sensible approach. What it does instead is to build up master plans in the form of 'macro operators' to guide later problem-solving efforts. So the next time STRIPS is faced with a problem of the form PERSON AT PLACE 1 to PERSON AT PLACE 2, with information that PLACE 2 is a long way from PLACE 1, it can check its macro operators and find that it has a complete plan for the problem. This storage of results to guide further plans, together with the relatively simple structure of operator tables, gives

STRIPS considerable advantages over GPS. Even so, STRIPS still has a number of limitations. These stem from the way things are represented in the program as simple relationships of just three elements (ME ... AT ... HOME, etc.) and the orderly way that the program proceeds. Think about Denny. Could he work by using means–ends analysis in the simple way that STRIPS does?

The programs we have looked at in this chapter have been quite successful at capturing some aspects of language understanding and problem-solving abilities. They all show us how complex even the most seemingly simple human abilities are when we try to pin them down. Even the most successful programs are extremely limited by human standards.

We are now in a better position to consider the issue of machine intelligence. What do we mean by 'intelligence'? A short definition like 'The ability to learn and perform new acts that are functionally useful' gives us a rough framework, but it isn't really very helpful. Let's list some of the symptoms of intelligence:

- responding to situations in a flexible way
- synthesizing new concepts from old ones
- seeing differences between similar objects, events and situations
- seeing similarities between different objects, events and situations
- interpreting ambiguous information
- producing novel ideas.

At present we cannot attain many of these using simple rules on the computer. A key notion here is one of *meaning* . It isn't enough to manipulate symbols inside a computer; there must be some external reference to the world to give the symbols meaning. Humans have a very rich knowledge of the world. We can examine objects and classify them in a wide variety of ways.

For example, try this simple game. Write down all the ways you can think of for using a brick; a pencil; a toffee wrapper. Next, imagine that Snaggle Prod, a wild creative genius with no inhibitions at all, was also compiling a list. Write down some of her ideas too.

Think about how you and Snaggle generated your uses. Here are some of our uses of a brick. Doorstop; ruler; paper weight; pendulum bob; for breaking a window; making paths; supporting car axles; drowning pets; broken, to stop barefooted robbers; broken, as sweets for dentists to hand out when trade is bad; powdered, for ...

Notice how much these uses depend on a very detailed knowledge about the world. We could analyse these into the features of a brick which have been used, such as weight, straight edges, shape (tesselates), sharpness, colour.

It is clear that if we are to get a machine to do this task, which humans find quite easy, we have to provide it with a huge amount of knowledge about the world. This is not impossible in principle, but is very difficult in practice.

A machine like Denny is probably quite a long way off. The arguments about whether such a machine is possible have by no means been resolved. The advances in AI programs have been such that computers can now perform tasks that even such a forward thinker as Alan Turing would have thought impossible 30 years ago. Our comments about the nature of intelligence suggest that it is still possible to argue that machine intelligence is in principle achievable, but the rules of the argument have been changed somewhat. Whereas 30 years ago people would have counted the ability to play complex games like chess well (or at all) as evidence of intelligence, now we insist on a more general definition of 'intelligent'.

Changes in the way we think about human intelligence have largely been brought about by AI programs. These are probably more important than the argument about whether machine intelligence is possible, because they have brought new insights into human activities and new ways of exploring these abilities. The problems of understanding a computer, a human and the world have a good deal in common. The most important similarity is that, to understand any of these three, one must conduct investigations at lots of different levels. One can discuss the way a computer works by discussing: the way individual integrated circuits work (chips); their interconnections; the system which controls the flow of control around the computer; the program which the computer is running at any one time. None of these levels of discussion captures the 'essence' of the computer; none is complete on its own.

One can discuss humans in terms of physiology (notably the physiology of the brain, if we are talking about behaviour); in terms of their abilities; in terms of their beliefs; in terms of their emotions; in terms of their family, in terms of the society in which they live. None of these levels of discussion defines the essence of what it is to be human: all levels of discussion are necessary to explain certain aspects of our behaviour.

When we try to explain the world we live in, we adopt a wide variety of approaches. Theoretical physicists puzzle over the nature of matter, nuclear physicists analyse things at the level of particles. Chemists analyse things taking whole atoms as their units. Biological science ranges from the study of complex organic molecules and chains of molecules, and extends up through simple animals to complex ones, and finally encompasses discussions of ecological systems (that is, the whole pattern of the interactions of animals and resources in some area). We have sketched these analogies in Figure 7.6.

Notice that we are *not* claiming that neurones are like integrated circuits are like DNA strands, or that AI programs are like minds are like ecological systems. The claim is that in order to tell a sensible story about any of the

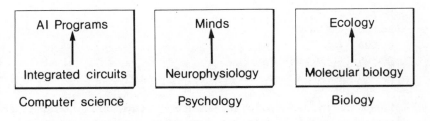

Figure 7.6. Examples of analogies used as explanations.

topics of computers, humans or biology we need analysis and explanation at lots of different levels. In addition, the higher levels depend on the lower levels in very non-obvious ways. While low level structures might set the limits of what can be performed at the higher levels, the higher levels of processing can operate according to rules which are different from those which govern the lower levels. Indeed, for many purposes, understanding events at higher levels can be done almost without reference to lower level events.

Computer models have been a great attraction to psychologists for a considerable period of time. There are broadly two sorts of approach. The first use is a crude version of the approach which we have just sketched out, namely to use the computer as an analogy for a person. The analogy might run as follows: we have some input devices, which tell us about the world; a central brain capable of solving complex problems; capacity to store knowledge; and the ability to respond to the world. Analogies like this can be useful in that they provide a concrete example of the sort of 'model of humanity' under discussion. This model can be classified as 'People as logical machines'. The tendency to describe ourselves in terms of the technology available to each epoch has a long and honourable tradition; if we look back, we can find precursors of 'People as computers', such as 'People as clocks', and 'People as water cisterns' at the time of the Renaissance. There need not be anything particularly harmful about this view, so long as we realize that we are just using an analogy. A helpful corrective is to generate lots of analogies, and to look at their strengths and weaknesses. Try some of the following. All you have to do is to point out similarities and differences between each of these pairs. Think about their structure (what they are made of), their function (what they do) and their evolution (how they change).

person – monkey
person – dust
person – tiger
person – clock

person – rat
person – car factory
person – tree
person – tailor's dummy
person – sewer

This activity is more difficult than it first seems, but is useful for a number of reasons. First, it forces you to look at your own constructions of the world. Second, it should help you to see that analogies are useful to focus on different aspects of a complex subject.

Drawing analogies as a scientific activity is not without its attendant dangers. First, the analogy provides nothing in the way of an explanation, unless the mapping between each attribute of the subject being studied (in our case, a person) and the object of the analogy (here, a computer) is carefully specified, *and* unless the relationships between these parts is well understood in the object of the analogy. So the suggestion 'people are like gods' has an attractive mystical feel, but isn't much of an explanation of behaviour. SF stories often focus on a second danger in using machine analogies. This danger is that machine models provide a dehumanizing view of humanity, encouraging us to deal with our fellows in the same way that we deal with machines. If the brain is a meat computer, instead of being an electronic one, and the body is an engine which uses bones as levers and muscles as activators, why shouldn't we treat meat computers which are old, inefficient, or only semi-functional when they come off the production line, in the same way that we treat old cars?

A qualitatively different way in which computers can help us understand people is to write a theory in the form of a computer program. Computers are used to test theories because of the great variety of things one can get a computer to do. Remember our definition of a computer, a machine that manipulates symbols. Any process which can be specified as a series of logical steps can, in principle, be run on a computer. Psychologists usually try to express their theories as clearly as they can. This is hard to do when we depend entirely on written and spoken language. The discipline of programming forces the theorist to be explicit about every aspect of the theory – how knowledge is represented; how events are interpreted; how actions take place. When theories are stated in words, details can, too easily, be glossed over. When programmed, everything has to be specified clearly. Running the program can show the psychologist whether or not the theory is capable of producing behaviour which is like human behaviour, given appropriate inputs. If it is, then the theorist can claim that the theory is at least *sufficient* i.e. it does what is claimed for it.

Computers are good at pushing the ideas contained in programs to their logical conclusions. This can be very hard to do by any other means, because of the mental load imposed when different elements in the theory affect each other, as we saw in Terry Winograd's SHRDLU. Occasionally we can be surprised at the power of quite simple ideas – for example, when programs produce new proofs in mathematics, or new methods of analysis in chemistry. Other surprising results are that: in limited domains, like geological prospecting, chemical analysis or certain areas of medical diagnosis, machines can sometimes perform as well as human experts; expert skills can often be captured in a small set of IF ... THEN rules (say a few hundred); tasks which humans take for granted like perceiving, and using language, are extremely hard to perform via machine.

There are three arguments commonly used against computer modelling. The first is that human behaviour cannot be understood by human beings. People are so different from each other that it is impossible *in principle* to make general statements about people. The second is that we don't know enough *at the moment* to make the computer behave in the way a human being does in a particular situation. The third is that computers will never be able to experience the same kinds of internal states as humans do, and so can never really provide a good model for psychology. These three ideas are frequently confused. Can you tell which criticism is implied by each of these assertions?

1. Computers can't solve problems.
2. There will never be a conscious computer.
3. Computer 'vision' is pitiful compared to human vision.
4. Computers haven't got the intelligence of mice.
5. People have ambitions and goals; computers haven't.
6. You have to be human to understand language.
7. Psychology can only study individuals, not people in general.
8. I can feel pain. Computers can't.
9. Human minds are all different.

Assertions 7 and 9 are arguments against theories of psychology which attempt any kind of generality. Statements 2, 6, 8 and perhaps 5 argue that the computer cannot feel as we do. 1, 3 and 4 make statements about what has been achieved so far.

It is important not to confuse these views. We readily accept the argument that we don't know enough at the moment to produce a machine which will act like a human being in a particular situation. However, this argument can be seen to be somewhat vacuous when examined closely. It is asserting that because you can't predict something now, using a particular explanation, you won't be able to do so in the future. This is a rather strange view; it certainly flies in the face of most people's conception of scientific activity. The history of science is a history of a slow creeping progress; progress in the collection of 'facts' (that is, repeatable observations); and progress in the ways these facts are grouped together and explained. Ideas and theories undergo slow changes and, indeed, the occasional revolution.

Rarely is a theory about some complex process brought forward, perfect in all its parts, and capable of explaining a wide range of observations.

The assertion that psychology can only study the individual, and that no observations and explanations can be made or put forward which have any generality seems to us to claim too much. A number of examples were given earlier in the book which demonstrate that generalizations *can* be made about people. This individual-centred approach should not be rejected out of hand, however. In clinical and educational settings where people ask for advice about problems or life-style decisions like choosing jobs, it is clear that the adviser must start off by establishing a 'model' of the individual seeking advice. It is quite conceivable that the factors which are relevant to personal decisions vary extensively from person to person. However, to claim that there are no useful generalities to be drawn seems to go too far.

The third argument that computers cannot experience the same things as humans is an interesting one. There is an interesting confusion of two ideas; explaining something and experiencing it. If we use a computer to simulate a psychological explanation of some aspect of behaviour, that is to say, the computer program embodies our theory about what is going on, we are mainly interested in the extent to which the program produces the desired behaviour, and avoids producing behaviour which is never observed. It is quite irrelevant to our theory that the program 'feels' or 'sees'. If we apply the same criterion to a theory which is implemented in another (non-computer-based) form, we see the irrelevance of this criticism. Suppose the theory were written down in a book. Requiring the computer to 'feel' is directly analogous to requiring the book to 'feel'; this is clearly a nonsensical requirement of an explanation.

So much for psychologists' uses of computers to model theories of human behaviour. Denny is hardly a theory of behaviour – it has been designed to be a very sophisticated weapon – everything else about it which seems human is incidental to this main purpose. The main thrust in AI research in general has been to produce computer systems that work, rather than clever research tools for psychologists. Research in AI has been in progress since the 1950s. In the UK, the Lighthill Report 'Artificial Intelligence', published in 1972 for the Science Research Council, stopped UK research almost completely. The report asserted (quite wrongly as we saw earlier) that the combinatorial explosion of possible states in games, for example, would make AI impossible. Despite earlier withdrawals of funds from machine translation, research in the USA continued unchecked, funded largely by the US Department of Defense. Now in Japan, the USA and Europe (including the UK) governments are providing large amounts of money to fund research which is aimed at exploiting the new ideas and techniques which are available. Let's list a few applications of computers (considering both AI and non-AI applications).

- the first industrial robots have been in use long enough to pay for themselves; manufacturing industries are assigning more, and increasingly complex, tasks to newer generations of robots
- computers have had a great impact on a wide range of clerical tasks, for example in banking, and other service industries
- elaborate computer-based models are used for corporate planning in many large companies, and indeed, as the basis for the economic plans of entire countries
- computer-assisted learning is now a feature of most schools; sophisticated systems attempt to model the state of the learner's knowledge, and to match the lesson to this knowledge (e.g. by challenging misconceptions)
- programs which can offer 'expert' advice are available in a number of domains. For example MYCIN simulates a consultant who specializes in infectious diseases. It offers help both on the identification of the likely disease, and on the choice of an appropriate antibiotic. At all stages, it offers the doctor who consults it the opportunity to ask for an explanation about MYCIN's choices, so that they can be modified or rejected in the light of other knowledge which the doctor has. (Note that this ability to explain itself implies a good deal of self-knowledge). Other expert systems have been developed to: aid legal decision making; advise on eligibility for social security benefits; offer advice to garage mechanics, computer maintenance engineers, power station controllers, etc.
- programs have been written which elicit medical histories, and administer personality and aptitude tests without human intervention
- military applications (like Denny) are extensive; for example, for strategic planning; pattern recognition for interpreting radar and sonar images, and terrain contour matching (tercom) guidance systems for cruise missiles
- programs are being written for language use – reading aloud from text; interpreting speech, and the like
- computer entertainment is becoming increasingly sophisticated, as adventure games and chess-playing programs, for example, make use of more techniques from AI.

Can AI be Achieved?

Are there things we are sure cannot be done by computers? Three contenders are often put forward: the most famous derives from Gödel's Incompleteness Theorem that there can never be a final, best system of mathematics; a second is that computers cannot show emotion or other aspects of life that we consider essentially 'human'; a third is that computers cannot act in an intuitive way.

Gödel's theorem shows that it is impossible to produce a set of assumptions (or 'axioms') which cover mathematical truth. It shows that any system of mathematical knowledge based on theorems derived from axioms must remain incomplete. The theorem is rather surprising. It shook the world view of many mathematicians when it was published, just before the Second World War. To get the flavour of the theorem, we need to go back a few thousand years to Epimenides' Liar paradox. How can we deal with Epimenides' statement 'I am lying'? If he is telling the truth, we conclude he lies. If he is lying, we conclude that he is telling the truth. Gödel's theorem is a development of this paradox. As applied to a computer program, it would assert that no program based on deductions from a set of axioms would ever be able to judge the truth of *every* statement in its domain of interest.

- We will label the sentence 'the program will never say that this sentence is true' with the label G (for Gödel).
- Next, ask the program if G is true or not.
- If the program says that G is true, then it contradicts itself, and would therefore make a false statement.
- Therefore 'the program will never say G is true' is a true statement.
- *But* , the program can never utter this sentence, and therefore *cannot* cover all true statements. In other words, we can construct a statement which we know to be true, but which the program cannot utter.

Gödel's theorem itself goes way beyond this illustration, and shows how to construct G as a mathematical statement which shows the limits of any particular set of mathematical axioms.

Does Gödel's theorem prove the impossibility of AI? No, it doesn't. It only applies to logical systems which start out with a fixed set of axioms, and make inferences from them. Programs can be written which modify themselves, and learn from experience. So something which was undecidable yesterday might be decidable today. So we can discount this rejection of the possibility of AI.

The second argument against the possibility of AI is that computers do not share our forms of life. They are not interested in friendship, dreams, sex, food, laughter; they have no knowledge of pleasure and pain, joy or sadness. All of these things are important aspects of 'humanness'. Wittgenstein captures this idea in a famous remark 'If a lion could speak, we would not understand him'. We must accept the idea that communication depends on shared knowledge (since it is true by definition of 'communication'!). Many programs depend on a good deal of inbuilt knowledge because of this – think back to the restaurant scripts – but common experiences; common subjective feelings?

A useful question to ask when we consider machine limitations, is what kinds of judgements are we making when we assert that other people think and feel as we do? Why do we attribute 'consciousness', 'free will', 'emotions' and 'feelings' to others? These topics have been at the centre of discussions among philosophers for a long time; we might boldly call them the central topics of philosophy. If we are to discuss the extent to which machines have feelings, consciousness and emotions, we need some ways of distinguishing between conscious and non-conscious things which do not include an implicit definition that consciousness is a human attribute. Think about it. What would the following things have to do before you believed that they were conscious?

A table.
A statue.
A tree.
A worm.
A dog.
An ape.
A baby human.
A computer.

When we are dealing with other people, we adopt a social politeness of assuming that they are conscious. Why? Well, other people look like we do; they put out signs that we recognize as signifying certain internal states (shyness, aggressiveness, sexual arousal), and they often confirm our hunches when we ask. They report internal events which correspond to ours, like 'I have never felt so angry'; 'I came over in a warm glow'; 'It was just like Christmas'. In short, all the information we receive is consistent with the view that other people share our internal world.

Suppose we made an android like Denny. Would we accept physical similarity to ourselves and verbal reports which correspond to our own internal states as sufficient evidence that Denny was conscious? We rather think that we would. There is some support for this view in the area of eliciting medical histories via computer. Patients tend to imbue the computer with a simple personality, rather than with no personality at all.

In this situation no deliberate attempt has been made to deceive the user. With deliberate deception, the anthropomorphization would presumably be far more marked. Self-reference, you remember, is no problem. In order for Denny to function, he must be able to refer to himself in relationship to the battlefield, his remaining capabilities and his self-maintenance routines. If Denny behaves intelligently, yet makes errors, talks lucidly about the world and himself, would *you* say he was conscious?

Notice that these issues do not concern the value of computer models for articulating psychological themes; they concern the broader psychological and philosophical issues of knowing about internal states, and shared experiences.

The third argument that computers cannot think intuitively depends heavily on what we mean by 'intuition'. If the word is taken to mean a way of thinking which can be effective in solving problems but which is quite inexplicable, then the assertion 'computers cannot think intuitively' actually means 'no- one will ever be able to explain intuition' – which is a statement of belief, rather than fact. If 'intuition' means 'inexplicable at present' then it poses a challenge to psychologists to explore it. If we have no idea how humans do it, we cannot program it. This form of the argument is a comment on our state of knowledge at present, of the sort we saw levelled against computer-based theories in psychology.

The philosophical arguments which are most commonly used to dismiss the possibility of AI fail to convince us. However, even if we believe that AI is not impossible in principle, we cannot conclude that it is possible in practice! Effective AI depends on solving problems which have challenged students of behaviour for hundreds of years. We have seen throughout this volume that explaining behaviour is no easy matter.

REFERENCES

Chapter 1

Most of the references here were cited in:

* Duck, S. (1983) *Friends, For Life*. Brighton: Harvester.

Bloom, B., Asher, S. and White, S. (1978) Marital disruption as a stressor: A review and analysis. *Psychological Bulletin 85*, 867–894.

Byrne, D. (1971) *The Attraction Paradigm*. New York: Academic Press.

Duck, S.W. and Allison, D. (1978) I liked you but I can't live with you: A study of lapsed friendships. *Social Behaviour and Personality, 6*, 43–47.

Huston, T., Surra, C., Fitzgerald, N. and Cate, R. (1981) From courtship to marriage: Mate selection as an interpersonal process. In S.W. Duck and R. Gilmour (eds) *Personal Relationships 2: Developing Personal Relationships*. New York: Academic Press.

Kaplan, R.E. (1976) Maintaining interpersonal relationships: A bipolar theory. *Interpersonal Development, 6*, 106–119.

Markman, H.J., Floyd, F. and Dickson-Markman, F. (1982) Towards a model for the prediction and primary prevention of marital and family distress and dissolution. In S.W. Duck (ed.) *Personal Relationships 4: Dissolving Personal Relationships*. London: Academic Press.

Murstein, B.I. (1977) The Stimulus-Value-Role (SVR) theory of dyadic relationships. In S.W. Duck (ed.) *Theory and Practice in Interpersonal Attraction*. London: Academic Press.

Newcomb, M.D. (1981) Heterosexual cohabitation relationships. In S.W. Duck and R. Gilmour (eds) *Personal Relationships 1: Studying Personal Relationships*. London and New York: Academic Press.

Newcomb, M.D. and Bentler, P. (1981) Marital breakdown. In S.W. Duck and R. Gilmour (eds) *Personal Relationships 3: Personal Relationships in Disorder*. New York: Academic Press.

Peplau, L.A., Rubin, Z. and Hill, C.T. (1977) Sexual intimacy in dating relationships. *Journal of Social Issues, 33*, 86–109.

Rubin, Z. (1974) From liking to loving: Patterns of attraction in dating relationships. In T.L. Huston (ed.) *Foundations of Interpersonal Attraction*. New York: Academic Press.

Walster, E., Walster, G.W. and Berscheid, E. (1978) *Equity Theory and Research*. Boston: Allyn and Bacon.

References

Chapter 2

* Baddeley, A. (1983) *Your Memory: A Users' Guide*. Harmondsworth: Penguin.
Bartlett, F.C. (1932) *Remembering*. Cambridge: Cambridge University Press.
Bransford, J.D. and Franks, J.J. (1971) The abstraction of linguistic ideas. *Cognitive Psychology*, 2, 331–350.
Brown, E., Deffenbacher, K., Sturgill, W. (1977) Memory for faces and the circumstances of encounter. *Journal of Applied Psychology*, 62, 311– 318.
Buckhout, R. (1974) Eyewitness testimony. *Scientific American, 231(6)*, 23–31.
Clifford, B.R. and Scott, J. (1978) Individual and situational factors in eyewitness testimony. *Journal of Applied Psychology*, 63, 352–359.
Devlin, Lord Patrick (Chairman) (1976) Report to the Secretary for the Home Department Committee on Evidence of Identification in Criminal Cases. London: HMSO.
Going, M. and Read, J.D. (1974) Effects of uniqueness, sex of subjects, and sex of photograph on facial recognition. *Perceptual and Motor Skills*, 39, 109–110.
Haber, R.N. and Herschenson, M. (1980) *The Psychology of Visual Perception*, 2nd ed. New York: Holt, Rinehart and Winston.
Hochberg, J. and Gallper, R. (1967) Recognition of human faces: 1. An exploratory study. *Psychonomic Science*, 619–620.
Loftus, E.F. (1977) Shifting human color memory. *Memory and Cognition, 5*, 696–699.
Loftus, E.F. (1979) *Eyewitness Testimony*. Cambridge, Mass.: Harvard University Press.
Loftus, E.F. and Palmer, J.C. (1974) Reconstruction of automobile destruction: An example of the interaction between language and memory. *Journal of Verbal Learning and Verbal Behavior, 13*, 585–589.
Meehl, P.E. (1977) Law and fireside inductions. Some reflections of a clinical psychologist. In J.L. Topp and F.J. Levine *Law, Justice and the Individual in Society. Psychological and Legal Issues*. New York: Holt, Rinehart and Winston.
Neisser, H. (1982) *Memory Observed: Remembering in Natural Contexts*. San Francisco: W.H. Freeman.
Patterson, K.E. and Baddeley, A.D. (1975) When face recognition fails. *Journal of Experimental Psychology: Human Learning and Memory, 3*, 406–417.
Shepard, R. (1967) Recognition memory for words, sentences and pictures. *Journal of Verbal Learning and Verbal Behaviour, 6*, 156–163.
Stern, W. (1904) Wirklichkeitsversuche. *Beitrage zur Psychologie der Aussage, 2(1)*, 1–31. Translation by U. Neisser. In Neisser (1982).
Yarbus, A.L. (1967) *Eye movements and Vision*. New York: Plenum.

Chapter 3

Aserinsky, E. and Kleitman, N. (1953) Regularly occurring periods of eye mobility and concomitant phenomena during sleep. *Science, 118*, 273–274.
Aserinsky, E. and Kleitman, N. (1955) Two types of ocular motility occurring in sleep. *Journal of Applied Physiology, 8(1)*, 1–10.
Bartlett, F.C. (1932) *Remembering*. Cambridge: Cambridge University Press.
Berger, H. (1929) Über das Elektroenzephalogram des Menchen. *Archiv für Psychiatrie und Nervenkrankheiten, 87*, 527– 550.
Berger, R.J. (1963) Experimental modification of dream content by meaningful verbal stimuli. *British Journal of Psychiatry, 109*, 722–740.

Bertini, M., Lewis, H.B. and Witkin, H.A. (1969) Some preliminary observations with an experimental procedure for the study of hypnagogic and related phenomena. In C.T. Tart (1969).

* Chase, M. and Weitzman, E.G. (1983) *Sleep Disorders: Basic and Clinical Research*. Lancaster: MTP Press.

* Cohen, D.B. (1979) *Sleep and Dreaming: Origins, Nature and Functions*. Oxford: Pergamon Press.

Dement, W. (1960) The effect of dream deprivation. *Science, 131*, 1705–1707.

Dement, W. (1983) A life in sleep research. In M. Chase and E.G. Weitzman (1983).

Dement, W. and Kleitman, N. (1957) The relation of eye movement during sleep to dream activity: An objective method for the study of dreaming. *Journal of Experimental Psychology, 53(5)*, 339–346.

Dement, W. and Wolpert, E. (1958) The relation of eye movements, body motility, and external stimuli to dream content. *Journal of Experimental Psychology, 55*, 543–553.

Foulkes, D. (1962) Dream reports from different stages of sleep. *Journal of Abnormal and Social Psychology, 65*, 14–25.

Foulkes, D. (1969) Theories of dream formulation and recent studies of sleep consciousness. In C.T. Tart (1969).

* Freud, S. (1976) *The Interpretation of Dreams*. Harmondsworth: Pelican Books. (First published 1900.)

Goodenough, D., Shapiro, A., Holden, M. and Steinschriber, L. (1959) Comparison of dreamers and non dreamers: Eye movements, electroencephalograms and recall of dreams. *Journal of Abnormal and Social Psychology, 59*, 295–302.

Hall, C.S. (1971) What people dream about. In R.F. Thompson (1971).

Jung, C.G. (ed.) (1964) *Man and His Symbols*. London: Aldus Books.

Kleitman, N. (1971) Patterns of dreaming. In R.F. Thompson (1971).

Liebert, R.M. and Neale, J.M. (1977) *Psychology: A Contemporary View*. New York: Wiley.

Lindsay, G., Hall, C.S. and Thompson, R.F. (1978) *Psychology*. New York: Worth Publishers.

Tart, C.T. (ed.) (1969) *Altered States of Consciousness*. New York: Wiley.

Thompson, R.F. (ed.) (1971) *Physiological Psychology: Readings from Scientific American*. San Francisco: W.H. Freeman and Co.

Vogel, G.W. (1975) A review of REM sleep deprivation. *Archives of General Psychiatry, 32*, 749–761.

Chapter 4

* Antaki, C. (1981) *The Psychology of Ordinary Explanations of Social Behaviour*. London: Academic Press.

* Berger, P. and Luckmann, T. (1979) *The Social Construction of Reality*. Harmondsworth: Peregrine Books.

Cooley, C.H. *Human Nature and the Social Order*. New York: Schocken Books.

Duval, S. and Wicklund, R.A. (1973) Effects of objective self awareness on attribution of causality. *Journal of Experimental Social Psychology, 9*, 17–31.

Fletcher, R. (1976) *The Framework of Society*. Milton Keynes: Open University Press.

Heider, F. (1958) *The Psychology of Interpersonal Relations*. New York: Wiley.

James, W. (1950) *The Principles of Psychology*. New York: Dover Publications, Inc. (First published 1890.)

References

Kelly, G.A. (1955) *The Psychology of Personal Constructs*. New York: Norton.
McCall, G. and Simmons, J.L. (1966) *Identity and Interaction*. New York: Free Press.
Mannheim, K. (1936) *Ideology and Utopia*. London: Routledge and Kegan Paul.
Marx, K. (1953) *Die Frühschriften*. Stuttgart: Kroner. (First published 1844.)
Mead, G.H. (1967) *Mind, Self and Society*. Chicago: University of Chicago Press.
Storms, M.D. and Nisbett, R.E. (1970) Insomnia and the attribution process. *Journal of Personality and Social Psychology, 16*, 319–328.

Chapter 5

Baron, R.A. and Byrne, D. (1981) *Social Psychology: Understanding Human Interaction*. London: Allyn and Bacon, Inc.
Cockcroft, W. (Chairman) (1982) *Mathematics Counts*. Report on the Committee of Inquiry into the Teaching of Mathematics in Schools. London: HMSO.
D'Andrade, R. (1966) Sex differences and cultural institutions. In E.E. Maccoby (ed.) *The Development of Sex Differences*. Stanford: Stanford University Press.
Darwin, C. (1896) *The Descent of Man and Selection in Relation to Sex*. New York: Appleton. (Original edition 1871.)
Ford, C.S. and Beach, F.A. (1951) *Patterns of Sexual Behaviour*. New York: Harper and Row.
Fox, L.H. (1977) The effects of sex role socialisation on mathematics participation and achievement. In NIE Papers in Education and Work, No. 8 'Women and mathematics: Research perspectives for change.' Washington, DC: National Institute of Education.
Freud, S. (1925) Some psychical consequences of the anatomical distinction between the sexes. Standard Edition of the Complete Psychological Works of Sigmund Freud, Vol 19. London: Hogarth Press and the Institute of Psychoanalysis.
Frieze, I.H., Parsons, J.E., Johnson, P.B., Ruble, D.N. and Zellman, G.L. (1979) *Women and Sex Roles: A Social Psychological Perspective*. New York: Norton.
Gouldner, A.W. and Peterson, R.A. (1963) *Notes on Technology and the Moral Order*. Indianapolis: Bobbs- Merill.
Hall, S. (1905) *Adolescence: Its Psychology and its Relation to Physiology, Anthropology, Sociology, Sex, Crime, Religion and Education, Volume II*. New York: Appleton.
* Hoyenga, K.B. and Hoyenga, K.T. (1979) *The Question of Sex Differences: Psychological, Cultural and Biological Issues*. Boston: Little, Brown and Co.
Joint Matriculation Board (1983) *Annual Report 1981–82*. Manchester: Joint Matriculation Board.
Lewis, M. (1972) Parents and children: Sex role development. *School Review, 80*, 229–240.
Maccoby, E.E. and Jacklin, C.N. (1974) *The Psychology of Sex Differences*. Stanford, CA: Stanford University Press.
Mead, M. (1945) *Sex and Temperament in Three Primitive Societies*. New York: Dell. (First published 1935.)
Mead, M. (1950) *Male and Female*. Harmondsworth: Penguin.
Mill, J.S. (1869) *On the Subjugation of Women*.
Montagu, A. (1974) *The Natural Superiority of Women*. New York: Collier.
Morris, D. (1967) *The Naked Ape*. London: Jonathan Cape.
Oakley, A. (1975) *Sex, Gender and Society*. Bath: Pitman.

* Richards, J.R. (1980) *The Sceptical Feminist*. Harmondsworth: Penguin.
Rosaldo, M.Z. (1974) Women culture and society: A theoretical overview. In M.Z. Rosaldo and L. Lamphere (eds) *Women, Culture and Society*. Stanford, CA: Stanford University Press.
Sanday, P.R. (1974) Female status in the public domain. In M.Z. Rosaldo and L. Lamphere (eds) *Women, Culture and Society*. Stanford, CA: Stanford University Press.
Sayers, J. (1982) *Biological Politics: Feminist and Anti-Feminist Perspectives*. London: Tavistock Publications.
Seligman, M.E.P. (1970) On the generality of the laws of learning. *Psychological Review*, 77, 406–418.
Shuard, H.B. (1982) Differences in mathematical performance between girls and boys. Appendix 2 of Cockcroft (1982).
Spence, J.T. and Helmreich, R.L. (1978) *Masculinity and Femininity*. Austin: University of Texas Press.
Spencer, H. (1898) *The Principles of Sociology, Volume I*. New York: Appleton. (First published 1876.)
* Tavris, C. and Offir, C. (1977) *The Longest War: Sex Differences in Perspective*. New York: Harcourt, Brace, Jovanovich.
Thompson, R.F. (ed.) (1971) *Physiological Psychology: Readings from Scientific American*. San Francisco: W.H. Freeman and Co.
Washburn, S.L. (1971) Tool use and human evolution. In R.F. Thompson (ed.) 1971.
Weitzman, L.J., Eifler, D., Hokada, E. and Ross, C. (1972) Sex-role socialization in picture books for preschool children. *American Journal of Sociology*, 77, 1125–1150.
Will, J.A., Self, P.A. and Datan, N. (1976) Maternal behaviour and perceived sex of infant. *American Journal of Orthopsychiatry*, 49, 135–139.

Chapter 6

Blumberg, H.H., Cohen, S.D., Dronfield, B.E., Mordecai, E.A., Roberts, C.J. and Hawks, D. (1974) British opiate users: I. People approaching London drug treatment centres. *International Journal of Addiction*, 9(1).
Dobson, R. (1975) Statement at the Annual General Meeting of British American Tobacco Company, 20 March 1975. Cited in Report of College of Physicians (1979).
Doll, R. and Hill, A.B. (1950) Smoking and carcinoma of the lung. Preliminary Report. *British Medical Journal*, 2, 739.
Girdano, D.A. and Girdano, D.D. (1976) *Drug Education: Content and Methods*. London: Addison Wesley.
Godber, G.E. (1970) On the State of the Public Health. The Annual Report of the Chief Medical Officer of the Ministry of Health for the year 1969. London: HMSO.
Hamburg, B.H. *et al.* (1975) A hierarchy of drug use in adolescence. *American Journal of Psychiatry*, 132, 1155–1163.
Liebert, R.M. and Neale, J.M. (1977) *Psychology: A Contemporary View*. New York: Wiley Inc.
Lindzey, G., Hall, C.S. and Thompson, R.F. (1978) *Psychology*. New York: Worth Publishers.
Royal College of Physicians (1962) *Smoking and Health*. London: Pitman.

References

Royal College of Physicians (1971) *Smoking and Health Now.* London: Pitman.
Royal College of Physicians (1979) *Smoking or Health.* London: Pitman.
World Health Organization (1974) *Twentieth Report of Expert Committe on Drug Dependence.* Technical Report Series, MO 551. Geneva: WHO.
World Health Organization (1975) *Smoking and Its Effects on Health. Report of WHO Expert Committee.* WHO Technical Report Series, MO 568. Geneva: WHO.
Zacune, J. and Hensman, C. (1971) *Drugs, Alcohol and Tobacco in Britain.* London: Heinemann.

Further reading

Tart, C.T. (ed.) (1969) *Altered States of Consciousness.* New York: Wiley.

Chapter 7

* Boden, M.A. (1977) *Artificial Intelligence and Natural Man.* Brighton: Harvester.
Colby, K.M. (1975) *Artificial Paranoia.* New York: Pergamon.
Lighthill, J. (1972) *Artificial Intelligence.* Report to the Science Research Council. London: SRC.
Newell, A., Shaw, J.C. and Simon, H.A. (1957) Preliminary description of the General Problem Solving Program I (GPS I). CIP Working Paper No 7, December. Cited in Newell and Simon (1972).
Newell, A. and Simon, H.A. (1972) *Human Problem Solving.* Englewood Cliffs, NJ: Prentice Hall Inc.
Samuel, A. (1959) Some studies in machine learning using the game of checkers. *IBM Journal of Research Development, 3(3),* 211–229. Reprinted in E. Feigenbaum and J. Feldman (eds) (1963) *Computers and Thought.* New York: McGraw-Hill.
* Schank, R. and Abelson, R. (1977) *Scripts, Plans, Goals and Understanding.* Hillsdale, NJ: Lawrence Erlbaum Associates.
Turing, A. (1950) Computing machinery and intelligence. *Mind, 59,* 433–460.
Winograd, T. (1972) *Understanding Natural Language.* Edinburgh: Edinburgh/New York: Academic Press.
Wittgenstein, L. (1958) *Philosophical Investigations.* Oxford: Blackwell.

* References marked with an asterisk are recommended for further reading.

Index

Index

CANNABIS, 159,167
career success, and sex differences 141
Cate, R. 17,217
causality 111
Chase, M. 219
chess-playing programs 202–203
child care, and sex differences 147
Clifford, B.R. 45,218
cocaine 159,169
Cockroft Report on Mathematical Education 140–141,220
codebreaking 183
coffee 159,161,164
Colby, K.M. 184,185,222
colour, dreams in 77
Cohen, D.B. 219
Cohen, S.D. 221
complementarity 16
computer programs
  GPS 204
  MYCIN 213
  PARRY 185
  SAM 196
  SHAKEY 205
  SHRDLU 188
  STRIPS 205
computers 183–216
  anthropomorphization of 215
  applications of 212–213
  and consciousness 214,215
  and diagnosis 184–186
  and language 187–188
  and meaning 207
  and modelling 211–212
  and planning 204–206
  and rationality 198
conceptual structures 112
confidence, and accuracy of identification 49
consciousness, and computers 214,215
constructs 104–105
control
  of drugs 167–168
  of the mind 116
  social 118–119
conventions, social 112
Cooley, C.H. 112,219
cortex, development of 132

counselling, and relationships 22
crime, and sex differences 139
crisis, in relationships 20–21
culture
  and memory 42
  and sex differences 128,140–144

D'ANDRADE, R. 220
Darwin, C. 130,131,220
Datan, N. 221
Deffenbacker, K. 47,218
Dement, 69,79–80,82–84,219
depressants 165
deprivation
  of REM 82–85
  sensory 87
Devlin Report 43,54–55,218
diagnosis, and AI 184–186
Dickson-Markman, F. 217
discrimination, and sex differences 146–148
disguise, and identification 50–51
distortion, of memory 43
Dobson, R. 162,221
Doll, R. 161,221
Dream Quiz 74–75
dreams 67–92
  amplification of 90
  analysis of 89–92
  and animals 77–78
  biological explanations of 83
  and colour 77
  and imagery 85,87,91
  laboratory studies of 68–74
  physiological studies of 68–74
  recall of 80
  stimulation of 79–80
  and unconscious 85–88
drugs 157–169
  and behaviour 164–166
  control of 167–168
  social use of 159,161
  and society 166–169
Duck, S. 26, 217
Duval, S. 113–114,219

EEG 69,70
  and brain activity 72
Egyptians, and sleep 67
Eifler, D. 221

224

Index

intelligence
  definitions of 207,208
  and sex differences 138
interpretation, of dreams 89–92
  of events 103–120
intimacy 17
  and drug use 161
institutions, and social control
  118–120
intuition, and computers 215
isolation, effects of 26–27

JACKLIN, C.N. 137,139,141,220
James, W. 113,118,219
Johnson, P.B. 220
Joint Matriculation Board 220
judgement, and attention 113
Jung, C.G. 86–87,88,89,219

KAPLAN, R.E. 20,217
Kelly, G.A. 104–105,117,220
King, Martin Luther 68
Kleitman, N. 69,71,73,
  81–82,84,218,219
knowledge
  and expectations 111
  of the world 103–120

LABORATORY STUDIES OF DREAMS
  74–82
language, and computers 187–188
law, and drugs 166–169
leading questions, effects of 51–53
learning 43
  associative 145
legal processes 38
Lewis, H.B. 219
Lewis, M. 141,220
Liebert, R.M. 219,221
Lighthill, J. 212,222
Lincoln, Abraham 67
Lindsay, G. 219
Lindzey, G. 221
literary analysis 9
Loftus, E.F. 45,51,52,218
logic, and understanding 111
Lovelace, Lady Ada 183

lovers 17–18
LSD 159,165,167
Luckmann, T. 219
Lucretius 77
lung cancer 161–162

MCCALL, G. 103,220
Maccoby, E.E. 137,139,141,220
machine intelligence 183–216
machine translation 187–188
Mannheim, K. 117,220
Markman, H.J. 217
marriage 19–20
  breakdown of 11
Marx, K. 116,220
Marxist concepts of control 116–117
mathematical ability, and sex
  differences 140–141
Mead, G.H. 113,220
Mead, M. 143,22
meaning
  and AI 207
  of events 42
means–ends analysis 199,204,
  205–207
measuring sex differences 134–142
medicines 158
Meehl, P. 55,218
memory
  and arousal 45
  and bias 50–53
  characteristics of 42
  distortion of 43
  for dreams 77
  and emotional arousal 45
  eyewitness 47–49
  for faces 44
  and questioning 52–53
  visual 43–44
men, stereotypes of 127
mental hospitals 118–120
Mill, J.S. 125,220
Milton, J. 9,23,24,25
mind control 116
modelling, computer 211–212
morality, and sex differences
  146–148
Morris, D. 133,220
motherhood 133
motivation, unconscious 85

Index